**north**

0  250  500

**Carlton Gardens**

Drummond St
Rathdowne St
Brunswick St
Victoria St
Victoria Pde
Gisborne St

Bowen St
RMIT
Bowen Lane
Mackenzie St
Latrobe St
Bennetts Lane
Little Lonsdale St
Lonsdale St
Albert St
Melbourne Central Station
Parliament Station
Parliament Gardens
Swanston St
Little Bourke St
Coverlid Pl
Market Lane
Exhibition St
Spring St
Macarthur St
Golden Fleece Alley
Bourke St
Russell St
Little Collins St
Bourke St Mall
Collins St
Treasury Gardens
Landsowne St
Howey Pl (Battle Alley)
Flinders La
Wellington Pde
Wellington Pde South
Hosier La
Flinders St
Flinders Street Station
Princes Bridge
Yarra River
Princes Walk

42, 43, 50, 49, 48, 44, 47, 46, 41, 45, 40, 37, 39, 38, 36, 35, 34, 33, 32, 21, 22, 20, 31, 24, 23, 25, 30, 26, 28, 27, 29, 19, 11, 12, 14, 16, 15, 13, 17, 18

# melbourne

Jeff Sparrow & Jill Sparrow

the vulgar press

First published 2001 by The Vulgar Press,
PO Box 68, Carlton North, Victoria 3054.
www.vulgar.com.au

Reprinted 2002, 2004

Distributed by Dennis Jones and Associates,
19a Michellan Court, Bayswater, Victoria 3153.

Copyright © Jeff Sparrow 2001
Copyright © Jill Sparrow 2001

All rights reserved. This book is copyright. Apart from any fair dealing for the purposes of study, research, criticism, review, or as otherwise permitted under the Copyright Act, no part may be reproduced by any process without written permission. Enquiries should be made to the publisher.

National Library of Australia
Cataloguing-in-Publication entry

Sparrow, Jeff, 1969–.
Radical Melbourne: a secret history

Includes index.

    ISBN 0 9577352 4 3.

    1. Radicalism – Australia – History. 2. Buildings – Victoria – Melbourne – History. 3. Melbourne (Vic.) – History. I. Sparrow, Jill, 1971– . II. Title.

994.51

Typesetting and design by
**Vulgar Enterprises of North Carlton**

Set in 10/14 pt Stempel Schneidler

Printed in Australia by McPherson's Printing Group, Maryborough

The Vulgar Press is grateful to the State Library of Victoria for its provision of the historical images in the book and its assistance with their reproduction. Many of the images are taken from the Library's collection. The State Library of Victoria is at 328 Swanston Street, Melbourne, Victoria, Australia 3000. Enquiries can be made via telephone: (03) 8664 7000 or <http://www.statelibrary.vic.gov.au>.

**State Library** of Victoria

# Contents

Illustrations **6**
Acknowledgements **8**
Foreword by Stuart Macintyre **10**
Introduction **14**

1. **First Cemetery** — Flagstaff Gardens **17**
2. **Unemployed Riot** — Flagstaff Gardens **21**
3. **Old Cemetery** — Victoria Market **24**
4. **New Theatre** — 293 Latrobe Street **27**
5. **Socialist Hall** — 283 Elizabeth Street **31**
6. **Orange Riots** — St John's Lane **35**
7. **Wharfies Riot** — 400 Flinders Street **39**
8. **Gaol and Stocks** — 455 Collins Street **43**
9. **Stock Exchange** — 380 Collins Street **47**
10. **Victorian Single Tax League** — 349 Collins Street **51**
11. **Cole's Book Arcade** — Howey Place **55**
12. **Town Hall** — Corner Collins and Swanston Streets **59**
13. **Burke and Wills Statue** — Corner Collins and Swanston Streets **64**
14. **Mechanics Institute** — 188 Collins Street **68**
15. **Anti-Fascist Protest** — 167 Collins Street **71**
16. **Unemployed Demonstration** — 140 Collins Street **73**
17. **Communist Party Office** — 3 Hosier Lane **79**
18. **Speakers Forum** — Yarra Bank **83**
19. **Melbourne Club** — 36 Collins Street **88**
20. **Parliament House** — Spring Street **91**
21. **Melbourne Anarchist Club** — Her Majesty's Theatre **97**
22. **Secret Society Riot** — Corner Market Lane and Little Bourke Street **101**
23. **Golden Fleece Hotel** — Coverlid Place **104**
24. **IWW Office** — 171 Little Bourke Street **109**
25. **Victorian Socialists League** — 177 Russell Street **113**
26. **Workers Art Club** — 175 Bourke Street **118**

| | | | |
|---|---|---|---|
| 27. | **Movement Against War and Fascism** | 145 Russell Street | **122** |
| 28. | **Andrade's Bookshop** | 201 Bourke Street | **125** |
| 29. | **Tivoli Theatre** | Tivoli Arcade | **129** |
| 30. | **Communist Party Office** | 224 Swanston Street | **132** |
| 31. | **Communist Party Office** | 252 Swanston Street | **136** |
| 32. | **Anarchist Bookery** | 213 Russell Street | **140** |
| 33. | **Communist Party Office** | 217 Russell Street | **144** |
| 34. | **Greek Club Bombing** | 189 Lonsdale Street | **148** |
| 35. | **Unemployed Workers Movement** | 260 Russell Street | **151** |
| 36. | **Cabinet Makers' Strike** | 264 Russell Street | **154** |
| 37. | **Salvation Army Picket** | 21 Bennetts Lane | **157** |
| 38. | **Public Library** | 328 Swanston Street | **161** |
| 39. | **Sir Redmond Barry Statue** | State Library Steps | **166** |
| 40. | **Guild Hall** | RMIT University | **169** |
| 41. | **Working Men's College** | RMIT University | **175** |
| 42. | **Gallows Hill** | Corner Franklin and Bowen Streets | **178** |
| 43. | **Eight-Hour Day Monument** | Corner Victoria and Russell Streets | **182** |
| 44. | **Old Melbourne Gaol** | Russell Street | **185** |
| 45. | **City Court** | Corner Latrobe and Russell Streets | **190** |
| 46. | **Turn Verein Hall** | 30–34 Latrobe Street | **195** |
| 47. | **Police Strike** | Old Russell Street Police Complex | **199** |
| 48. | **Progressive Spiritualist Lyceum** | Corner Victoria and Lygon Streets | **204** |
| 49. | **Matteotti Club** | Horticultural Hall | **208** |
| 50. | **Trades Hall** | 54 Victoria Street | **212** |
| | | Further Reading | **220** |
| | | Index | **222** |

# Sources for illustrations

All contemporary images are by Peter Ewer.

The map used throughout is created by Chris Lee Ack.

The following is a sequential list of sources for the historical images used in the book. They are listed according to page number. When two or more images are on one page, they are listed from top to bottom.

3. *The Argus*, 2 October 1928, Newspaper Collection, State Library of Victoria

19. McCrae Family Papers, La Trobe Australian Manuscripts Collection, State Library of Victoria

22. McCrae Family Papers, La Trobe Australian Manuscripts Collection, State Library of Victoria

25. Hall Press Clippings, La Trobe Collection, State Library of Victoria

28. New Theatre Collection, Performing Arts Museum, Victorian Arts Centre.

28. New Theatre Collection, Performing Arts Museum, Victorian Arts Centre.

33. *The Socialist*, 31 August 1907, Newspaper Collection, State Library of Victoria

34. Communist Party of Australia Collection, Melbourne University Archives

36. *The Herald*, 10 July 1845 Rare Books, State Library of Victoria

41. *The Argus*, 2 October 1928, Newspaper Collection, State Library of Victoria

44. La Trobe Australian Manuscripts Collection, State Library of Victoria

48. *The Australasian*, 13 June 1903, Newspaper Collection, State Library of Victoria

52. *Beacon*, 1 July 1984, Newspaper Collection, State Library of Victoria

54. *Beacon*, 1 July 1894, Newspaper Collection, State Library of Victoria

56. La Trobe Picture Collection, State Library of Victoria

56. La Trobe Picture Collection, State Library of Victoria

60. *Bulletin*, 13 September 1890, Newspaper Collection, State Library of Victoria.

61. *The Argus*, 6 November 1923, Newspaper Collection, State Library of Victoria

65. La Trobe Picture Collection, State Library of Victoria

67. La Trobe Picture Collection, State Library of Victoria

70. *Illustrated Sydney News*, 23 December 1854 La Trobe Picture Collection, State Library of Victoria

72. *The Herald Sun*, 31 January 1929, Newspaper Collection, State Library of Victoria

75. *Melbourne Punch*, 21 June 1906, Newspaper Collection, State Library of Victoria

78. *Bulletin*, 28 January 1906, Newspaper Collection, State Library of Victoria

81. *Workers Voice*, 13 November 1936, Newspaper Collection, State Library of Victoria

84. Communist Party of Australia Collection, Melbourne University Archives

84. Personal collection of Verity Burgmann

89. La Trobe Australian Manuscripts Collection, State Library of Victoria

92. *The Illustrated Australian News*, La Trobe Picture Collection, State Library of Victoria

95. *Bulletin*, 10 December 1892, Newspaper Collection, State Library of Victoria

98. La Trobe Picture Collection, State Library of Victoria

99. *Labor Call*, 9 July 1908, Newspaper Collection, State Library of Victoria

102. *Weekly Times*, 21 January 1893, Newspaper Collection, State Library of Victoria

102. *Weekly Times*, 21 January 1893, Newspaper Collection, State Library of Victoria

107. *Melbourne Punch*, 14 July 1890, Newspaper Collection, State Library of Victoria

111. Personal collection of Verity Burgmann

115. La Trobe Picture Collection, State Library of Victoria

119. Merrifield Collection, La Trobe Australian Manuscripts Collection, State Library of Victoria

120. Merrifield Collection, La Trobe Australian Manuscripts Collection, State Library of Victoria

124. *The Sun*, 26 February 1935, Newspaper Collection, State Library of Victoria

126. *Tocsin*, 26 September 1901, Newspaper Collection, State Library of Victoria

127. Personal collection of Verity Burgmann

130. *Truth*, 31 March 1928, Newspaper Collection, State Library of Victoria,

131. *Truth*, 31 March 1928, Newspaper Collection, State Library of Victoria

133. Merrifield Collection, La Trobe Australian Manuscripts Collection, State Library of Victoria

137. *Pix*, 15 July 1939, La Trobe Picture Collection, State Library of Victoria

138. *Pix*, 15 July 1939, La Trobe Picture Collection, State Library of Victoria

143. *Commonweal*, 22 October 1892, Newspaper Collection, State Library of Victoria

146. *The Sun*, 20 May 1933, Newspaper Collection, State Library of Victoria

147. *Truth,* 3 October 1931, Newspaper Collection, State Library of Victoria

149. *The Argus*, 2 December 1928, Newspaper Collection, State Library of Victoria

152. Reproduced with the permission of Pat Counihan

153. *The Age*, 9 August 1933, Newspaper Collection, State Library of Victoria

155. *Weekly Times*, 21 January 1893, Newspaper Collection, State Library of Victoria

155. *Weekly Times*, 21 January 1893, Newspaper Collection, State Library of Victoria

155. *Illustrated Australian News*, 1 September 1893, La Trobe Picture Collection, State Library of Victoria

158. Salvation Army Archives

159. *The Bulletin,* 6 August 1930, Newspaper Collection, State Library of Victoria

165. *The Bulletin*, 26 July 1890, Newspaper Collection, State Library of Victoria

167. La Trobe Picture Collection, State Library of Victoria

172. La Trobe Australian Manuscripts Collection, State Library of Victoria

173. Personal collection of Verity Burgmann

177. *Melbourne Punch,* 12 July 1887, Newspaper Collection, State Library of Victoria

179. La Trobe Picture Collection, State Library of Victoria

181. La Trobe Collection, State Library of Victoria

181. La Trobe Collection, State Library of Victoria

183. *Socialist*, 21 April 1906, Newspapers Collection, State Library of Victoria

184. La Trobe Picture Collection, State Library of Victoria

188. *Weekly Times*, 2 February 1905, Newspaper Collection, State Library of Victoria

189. *The Sun*, 15 April 1924, Newspaper Collection, State Library of Victoria

192. La Trobe Picture Collection, State Library of Victoria

193. *Socialist*, 4 July 1919, Newspaper Collection, State Library of Victoria

197. La Trobe Picture Collection, State Library of Victoria

201. *The Herald,* 5 November 1923, Newspaper Collection, State Library of Victoria

207. *Weekly Times*, 12 August 1899, Newspaper Collection, State Library of Victoria

209. Italian Historical Society– CO.AS.IT

210. Italian Historical Society– CO.AS.IT

211. Italian Historical Society– CO.AS.IT

213. Personal collection of Verity Burgmann

217. *Labor Call*, 7 July 1908, Newspaper Collection, State Library of Victoria

# Acknowledgements

This book would not have happened without the work of many people.

Mick Armstrong co-ordinated the secret history tours which inspired it, and commented helpfully on the manuscript. David Hudson generously shared a passion for history, a sense of humour and an eagle eye for errors. Louise Craig was an excellent copyeditor and proofreader. Gerard Morel worked with us on the project from its earliest days, assisting in every aspect of the process.

Thanks are also due to Peter Ewer for work above and beyond the call of duty in producing the photos that appear throughout the book, and to Chris Lee Ack for designing the elegant map that accompanies it.

Gill Smith and Jim Davidson gave us useful advice on both the manuscript and the publishing industry. Di Websdale-Morrissey and her non-fiction class at RMIT workshopped great slabs of the book throughout 2000. Linda and Jim Sparrow provided constant encouragement and useful comments on early drafts, and helped produce the Index. Donalee Weis did a terrific job in completing the Index.

Bob James generously corresponded with us about David Andrade. Wendy Lowenstein helped with information about Jim Coull and Chummy Fleming. Gianfranco Cresciani shared his knowledge of the Matteotti Club. Angela O'Brien gave us access to both her thesis and her collection of New Theatre archives.

We owe a debt of thanks to Stuart Macintyre for his detailed reading of the manuscript and his splendid Foreword. Verity Burgmann gave us her helpful comments on the book, as well as a great deal of encouragement (and access to some fantastic photos!). Jerome Small made available his historical knowledge and his political judgement; we thank him for both.

Researching the book was made infinitely more simple by the resources and staff of the State Library of Victoria. In particular, we would like to thank Dianne Reilly for permission to use photographs from the Library's collections, Peter Mappin for bearing patiently with the ever increasing volume of historical material which we gave him to photograph, Euan McGillivray for enthusiastically supporting our project and organising State Library support, and the staff from the Picture, Manuscripts, Newspapers, La Trobe and Off-Site Delivery teams.

We also acknowledge the assistance of the Jeff Goldhar Project, and thank Tom O'Lincoln for administering it.

Without the support of Ian Syson, this project would not have been possible. His patience, good humour and encouragement made the process of publication as painless as possible.

Lastly, we'd like to thank our comrades in Socialist Alternative, who taught us how to appreciate history in the course of the struggle to make it.

Jeff Sparrow and Jill Sparrow

# Foreword

The spectre that haunted nineteenth-century Europe inhabited its cities. The Parisians who stormed the Bastille in 1789 sounded the death-knell of the *ancien regime*. Barricades went up in most capital cities in 1848, driving the rulers from their seats of government. In 1871 the Paris Commune briefly seized power from rulers who withdrew to Versailles. The opening of fire on a demonstration of workers in St Petersburg brought uprisings across Russia in 1905; the rising in Dublin in 1916 gave birth to the Irish Republic; the storming of the Winter Palace in 1917 signalled the Russian revolution.

The metropolis was a site of protest because it was the centre of authority. Courts sat, laws were made and administration conducted in the capital. Just as those who exercised power congregated there, so did those who wished to challenge it. Cities became the incubators of radical and revolutionary movements as they expanded in size and reach. The growth of industry produced dense concentrations of working people. Advances in transport and communications spread dissident doctrines. Movements of population created restless, cosmopolitan communities.

The cities of the new world, while they were thought to offer an escape from the class conflict of the old, quickly reproduced these forms. Less than half a century after it was chartered as a city, repression of protest in the immigrant industrial and transport centre of Chicago gave rise to the international commemoration of May Day.

The development of Melbourne was no less dramatic. It was established as an illegal frontier trading post in the 1830s. There followed a pastoral boom and then a gold rush, so that by 1857 the trade union leader, Charles Jardine Don, could invite an audience at Williamstown to gaze across the harbour at a city of nearly 100,000 inhabitants:

> Look at yonder city, illuminated by its magic lamps, its windows glittering with wealth, a city with palaces worthy of kings and temples worthy of gods, which labour has placed there in the short space of a quarter of a century.

Don is remembered in this guide to radical Melbourne for his part in winning the eight-hour day and subsequent decline as a parliamentary representative of labour. But he was also a regular speaker at the Eastern Market, where radicals harangued the crowds that came together in flickering torchlight at the end of the working day. The atmosphere at this time, following armed rebellion on the goldfields and intense argument over the forms of self-government, was recalled by a participant:

> You saw men who had fought in the streets of Paris; political refugees from Frankfurt, Berlin, Vienna and Buda Pesth, and Carbonari from Italy. Mostly young, ardent, enthusiastic and animated by more or less Utopian visions of reconstructing the political and social institutions of mankind so as to bring about an era of universal peace and prosperity, these heterogeneous exiles flung themselves heartily into the popular movements of the day.

The crowds that gathered at the Eastern Market in Bourke Street frequently marched up the hill to the new Parliament House to demand that it accept their democratic demands. Parliament House remains, though still incomplete, as a building that proclaims the majesty of government. The Eastern Market was demolished for the Southern Cross Hotel, the name recalling the flag the diggers hoisted at their Eureka Stockade, though more often recalled as the place besieged by the city's youth when the Beatles stayed in it during the 1960s. It has since been sentenced to obsolescence by the hospitality industry.

Melbourne's radical history is not immediately apparent to the visitor or even to the resident. The radical impulses of the formative decades were absorbed into Victorian liberalism, which became increasingly comfortable as the city prospered. Prosperity tilted into the speculative excess of Marvellous Melbourne in the 1880s, and then collapsed in the depression of the 1890s. The angry protests at the turn of the century were harnessed, in turn, by the rise of a Labor Party that sought gradual improvement by parliamentary reform. As the following directory of radical movements makes clear, there were numerous dissidents in Melbourne who offered alternative remedies and frequently found a responsive audience. Their influence extended into the trade unions and the Labor Party, which in Victoria has drawn much of its energy from ideological ferment.

But Labor in this state has usually been an oppositional force. During the period covered here, there were Labor ministers in Treasury Place for less than five years – in every other Australian state, Labor held office for more than twice as long. At least until the 1970s, Victoria was the jewel in the Liberal crown, and Melbourne the stronghold of conservative orthodoxy.

The following survey takes the reader around the city to places of conflict that have effaced their stormy past. The tour begins at the Flagstaff Gardens and the Victoria Market, with a reminder of their earlier roles as burial grounds for those indigenous Australians who died in the violent occupation of the new colony. The authors also draw our attention to buildings that once served as the premises of radical organisations. Few of those organisations have survived, and the buildings themselves have mostly been replaced by new ones too expensive for dissidents to rent. The tour also takes in city landmarks that the radicals contested: the Town Hall, the Scots Church, the Melbourne Club, Parliament House, the Public Library, the old City Court. They remain intact, if now dwarfed by the corporate towers that have displaced them in the city's political topography.

Jeff and Jill Sparrow conduct their tour through the streets of central Melbourne as a guide to the city's radical traditions. They assemble us on the high ground of the Flagstaff Gardens to the north-west, which originally overlooked the bay and displayed flags to signal the arrival of ships. After taking us briefly to the present Victoria Market, formerly the outlying cemetery of the new settlement, they come back south into the heart of the city with its regular design of straight lines and right angles.

The grid plan was laid out very early, aligned to the bank of the river, and the first land sales were conducted off the plan. It was a new-world city, planned and orderly, and it dismayed the bush poet John Shaw Neilson when in failing health he was found a job there in the 1920s. Neilson hated 'the dreadful noise of the city', and also its unbending character:

> *No curve they follow in Stony Town;*
> *but the straight line and the square.*

The arrangements also remind us of the wide thoroughfares that were driven through dense residential quarters in European cities during the nineteenth century, both to facilitate the movement of troops and to open up warrens of teeming humanity to public scrutiny. But the apparent openness and uniformity of central Melbourne was belied by the small streets and lanes that ran off the main streets, and also by the variegation of different districts within the grid.

The Sparrows conduct us down the central axis of the city towards the river, where early trade was centred and the first gaol stood. We then return to the western half of Collins Street, where the banks and Stock Exchange were established. These are remembered as sites of angry invasion. The tour proceeds east along Collins Street, past the Town Hall, the Mechanics Institute and the principal Protestant churches, to the entertainment district. We are reminded of the open-air forum of the Yarra Bank, to the south, and then move up to the citadels of privilege, the Melbourne Club and Parliament House. That takes us further north into more theatres and then the demi-monde of Chinatown in Little Bourke Street, fringed by bawdy houses and taverns.

This turns out to be the densest thicket of radical activity, with the Socialist League, the anarchists, the Wobblies, the Communist Party and its various offshoots – the Unemployed Workers Movement, the Workers Art Club and the Movement Against War and Fascism – all taking advantage of its cheap rents. The milieu is recalled by Judah Waten's novel *Scenes of Revolutionary Life*. A small group of comrades operate in the 1920s among Chinese restaurants, brothels, pawnbrokers, lodging houses, a temperance hall and evangelical chapels, including the Salvation Army citadel, remembered here for an unemployed protest.

Our walk heads west to the more respectable ambience of the Working Men's College, the State Library, and its founder, Redmond Barry. The Old Melbourne Gaol, built in the 1840s, is visited, not just for Ned Kelly – sentenced to execution by Barry – but for other victims of capital punishment. A pause at the City Court reminds us that it was once illegal to fly the red flag. The Russell Street police station recalls the police strike of 1923. In this quarter there were also the premises of radical immigrants and the once-influential Spiritualists. Further north, as the city gives way to the suburb of Carlton, the eight-hour day monument leads on to Trades Hall, which serves both as the workers' parliament and the gathering point for many marches. We might stop at this point for coffee

# FOREWORD

and cakes at the New International Bookshop in its nearest corner.

Our guides on this tour have provided a lively commentary. They have a close familiarity with Melbourne's radical history. To each place they attach a story, sometimes of peaceful protest and sometimes of violent confrontation. We find sectarian violence spilling into the city's streets, strikebreakers enrolling at the Town Hall, gun lofts in Parliament House, Chinese workers on strike, a Greek Club in Lonsdale Street bombed, military police raiding Trades Hall.

Some of these places are sites of injustice, as in the execution of Aborigines turned off their land. Some are reminders of lost resources, such as the remarkable Book Arcade of E.W. Cole or Will Andrade's bookshop in Bourke Street with its stock of free-thought and anarchist literature, theatrical and conjuring supplies, and contraceptives.

Well-known Melburnians appear: Redmond Barry in the Melbourne Club, the Mechanics Institute and Public Library, as well as on the bench; Alfred Deakin in the Spiritualist Lyceum; Squizzy Taylor possibly involved in a raid on a union safe; Tom Blamey, doubling as police commissioner and leader of a clandestine right-wing organisation.

But in this tour they are of less account than the rebels. As we retrace the habitat of radical Melbourne we learn of the dissidents. In the closing decades of the nineteenth century the Andrade brothers sit alongside the ascetic J.A. Andrews and gentle Chummy Fleming in the anarchist ranks. Then there was Monty Miller, who claimed to have fought at the Eureka Stockade and ended up a member of the Industrial Workers of the World.

In the early years of the new century, ambitions turn to the potential of organised labour. Hearty Tom Mann has come from England to lead the Victorian Socialist Party. William Maloney, the 'little doctor', acquires muscles at the Melbourne Deutscher Turn Verein, opens a free medical practice at Victoria Market and wins election to the federal seat of Melbourne in 1904. The Wobblies warn of the perils of parliamentary socialism and irreverent Bill Casey achieves immortality with his song 'Bump me into parliament'.

The labour movement splits during the First World War over the issue of conscription, and militant women such as Jennie Baines and Adela Pankhurst defy the wartime controls on protest. Percy Laidler and Bertha Walker search for an alternative to reformism, and a new revolutionary party emerges in the 1920s, the Communist Party. We see one of its youthful enthusiasts, the artist Noel Counihan, bunking down at the Workers Art Club, the Czech publicist Egon Kisch defying government bans, and the high-minded apologist Ralph Gibson rushing from one meeting to the next.

All this in just fifty places that span the creation of Melbourne to the outbreak of the Second World War. I wish there was time to extend the tour beyond Spring Street to the Higinbotham statue, or to take in the Bourke Street shopping emporia, whose plate-glass windows were smashed by the Women's Peace Army during the First World War. Since the Second World War, the radical topography of Melbourne has been expanded further. Perhaps the Sparrows will organise another tour after this inspiring walk around our city.

Stuart Macintyre

# Introduction

> God spare the people of Melbourne from ever again witnessing such an awful sight! Scores of our brave volunteers, who a few short hours before had been in the full pride of life and manhood, were lying in the filthy gutters of Flinders Street, the running waters of which were thickly stained with blood, the fearful groans of the wounded and dying were mingled with the coarse 'hourra' of the triumphant Russians . . .

Thus do the Tsar's armies complete their conquest of Melbourne in *The Battle of the Yarra*, a melodramatic novella published in 1883 with the stated aim of waking the populace to arm against the Asiatic hordes coveting the city.

The pioneer suffragette Harriet Dugdale also released a book that year. Her novel, A *Few Hours in a Far Off Age*, tells of Port Phillip Bay, not as a battleground, but as an earthly paradise, constructed with energies unleashed by women's entry into politics. Indeed, the happy people of Dugdale's 'Alethia' only dimly recall the city upon which their utopia now stands:

> It was supposed that somewhere near the west end of Alethia the old bright – and you would say very wicked – city of Melbourne had flourished for thousands of years in those far-off ages.

A site for racial war or a feminist paradise? Melbourne's past contains numerous struggles over the nature of its future. Though the sleazy entrepreneurs who led white settlement imagined Port Phillip merely as a source of rich pasture, others dreamed a different dream. The details of the Jerusalems each generation imagined springing forth beside the Yarra varied over time, but the yearning for them remained constant. And the struggle between those agitating for change and the defenders of the established order raged as sharply in the world's most liveable city as anywhere else in the world.

This book presents a guide through the first hundred years of political radicalism in Melbourne, focusing on the structures, streets and public places that remain today. It concentrates on identifying the physical traces of radical Melbourne, in the hope that geographical familiarity will provide a bridge between the struggles of the past and the people of the present.

Why is a guide necessary? In one sense, the legacy of Melbourne's past stands forth during even the most cursory stroll through the city. Yet the history we first encounter records power rather than resistance. Melbourne's rigid street grid honours a Captain Lonsdale, a Superintendent La Trobe, a Governor Bourke and a gaggle of other colonial grandees. The statues throughout the town and surrounding gardens laud establishment figures of an almost uniform bastardry – the hanging judge Redmond Barry, the war criminal John Batman, the more-or-less overtly fascist Thomas Blamey, the imperialist Charles 'Chinese' Gordon as well as the obligatory King (George) and Queen (Victoria).

This is in the nature of cities. The landscape of any metropolis inevitably celebrates the legacy of the rulers rather than the ruled – a point noted by no less an authority than V. I. Lenin, when he and Leon Trotsky briefly met in exile in London. Trotsky recalled:

> From a bridge, Lenin pointed out Westminster and some other famous buildings. I don't remember the exact words he used, but what he conveyed was: 'This is their famous Westminster,' and 'their' referred of course not to the English but to the ruling classes.

So it goes in Australia. Melbourne, it should be remembered, takes its name from the British Prime Minister who transported five men from the town of Tolpuddle for the crime of forming a trade union.

*Radical Melbourne*, then, tries to present a secret history of the city.

On the one hand, it focuses on secret places – those buildings too lowly or dilapidated or unassuming to accumulate associations with the powerful. Certain sections of Melbourne have cultivated a sufficiently unsavoury reputation for long enough to avoid renovation or demolition – and such areas naturally attract the outcasts and the rebels. The cheap rent in Russell Street, for instance, provided an opportunity for radicals of all persuasions to establish their headquarters from the late nineteenth century onwards, while the area's notoriety today ensures that many of the original buildings remain there to be rediscovered.

But *Radical Melbourne* also tries to give a history of places *with* secrets. Lenin, for instance, would doubtless have assigned RMIT's Storey Hall to the ruling class. The main function room of a multi-million dollar educational institute, it's today most often employed for the tedious pageantry of university official-dom. Yet in the revolutionary year of 1917, the speeches ringing throughout the hall came not from pompous Vice-Chancellors but socialist feminists, who had transformed the building into a commune for striking waterside workers. And, with the history of the Women's Political Association embedded in your consciousness, it becomes hard not to see the Storey Hall as belonging at least as much to working people as to any university.

*Radical Melbourne*'s Melbourne centres on fifty sites – a more or less arbitrary number, but sufficient to provide an overview of the diverse forms in which protest and resistance have manifested at various times within the city.

To keep the book to a manageable length, we have worked within a number of constraints. Firstly, we only cover sites within the CBD. A history exploring the suburbs would entail a separate volume, and so we've reluctantly confined ourselves to a comparatively small area.

Secondly, we've limited our scope up until 1939 – a date coinciding with the outbreak of the twentieth century's second mass slaughter, as well as marking (more or less) a hundred years of white settlement. We've done nothing on pre-contact Aboriginal sites, partly because we don't feel qualified and partly because it's a topic already covered elsewhere. Similarly, we've chosen not to record struggles from the postwar period, since doing any kind of justice to them would have entailed a book of intimidating length.

Further, we set ourselves a rule of thumb to include sites where some trace of an original structure remained. We bent this slightly on occasions to allow us to keep material relating to older struggles – but we've tried to ensure that each of our fifty sites retains some physical marker that can be seen today, even if it is only a street sign.

*Radical Melbourne* is intended for use charting a trip through the city, but also as a book to be read in one sitting at home. The sites are thus arranged geographically rather than chronologically, numbered in a sequence that would allow someone to walk from the first to the last in the most direct way.

Nonetheless, *Radical Melbourne* is neither an academic history, nor an alternative tour guide for jaded walkers. We wrote the book because we believe that the struggles it documents *matter*; that in this new millennium, with the left realigning itself in opposition to an ever more destructive world order, young radicals need to acquaint themselves with the victories and defeats of the past. The secret history of this city seemed to us an inspiration. We hope that the activists writing their own history amongst the Nike billboards and Optus towers of present day Melbourne share our enthusiasm, so that *Radical Melbourne* can play some part in encouraging future cities based on visions of freedom rather than visions of fear.

# 1. First Cemetery

## Flagstaff Gardens

The park that is now the Flagstaff Gardens performed a dual role in early Melbourne. The little hill at the northern end provided a vantage point for communication with Williamstown, while the lower area served as the town's first cemetery. Today, half a dozen bodies still lie beneath it – including two men whose deaths sparked one of Melbourne's earliest massacres.

In July 1836, a settler by the name of Charles Franks took a large herd of sheep to Mount Cottrell on the Werribee River, where he established a station. On the ninth of that month, one of the settlement's founders, John Pascoe Fawkner noted in his diary:

> Mr Gellibrand [another colonist] had been to the Point in the night and reported that Mr Franks and his men were missing.

The subsequent investigation revealed that Franks and a shepherd called Flinders had been clubbed to death, presumably by the local Aborigines.

It is not difficult to reconstruct a motive for the attack. One of the colonists acknowledged that 'Franks had a great aversion to the native blacks, and would not give them food, thinking it the best way to prevent them from frequenting the station'.

Indigenous society depended upon communality. Hunter-gatherer production entailed the consumption of resources as they were acquired, with any surplus distributed to those in need. This was not a matter of simple etiquette – in a society without facilities for storage, individual 'generosity' formed the fundamental moral imperative around which social organisation cohered.

Franks ran five hundred sheep, far more than he could ever personally consume. By refusing to offer them to those around him, he committed a grievous offence. As the settler J.D. Wood noted (albeit much later and in a different context): 'greediness in us, is with the [Aborigines] a great crime, their ignorance prevents them having a knowledge of the cost of our property'.

Earlier that month, the colonists had established their cemetery, after the death of Willie, the infant son of James Goodman. Following that service, Fawkner described the area that would become Flagstaff Hill:

Here is only one grave in a Burial ground of ten acres, the first natural death in this new Settlement.

He then added:

How many more would there be committed to the dark house within the Next Five years, how many will Strong drink hurry there prematurely, I fear a great many . . .

At the time, Fawkner himself operated a hotel, making good money out of the river of strong drink that flowed through the colony. Still, that was Fawkner all over. Standing barely five feet, he compensated for what he lacked in inches with a surfeit of gall – as would become apparent in his response to Franks' death.

A few days after receiving Gellibrand's report of Franks' disappearance, Fawkner recorded that the bodies of the missing men had been recovered. But he could not resist a jibe against another of the settlers: 'Taylor (the brute) refused to lend his Cart for this purpose.' The next day he noted that 'the bodies of Mr Franks and his man [Fawkner nowhere mentions Flinders' name] were buried this day'. He recorded those present at the service and commented that 'Mr Jas Smith read the service very feelingly'. And then – with typical Fawknerian spite – he added: 'A man refused to dig the 2 graves for 20/- a day's work.'

The pioneer grave memorial, Flagstaff Gardens.

Despite the internal tensions of the colony, there remained the one point on which all the colonists could agree – the need to punish the blacks.

Determining how this might be best done proved rather ticklish. After all, the settlement in Port Phillip had been launched without government approval, and the colonists remained desperate to convince the authorities to legitimise their land claims. Overtly provoking a fresh war with the Aborigines would not help matters, and they decided to maintain a fiction that their goal in hunting down Franks' killers consisted of the enforcement of indigenous law.

So on 10 July, Fawkner wrote in his diary (a document clearly intended for publication) that 'we enlisted as many Natives as would consent to go and agreed to send them out to deal with the Murderers as they think according to their Rules they should be treated'.

A sketch of Flagstaff Hill in the 1840s.

This was a complete nonsense. Gellibrand let the cat out of the bag by recording: 'Several parties are now out after the natives and I have no doubt many will be shot and a stop will be put to this system of killing for bread.'

What made Gellibrand so certain? Because he knew his fellow colonists and the experience they had acquired in the business of shooting down natives. John Batman, the other contender for the title of founder of the city, had led many sorties during Tasmania's Black Wars. On 1 September 1829, he had encountered a group of seventy Aboriginal men, women and children. When they tried to run, Batman opened fire, killing (by his own estimate) some fifteen people. His account includes an unselfconscious description of how, after the massacre:

> We left the place for my Farm with the two men, woman and child, but found it quite impossible that the Two former could walk [they were both suffering gunshot wounds], and after trying them by every means in my power, for some time, found I could not get them on. I was obliged therefore to shoot them.

By 1836, Batman's syphilis was beginning to trouble him and the old war criminal bowed out of the operation in favour of his equally brutal brother, Henry. Now, elsewhere, Fawkner had recorded of the Batmans: 'I believe [Henry Batman] to be a rogue and Cheat and fear John B. is not much better'. Yet he had no objection to unleashing this cheating rogue upon the natives. And on 16 July, two parties of settlers caught up with the Aborigines.

Fawkner writes:

> This day the Party sent out a few of the Blacks to fall in with them and the Native Blacks took full satisfaction on the Murderers & they found several Huts and some of the Property in each Hut.

The violence peeking slyly from behind Fawkner's euphemism of 'full satisfaction' leads one to suspect that the account subsequently given in the Tasmanian paper *The Cornwall Chronicle* is not exaggerated. It describes how the

> avenging party fell upon the guilty tribe about daylight in the morning, having watched them the previous night, and putting into effect a preconcerted plan of attack, succeeded in annihilating them. This tribe, which we now presume to be no longer troublesome, were it appears, a particularly treacherous people – less numerous than any of the others, and despised by all.

At least ten people died in the massacre, a calculatedly disproportionate retribution intended (in the time-honoured technique of occupying powers) to demonstrate the futility of further resistance. When the first Police Magistrate took office later that year, he made some desultory investigations into the matter, but – naturally – Henry Batman and his murderous band were never brought to justice.

Today, a monument and plaque commemorate the presence of those buried in the Gardens. But there is no acknowledgement of the scores of people murdered in their names.

# 2. Unemployed Riot

## Flagstaff Gardens

A post near the top of the hill in Flagstaff Gardens marks the point where the original flagstaff once stood. A sign explains how the colonists had erected a pole by which flag signals could be exchanged with the Harbour Master at Williamstown. The latest shipping intelligence displayed near the keeper's octagonal timber cottage made the hill a popular rendezvous in a colony understandably obsessed with news from beyond its own narrow bounds.

But on 19 April 1842, the breaking story was entirely local. The government had reduced the wages of immigrants working on the road from Melbourne to Sandridge (Port Melbourne), and all but six of the men had walked out on strike.

As the journalist and historian Edmund Finn – who in 1880 used the name 'Garryowen' to publish a definitive account of early Melbourne – documented:

> It was announced that the wage was to be reduced from 20s to 18s per week, and there was a general strike instanter. Pitching aside wheelbarrows and shouldering picks and shovels, the men formed into line and marched about 200 strong upon the town. Preceded by a giant of a fellow with a large loaf of bread stuck on the top of a ti-tree, they crossed by punt, and this, the first popular demonstration that ever turned out in Melbourne, tramped through Collins Street and pulled up at the office of the Superintendent [La Trobe].

The dispute arose against a backdrop of an economic collapse brought on by speculation in property and a fall in wool prices. By May 1841, squatters like Henry Meyrick moaned: 'Melbourne is in a miserable state; the land sales have run away with every farthing of cash'.

Amidst the growing distress, state-sponsored infrastructure projects such as road construction provided the main source of employment for immigrants. But the colonial authorities had come under pressure to cut expenditure, both to save money and to drive down wages in the private sector.

The local newspapers responded to the strike with astonishment, rage – and not a little racism. *The Port Phillip Patriot* spoke of the 'corps of bogtrotters in government employ', while *The Port Phillip Herald* thundered:

We may safely say that such another specimen of ignorance, and every thing that can render human nature degraded, could scarcely be again witnessed in any other part of the globe. They [the strikers] have come from the inland – almost impervious recesses of the mountainous districts of the south of Ireland, knowing little except what untutored instinct teaches, and directed by no other law than the impulses of a savage passion.

Superintendent La Trobe – the man most directly responsible for the wage cut – seems to have been equally fearful of the immigrants' passions. When the strikers made their way to his office (on the south side of the hill since levelled in the construction of Spencer Street railway station), the Superintendent was nowhere to be found.

Undaunted, the protesters ('in a state of excitement, and bent on mischief') continued along William Street. They paraded past the newly constructed St James's Church on the north-west corner of Collins Street and, says Garryowen:

> grew much excited and, muttering about what they would and would not do, passed along William Street towards the Flagstaff Hill. Tidings of the menacing turn of the movement were conveyed to the police, where Major St John (the Police Magistrate) happened to be sitting.

The original flagstaff, today marked by a post.

Now, elsewhere in his memoirs, Garryowen describes the police of the day as 'mostly a miserable set of broken-down cripples'. But, even within such company, Magistrate St John's avarice commanded attention. A retired military officer of aristocratic origin, St John earned the nickname 'Tippo' ('Tip oh!') from his habit of demanding gratuities. John Fawkner later complained: 'He takes bribes from all conditions of men – from the half-dozen eggs, or the pound of butter, up to a cow or a calf, horses, grog, wines, champagne, brandy and gin'.

Nonetheless, with the industrial peace disturbed, the newspapers happily portrayed St John as a champion of law and order. *The Herald* continues:

> The Major hastily adjourned the Court, and putting the Riot Act into his pocket, mounted his Bucephalus, and galloping after them, overtook these gentry [the strikers] on the outskirts of the town. The matter spread like lightning through the town and parties were seen in all directions hastening to 'the row'. The Major rode in amongst them, and enquiring their com-

plaint, was told that the reduction in their wages deprived them of the means of getting bread . . . A few of the more refractory spirits breathed 'battle, murder and sudden death'. In fact, we heard one fellow exclaim – 'wouldn't it be better to fight an' die, than to live and starve', which sentence he punctuated by sundry gyrations with a black-thorn shellelagh.

What happens next? Here, a few discrepancies arise. *The Herald* has St John quelling the riot single-handedly with his 'good humour and coolness'. *The Patriot*'s account is less heroic and more realistic – the magistrate confronts the mob in the company of his 'myrmidons' (servants).

But, from what we know of policing (then and today), we suspect Garryowen's version to most closely resemble the truth. He relates that, when the striker made his speech, the Magistrate:

> took the fellow near the butt end of the ear with the hammer of his riding whip, and 'floored' him. The pluck and promptitude of the act, and a few conciliatory words well seasoned with promises, caused the assemblage to quietly disperse.

The pioneer grave memorial, with the original flagstaff site to the right.

Whatever the case, the strike was over. When an overseer could not identify any ringleaders ('they appeared to rise en masse'), warrants were simply issued for the first four names appearing on a list of immigrants.

Over the following few weeks, the powers-that-be seemed to be seriously concerned that the men's example might spread. *The Herald* editorialised:

> The disgraceful exhibition, on Tuesday last, by the ignorant and impudent mob who paraded the streets of our town, calls in the most imperative manner upon Mr La Trobe to adopt some stringent measures by which such a lawless display may be prevented in future.

Others went further still. The squatter H.B. Morris not only damned the immigrants, *and* the government for employing them, but went on to condemn the very idea of building a path to Port Melbourne as a proposal solely of interest to those who wanted to be able to return safely after getting drunk at the beach!

As it happened, the immigrants did not strike again. Nor were their wages restored. In that sense, the men were defeated. Yet the fact that the action took place was in itself something of a victory, in a city in which unionism (or 'combination') was illegal. The parade through Melbourne in 1842 became the first in a long line of workers' rallies that developed as the city grew. The Flagstaff Hill – the demonstrators' ultimate object – remains a good place to remember it.

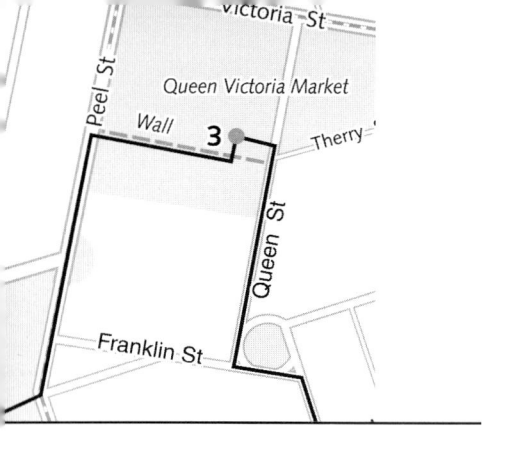

# 3. Old Cemetery

## Victoria Market

As you make your way into the Victoria Market on a Saturday morning, you can't help but tread over the corpses of some nine thousand of early Melbourne's citizenry. Why? Because much of the land occupied by today's market once formed the city's major cemetery – and most of the bodies interred have never been removed.

In Port Phillip's formative years, the few burials in the colony took place in the Flagstaff Gardens. The area proved too small and, in 1838, the city authorities assigned eight acres for use as a cemetery in the area bordered by Queen, Franklin, Peel and the now non-existent Fulton Streets. The administrators neatly divided the space into separate portions for the main religious denominations.

The first burial on the site took place in 1837, when John Smith – a shepherd working in the Geelong district – died after an attack by local Aborigines. When John Batman eventually succumbed to syphilis, his became about the thirtieth interment. Many believed that Batman subsequently haunted the cemetery, using it as a base for ghostly appearances in front of his old enemy, John Pascoe Fawkner. When confronted with the story, however, Fawkner flatly denied any contact with an ectoplasmic Batman. 'Ho! Ho! Take my word Batman would not be such a fool to play me such a trick, even if he could; and if he tried it on with me I would make it warm for the fellow.'

With the growth of the city, the allocated space quickly filled, though burials in family owned plots continued until 1917. The authorities decreed that commerce should take priority over sentiment, and in 1878 gave stallholders the use of the northern part of the cemetery as a market. Forty-five bodies buried on those grounds were exhumed and then reburied in the Carlton cemetery.

In 1920 the market took over the rest of the site. Identifiable graves (around nine hundred) were exhumed, with most of the bodies reinterred in the Pioneers Section of the Fawkner Memorial Park. The graves for which no records existed remained where they were.

In other words, the earth beneath the market is riddled with bodies, a fact that has caused continual headaches for market administrators. In earlier days, authorities simply tried to ignore the problem – a minor scandal erupted in 1930

The northern wall of the cemetery as it appeared after 1878.

The same structure today runs through the Victoria Market from west to east.

when *Truth* magazine discovered that a steam shovel performing extension work had dumped piles of bones in a North Melbourne tip (an event it recorded with the headline: 'Remains of Early Settlers Tossed Callously Aside to Rot in Mud'). More recently, when renovators encountered graves in October 1991, archaeologists advised that the ground remained so crowded that it would be difficult to dig more than one and a half metres without disturbing human remains. To make matters worse, in the cemetery's early days, its boundaries were loosely defined – bodies have been discovered as far away as the deli buildings on Therry Street.

Cemeteries necessarily manifest a certain tendency towards egalitarianism, embracing the poor and despised alongside the (equally dead) great and powerful. In Melbourne, however, the authorities tried to give any such necropolitan democracy as little rein as possible.

So, while the Old Cemetery did accept the bodies of the first men executed in Melbourne, it allowed them only anonymous plots on unconsecrated ground. We know that when the Aboriginal resistance fighters Robert Smallboy and Jack Napoleon Tunermenerwail died on the Russell Street gallows on 20 January 1842, the executioner took their still-warm bodies by cart to the cemetery, where they were interred just outside the fence at the north-eastern corner of the ground. The bushrangers Charles Ellis, Martin Fogarty and Daniel Jepps joined them on 28 June 1842, followed by another Aboriginal man identified only as 'Roger' on 5 September 1842.

What happened to the bodies of the executed men remains unclear. The area became a general burying ground for Aboriginal and Quaker dead. These bodies were later exhumed, although the work was not terribly thorough – in November 1990, building works for a fire hydrant uncovered two Aboriginal graves.

According to Garryowen, popular belief through the 1840s held the condemned graves to be haunted:

> Herein were deposited the remains of the blackfellows, and nothing further was heard of them for more than five months, when they were joined by the white fellows, and shortly after it began to be rumoured that on certain nights of the week (Tuesdays and Fridays) the most unearthly doings were indulged in by the ghosts of the five defunct individuals, who had the outside graveyard to themselves but who, so soon as the night was well in, jumped out of their graves, and plunged into vagaries of a most astounding character, a species of pedestrianism which might be termed a combination of corroboree and hornpipe. The blackfellows in opossum rugs, and the whites in shrouds romped about in wild confusion, kicking and sparring at each other, prancing along by the northern boundary . . .

Most of the 1878 northern cemetery wall still remains – as the brown and cream arched brick wall which runs through the middle of the market. If you stand just to the north of the wall (at the Queen Street end), you are fairly close to where the condemned men must have been laid.

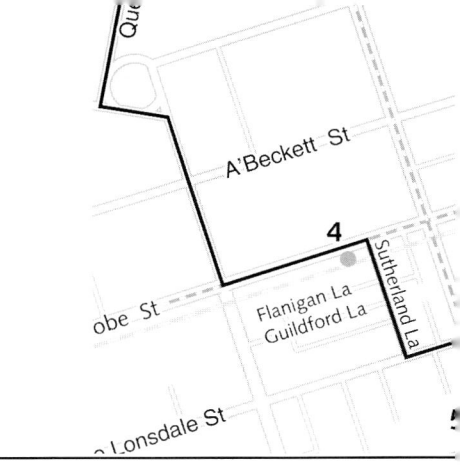

# 4. New Theatre

## 293 Latrobe Street

Even today, Melbourne is not a town that you associate with artistic experimentation. Yet for a brief period in the late 1930s, the tiny loft nestled beside the Duke of Kent provided a space for a remarkable attempt to create an innovative and political theatre.

In 1939, *The Age* announced:

> Tucked away in a city back-water, the New Theatre is unknown to many Melbourne playgoers, but to those who are aware of its existence it provides a centre of intellectual recreation. The New Theatre has a purpose – an aim apart from, and yet closely bound to, the art of the drama. The aim is not the box office, nor is it the manufacture of dramatic drugs. The aim is the restoration for the theatre of its historic right of social criticism.

New Theatre came as the culmination of various attempts, mostly associated with members of the Communist Party, to establish distinctively working class drama in Melbourne. In the early 1930s, the Workers Art Club had performed a number of sketches and one-act plays. Many of its members subsequently joined the Workers Theatre Group, which presented a series of agit-prop scenes at union meetings, factory gates and suburban halls, before making its public debut in Central Hall with a play by the American communist Clifford Odets, *Waiting for Lefty*.

This portrayal of a New York taxi strike did not follow the saccharine conventions to which most Australian theatre goers were accustomed (the final scene culminated with actors leading the audience in chants of 'Strike! Strike!'). But, much to everyone's surprise, the reviews it generated proved overwhelmingly positive.

The Workers Theatre Group (and its Sydney sister organisation) quickly followed with another Odets piece, *Till the Day I Die* – a bleak account of Nazi brutality in contemporary Germany. Unfortunately, the Sydney production came to the attention of the German Consul-General, who promptly complained to Attorney-General Robert Menzies. In response, Menzies pressured the state government to ban the play on the ground that it might be offensive to a friendly power – Nazi Germany!

The Sydney cast received notification of the censor's decision on opening night. One member later recalled:

> . . . at interval time an impassioned speech was made . . . about the undemocratic procedures of the Government and we said, 'Well, never mind. We won't let you down, you've paid your money, so we'll put on another play. It's called *We'll live tomorrow*, or something like that. So up went the curtain and on went the banned play. We knew there were plenty of police in the hall. And we continued, wondering what the police were going to do, until finally the Inspector in charge came backstage and said, 'Right-oh boys! We know this is the banned play. Bring the curtain down!'

In Melbourne, Workers Theatre tried to beat the ban by staging a private performance at the Collingwood Town Hall. When six thousand people assembled, they discovered the doors bolted and locked, and over twenty police on hand to ensure no play took place. *The Argus* reported:

> An amazing scene followed the announcement that the play would not be produced, as a disappointed crowd of several thousands had to be turned away. Efforts to produce the play on a vacant allotment near by were abandoned on the advice of the police . . . The producer Catherine Duncan told the crowd: 'The Collingwood Council, the Government and the censors need not think for one moment that we are going to accept their dictum. We will fight for freedom of expression in Australia even if takes till the day we die.'

A few months later, a sympathetic Brunswick Council allowed a performance in its Town Hall. Nonetheless, the New Theatre – as the group now called itself – recognised the need for its own space.

A solution presented itself in the shape of an old tin-roofed loft above a disused garage next to the Duke of Kent Hotel on Latrobe Street. Supporters financed its renovation by purchasing 'planks' in the stage at two shillings each. Volunteers then worked day and night to transform makeshift materials into a theatre, with a bolt of hessian enabling the production of stage drapes and old wooden benches providing seating for an audience. Though the space had only one toilet, health regulations (and censor-

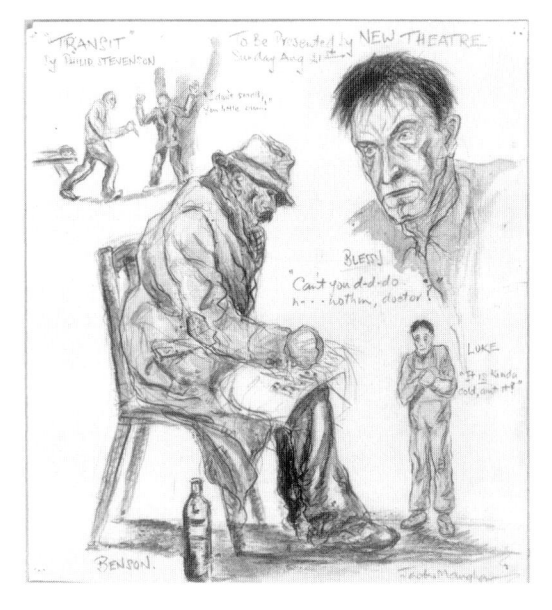

Top: director Jack Maughan's sketches for New Theatre's *Transit*. Above: Eric Reimor in the same production.

ship laws) were circumvented by proclaiming the space a private club, with entry by membership badge. Patrons had to find their way to a rear entrance in the narrow Flanigan Lane – today, if you look closely enough on the stone walls of the lane, you can still see a roughly painted sign pointing the way.

By November 1937, the Communist Party paper *Workers Voice* could declare:

> What seemed a large and extremely unpromising room has been changed into a trim theatre, with dressing room space, spotlights, a proper proscenium and a professional-looking curtain.

Another reviewer commented upon:

> a well equipped stage and seating accommodation for about 140. Excellently drawn murals decorate the tinted walls, and I understand that everything except the tip-up seats is the work of the members.

Over the next months *Till the Day I Die* and *Waiting for Lefty* played on alternate Sunday nights. The Flanigan Lane theatre subsequently staged pieces by Langston Hughes, Katharine Susannah Prichard and Bertolt Brecht (in the first-ever Brecht performance in Melbourne).

Most of those involved in New Theatre were Communist Party members. Many, like Jack Maughan (one of the early New Theatre's leading directors), had played a role in previous attempts to fuse politics and culture (such as the Workers Art Club). Though the CP officially supported the project, many of its leaders tended to regard the New Theatre crowd as suspiciously bohemian. After all, rehearsals at Flanigan Lane often involved passionate (and unauthorised) debates about politics and dramatic theory. As one member recalled:

> We were regular students of the International Theatre Magazine. We ran a Wall Newspaper on such themes as propaganda and Art, Gorky plays and social realist theatre and similar subjects such as Stanislavsky's 'Method Acting'.

Early in 1939, authorities declared the Flanigan Lane theatre unsafe and closed it down, in an action almost certainly motivated by political imperatives (the Communist Party itself would be declared illegal in the next year). New Theatre moved elsewhere, continuing into the 1990s as one of the longest running theatre groups in the country.

What were the Flanigan Lane performances like? Opinions

Top: the still-visible sign directing patrons to the theatre (corner of Guilford and Sutherland Lanes). Above: the Duke of Kent Hotel (the New Theatre was in what is now the hotel's beer garden).

varied. *Workers Voice* declared the theatre's opening night to be 'more than satisfying'. The right-wing *Argus* commended New Theatre's *Transit* (directed by Jack Maughan), while Geoffrey Hutton of *The Age* described New Theatre as 'hard to find but worth finding'.

On the other hand, the writer Vance Palmer (generally not unsympathetic to the left) commented in February 1938:

> The players at the New Theatre, for instance, are so raw; have seen so few decent productions; and are inclined to think that any hit-or-miss performance is good enough. I saw them the other Sunday evening in two original plays, both very short things and worth doing decently, but the evening was not enlightening. There is plenty of potential talent, but that is all that can be said.

Palmer's comments highlight the novelty of Flanigan Lane – a theatre performing shows not only *about* working people but, in many cases, *by* them. The players *were* raw. Often they were unemployed, exchanging their threadbare rags for stage costumes. Leila Maughan, one of the stalwarts of New Theatre, remembers bringing in a billy tin of soup each week to enable hungry cast members to manage through rehearsals.

The achievement of New Theatre, then, lay not simply in what the shows meant to the audience but also in what they meant to the performers. Years later, Ethel White summarised her experience with Sydney New Theatre:

> They put on a play called, *Till the Day I Die*, by Clifford Odets. It was about the rise of Nazism. Nobody knew much about what went on in Europe in those days. It was all so far away and you didn't read about it in the papers, either. New Theatre opened a whole new world to me.

Flanigan Lane still stands, the tiny space now incorporated as a beer garden in the Duke of Kent Hotel. If you ever have a drink there, look around and remember the theatre that opened up a new world for people in the 1930s.

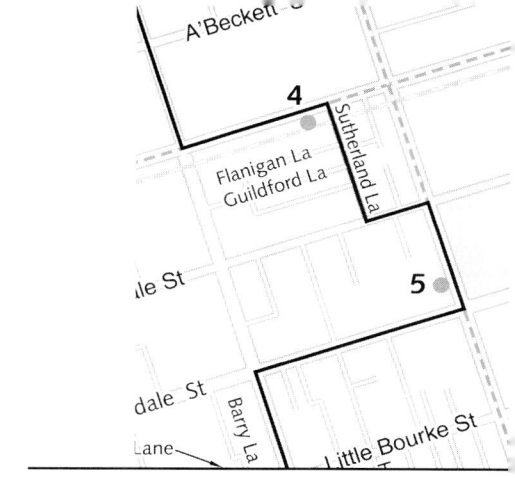

# 5. Socialist Hall

## 283 Elizabeth Street

In June 1906 a choir of twenty women performing labour songs led a crowd of unemployed to the Exhibition Building, where the Victorian Parliament had temporarily relocated. As the Governor's carriage entered for the opening ceremony, the assembly greeted him with a loud 'hoot' (an expression of noisy disapproval which seems to have disappeared from the repertoire of today's left). Later, when the official party tried to leave, the demonstrators were waiting.

*The Argus* reported that as the Governor appeared:

> Mutterings recommenced in the crowd, which by this time had increased to about 300 persons, and Sub-Inspector Davidson remarked, 'The first man who hoots will be arrested.' The moment the Sub-Inspector turned his head towards the Governor, a young man with a collar fully 3 inches high, a fringe of similar dimensions and a boxer hat on the back of his head, removed a cigarette from his mouth and cried, 'A good hoot for plutocracy.' Over 100 persons responded.

The subsequent detention of a demonstrator served only to inflame the crowd.

> 'Who have they arrested?' demanded Mrs Kirk, one of the Socialist Party's choir.
> '"Comrade" Pitt,' replied somebody, disconsolately.
> 'Comrade Pitt,' cried Mrs Kirk, her eyes shining like those of another Demoiselle Theroigne. 'Liberty! Liberty or death!'
> 'Liberty or death,' echoed the other members of the party.
> 'Liberty or death,' repeated a lady with a blue sash, unrolling a homemade banner bearing the words.

Thus emboldened, Mrs Kirk and the other women led the unemployed in a 'more or less military formation' through the city to Elizabeth Street, before halting opposite St Francis' Church. Here was the headquarters of the Victorian Socialist Party, the organisation leading unemployed agitation in the state. In the Socialist Hall, the marchers held an impromptu meeting to discuss bail for

Comrade Pitt, food for the unemployed and sundry other matters, before rising to sing the 'Marseillaise', with 'an old white bearded man of about 80 years of age leading the chorus in the front row'.

The Victorian Socialist Party had been formed in 1906 by the British labour leader Tom Mann, after his Social Questions Committee had uncovered the frightening extent of poverty in Melbourne. The VSP's paper, *The Socialist*, summarised the dire situation (and its view of its cause) in a verse entitled 'The Bootmaker's Son':

> *Hi, Sonny. Why have you got no boots on?*
> *Because I have not got any.*
> *Why have you not got any?*
> *Because we have no money to buy them.*
> *Why have you got no money?*
> *Because father is out of work.*
> *Why is your father out of work?*
> *Because there are too many boots.*

With Mann already one of the best known radical leaders in the country, the organisation grew in spectacular fashion. Within twelve months, the VSP boasted its own newspaper, a membership of two thousand, Sunday night mass meetings involving up to a thousand, and sixteen regular outdoor stumps each week.

The prominent role played by the Socialist Party choir in the Parliament protest exemplified the importance the VSP attached to art, culture and recreation. The considerable vocal talents of Elsie Mann – Tom's partner – proved a drawcard at early meetings (as she once put it: 'I sing them in and Tom talks them out'), and the VSP quickly formed an orchestra, choir and brass band. More fundamentally, though, the VSP aimed – as Mann later wrote – to fulfil 'the requirements of its members in every phase of life's activities'. So it operated a Socialist Co-operative bakery where socialists purchased their bread, and a shoe shop where they bought their boots. It offered working people classes at Socialist Hall in public speaking, economics, history, English and Esperanto, alongside weekly discussions of religion, philosophy, performing and creative arts, natural and physical sciences, animal husbandry, language, literature, history and current affairs. It organised its members into a dramatic club, a gym and a library, and took them to dances, May Day celebrations, nature excursions and picnics – leaving those too ill to participate to be consoled by the 'sick comrades' committee'.

The VSP also tried to promote physical fitness through athletics, football and cricket clubs. As an activist pointed out: 'If we turn out a slouching, weedy, undersized and underdeveloped race, we might as well forget any attempt at propaganda.' The Ruskin football club, in particular, aimed to 'help the Party shed some of its scrawny character by becoming a bit more manly'. In its pursuit of manliness, the team managed to lose every fixture in its first season, an achievement which left its spirits remarkably undampened. Indeed, after one match where the comrades received a seventeen-goal drubbing, *The Socialist* responded with a neat display of dialectics: 'To the superficial, this may seem disastrous and cause for depression but for those in the ranks the way Ruskins finished in the last quarter, when only one goal was kicked against them, was a revelation.'

The children of members attended the Socialist Sunday School in the Elizabeth Street hall, to learn ethics, callisthenics and the Ten Commandments of socialism (number one – 'love your school-fellows who will be your fellow-workmen in life'). By September 1906, these classes had proved so popular that a Young Comrades Contingent of the Socialist Army was formed to cater for children up to the age of 16. Headed by a superintendent known as 'Uncle Remus' (who, on picnic days, would don a comical tropical hat and long whiskers), the Young Comrades affirmed a pledge that ran: 'I am very sorry that there is so much suffering through poverty. I believe socialism will cure this evil and make it possible for all to be happy.'

At its height, the VSP even encouraged its members to baptise their children within the Party. During the Sunday meetings, parents brought their infants to the lectern and were asked: 'Is it your desire that your child shall be dedicated to the socialist cause?' Upon responding, 'That is our desire,' they received an inscribed red ribbon. Though *The Argus* described the ceremonies as 'burlesquing the holiest and most significant formulary in Christian life', in truth the socialist baptisms simply aimed to provide a secular alternative to rituals that played an important role in ordinary people's lives.

After all, for all the sports and social activities, the Socialist Party existed first and foremost as a political organisation. To this end, its major asset remained the towering presence of Tom Mann, a self-educated theorist capable of delivering lectures almost every Wednesday night on a startling variety of topics. He ranged freely from the development of prehistoric man to the nature of the solar system, usually concluding his oration by pulling 'a big red handkerchief from his fob pocket and shouting "three cheers for the social revolution".'

In October 1906, the Prahran council presented the VSP with a golden opportunity to put its rhetoric into practice when it barred socialist orators from speaking on public streets. Initially, the party met the challenge head on. On 6 October,

Top: the VSP's Co-operative Store. The Socialist Hall is just visible to the right of the frame. Above: the Hall today. The meeting room is now a display area for tents.

A VSP postcard celebrating the Prahran Free Speech Fight. Lizzie Ahern sits on the left with Tom Mann behind her.

Joe Swebleses, a 24-year-old cigarette maker from Abbotsford, politely replied to the policeman who asked him to move along: 'You have your duty to do, and I have mine'. He received a two-week gaol sentence.

As in most aspects of the VSP's work, women played a leading role in the Prahran fight. In the month following Swebleses' conviction, numerous VSP women – including the noted orator Lizzie Ahern, who later gave her occupation to the wedding registry as 'socialist agitator' – joined the male socialists in accepting prison sentences varying from three days to five weeks.

The VSP responded with a massive propaganda campaign, producing five thousand postcards displaying photographs of the imprisoned socialists, and then inviting the public to the Town Hall to watch 'the sensational Socialist march when 20 socialists will parade in gaol costume.' Though the publicity swelled the VSP's numbers, the council remained intransigent, and by December 1906 the party had decided to hold street meetings elsewhere.

Indeed, it became increasingly clear that a gulf remained between the party's often radical pronouncements and its official orientation towards Labor Party reform (as the VSP Executive put it, 'getting the Labor movement on to the straight-out openly-avowed socialist track'). Inevitably, tensions developed between those who wanted to moderate their demands so as to influence friendly ALP members, and those who wanted the VSP to break entirely with Labor.

Tom Mann returned to England in 1909. By the time of his departure, the organisation had already moved into decline, a process only accelerated by his absence. Under a new leadership, the party lurched substantially to the right. Its subsequent fortunes only changed during the mass campaign against conscription during the First World War – at which point it shifted out of the Elizabeth Street hall to a building in Exhibition Street.

A large number of the VSP's cadre found their way to other organisations. But many never forgot the early years of the Socialist Party. Years later, one member wistfully recalled:

> The street corner meetings, the riverside and bay picnics, the sing-songs around the camp fires, the Yarra Bank gatherings (south side then), the May Day processions, the Prahran Free Speech fight . . . the sheer thrill of the fight for liberty when life was young and blood was red and hopes were sanguine. All were young, most in years, all in spirit. All were in love with life and the zest of battle. All were students, some very poor in the material things, devoting to the books of Marx and Engels and Kropotkin and Jack London and Upton Sinclair hours of reading that were robbed from sleep.

# 6. Orange Riots

## St John's Lane

> Tuesday 14th July, 1846, was about the most disquieting day ever passed in Melbourne. The morning appeared muffled-up like an invalid in flannel, with a dense fog, and this atmospherical condition was fitly companioned by the angry gloom that pervaded the numbers thronging the streets from an early hour.

Thus did Garryowen describe Melbourne in the midst of the Orange riots of 1846.

The early emergence of the Protestant Loyalist society known as the Orange Lodge involved more than the old enmity between Catholics struggling for freedom in the south of Ireland and the Protestants loyal to the British empire in the north. In Melbourne, the ancient struggle between the proto-fascist Orange Order and the Nationalist Green often served as a screen behind which new and local interests contended.

The first election of Port Phillip representatives to the New South Wales Legislative Council in 1843 saw a contest between the Protestant Henry Condell and Edward 'Circular Head' Curr (the nickname came not from the shape of his cranium, but the region in Van Diemen's Land from which he originated). The victory of Curr, a Catholic, had been widely predicted and so when Condell emerged victorious on polling day, with 295 votes to his opponent's 261, the result caused a sensation. A crowd of perhaps two hundred Catholics (many of whom had been excluded by the restrictive franchise) gathered, and menaced two prominent Protestants in Elizabeth Street, before being dispersed by the police.

The fracas provided the pretext for the formation in late 1843 of a local Orange association by wealthy Protestants, including William Kerr, the editor of *The Port Phillip Patriot*. Unsurprisingly, Kerr's *Patriot* did its utmost to inflame sectarian tensions in the colony, especially after the emergence of George Cavenagh's pro-Catholic *Herald* challenged the circulation of both *The Patriot* and *The Gazette*. As Garryowen put it, the three newspapers were 'soon up to the ears in the muck, pounding and pelting and abusing each other mercilessly.'

In 1845, the Orange Lodge announced its intention to march in celebration of

> # THE GREATEST SPORT
> ### UNDER THE SUN!!
> THE grandest HURLING MATCH ever witnessed, even in "Old Ireland," will come off on Saturday next, at twelve o'clock, on
> ### BATMAN'S HILL,
> between all the MUNSTER men in the province. The TIPPERARY, CLARE, and LIMERICK boys on one side, and the sons of WATERFORD, CORK, and KERRY, on the other.
> 
> All strapping young fellows are particularly requested to attend, and to be sure and bring good *shillelaghs*, *hurlies*, &c., &c., with them.
> 
> ☞ Mononia expects every man to be early in the field.

The Catholic response to the proposed Orange march in 1845.

the anniversary of the Battle of the Boyne, a famous slaughter of Catholics by Protestants. In the face of this obvious provocation, Superintendent La Trobe swore in a force of a hundred special constables. The local Catholic community took its own precautions – advertising a hurling match, and using the game as a pretext for hundreds of southern Irish with home-made clubs to congregate on Batman's Hill (today's Spencer Street Station).

Not surprisingly, the Orangemen chose not to parade and the anniversary passed without incident. *The Patriot* went so far as to deny there had ever been any intent of marching, claiming that whole issue had been a beat-up by Cavenagh in his newspaper:

> Frequently as our witless contemporary *The Herald* has, from the sheer gullibility of its conductor [Cavenagh], been made the laughing stock of the whole community, never before Friday last, the anniversary of the Battle of the Boyne, was the outrageous silliness of the man, so prominently brought before the public.

Yet events the next year vindicated Cavenagh, when the expected clash did in fact take place.

In 1846, the Boyne anniversary fell on a Sunday. The Orange Lodge chose to mark the following Monday with a banquet in the Pastoral Hotel on the corner of Queen and Little Bourke Streets. In a calculated insult to Catholics, it hung banners celebrating the Boyne massacre from the tavern windows.

By about 4.00 p.m., the angry crowd outside stretched along Queen Street from Bourke to Lonsdale Streets. The Orangemen in the pub and the four hundred people on the street brandished firearms and other weapons. In a last ditch attempt to avoid violence, the mayor pleaded with the licensee to remove the banners.

The Lodge members refused the mayor's overtures and (according to *The Herald*):

> a volley of shots was fired from the windows upon the assemblage in the street, one of which was apparently aimed at the Rev. Mr Geoghegan... and it fortunately erred, but still unfortunately struck Mr David Hurley, Grocer, Bourke-street, in the shoulder. Another man named Jeremiah Donohue... received a ball in the thigh.

The arrival of the military – who stormed the hotel with bayonets fixed – ended the battle. The southern Irish celebrated the removal of the Protestants to the watch house, as special constables were again sworn in. For the rest of the night, police and soldiers patrolled the town.

The next morning, the Orangemen faced the magistrate in the weatherboard police office at the corner of Collins and William Streets. Their supporters from the Orange Lodge gathered at the Bird-in-Hand Hotel in Flinders Lane and muttered of plans for a rescue. Again, the mounted police were called. After the reading of the Riot Act, the Bird-in-Hand was closed – along with all the shops and hotels in the city.

Meanwhile, several hundred southern Irish gathered on the grassy, open spot that extended between Lonsdale Street and the Flagstaff Gardens, brandishing an irregular arsenal of guns, clubs and knives. Superintendent La Trobe once more produced the Riot Act; the men dispersed without arrest.

For the rest of that day, the military bivouacked in the Royal Exchange Hotel in Collins Street, making occasional sorties out to patrol the surrounding streets. All through the evening, residents of outlying suburbs were still assembling near the Russell Street prison (today's 'Old Melbourne Gaol').

Garryowen recalled:

St John's Lane today.

> Tales of blood were circulated in all directions, each moment increasing in exaggeration. The peacefulness of the localities were [sic], therefore, disorganised; arms were taken up, but upon reaching within a mile of the town and hearing that all was safe, they had the good sense to return to their respective pursuits.

Though about sixty members of the Orange Lodge remained sufficiently unabashed to hold another dinner the next day, the sectarian tensions gradually subsided. La Trobe leant on the Crown Solicitor not to prosecute the arrested Orangemen, and at the same time urgently demanded more men and greater weapons from his superiors. That year, the Governor passed the Party Processions Act, making it illegal to conduct meetings with offensive weapons or banners. A variant of the Act remains in force today.

The Pastoral Hotel is long gone, and the Bird-in-Hand didn't survive redevelopment. So what trace remains today of the episode?

In the 1840s, the entire block on the south-east corner belonged to one John Smith, who constructed Melbourne's first permanent theatre there. To offset the building costs of the Queen's Theatre, he opened a hotel, St John's Tavern, on the northernmost portion.

During the Orangemen's celebration in 1846, a certain Thomas O'Brien was sitting in the bar, enjoying a beer. Let us allow Garryowen to conclude the story:

> Mrs Smith, the landlady, fancied she saw the barrels of guns thrust from one of the Pastoral windows opposite, and calling on a waitress to do likewise, she threw herself flat on the floor outside the bar counter. They had hardly done so when a bullet whistled through the window, passed over the prostrate women, and entering O'Brien's jaw dislodged four of his teeth, ran up his tongue and stuck near the root. The man was removed in excruciating agony to his home in Little Flinders Street, and he was so bad next day that his dying deposition was taken. Life and he had no intention of so speedily dissolving partnership, for he rallied considerably. Meanwhile the bullet formed an abscess, which burst on the tenth day, when the ball was extracted; but instead of rolling out of his mouth it passed the other way, and he swallowed it. It remained in his system for a year, and in July, 1847, Dr D.J. Thomas succeeded in ridding him of so unwelcome a lodger.

Today, there's a single hotel, the Wig's Cellar, on the west-side corner of the intersection and north of where Mrs Smith's tavern once stood. The pub itself is more recent than our story. But behind it run two dark, evil-smelling lanes. The second of the two is unmarked by any signage. On the map it stands forth as St John's Lane – a permanent reminder of the pub where sectarianism cost Mr O'Brien four of his teeth.

# 7. Wharfies Riot

## 400 Flinders Street

The pleasantly unadorned Victorian structure on the corner of Flinders and William Streets is one of Melbourne's oldest buildings. Nearby, the Yarra forms a natural pool known as the Turning Basin – the highest point that ships can reach in the river. In 1840, Melbourne's authorities constructed a bluestone Customs House on the site. Until the imposition of income tax in 1915, customs duties provided 80 per cent of government revenue. As the colony grew, so did the Customs House – renovated in 1855 and substantially rebuilt in the 1870s.

As well as collecting customs, the premises provided a useful centre for sundry administrative tasks. Thus, when it came time to register scabs for work on the waterfront in 1928, the Customs House (a short distance from the Yarra berths) seemed the logical choice. As a result, the building became the epicentre for one of Melbourne's most ferocious riots.

In June 1928, the Commonwealth Court of Conciliation and Arbitration imposed a harsh new set of work rules, wages and conditions on Australia's waterfront. When, in response, the wharfies walked off the job, Prime Minister Bruce (himself a shipowner) responded with the Transport Workers Act. Christened the 'Dog Collar Act', Bruce's legislation forced wharfies to register (for a shilling – the price of a dog licence) for work. The licence could be rescinded (rendering its owner unemployable) if foremen's orders were disobeyed, even if those orders breached safety or award conditions. Worse still, in an overt invitation to discriminate against unionists, the cards were coloured – brown for 'volunteers', pink for union men.

On 1 October, the first so-called 'free labourers' were supposed to sign up at the Customs House. When they arrived at nine that morning, a thousand or so stevedores, coal lumpers and wharf labourers lay in waiting.

The unionists surrounded the building on all sides. At first, they simply jeered at those signing on to take their jobs. New words fitted themselves to an old hymn and the men roared out:

> *The Lord above, send down a dove,*
> *With wings as sharp as razors*
> *To slit the throats of bloody scabs*
> *Who cut down poor men's wages.*

Above: the Customs House today, lending dignity to the view from the Casino. Opposite: the battle outside the Customs House.

But by about ten o'clock it became clear that the 'volunteers' would not be dissuaded, and the mood grew uglier. Some unionists pelted the newly licensed men with rotten oranges from the nearby Western Market. Others armed themselves with billets of wood, coal shovels and hammers, and set about the scabs. *The Argus* reported:

> the first serious incident occurred when a man who left the Customs House by the William Street door after he had received his licence was pursued by a mob of hooting strikers. He sought refuge on the lorry of a carriage contractor which was travelling towards Flinders Street and the vehicle was immediately besieged by strikers, one of whom jumped on to the lorry and, selecting a large shovel lying inside, attempted to batter the head of the volunteer with it.

A police baton charge rescued the scab, but from then, the clashes developed into a fully-fledged riot.

For the most part, the numbers of police – and their willingness to use their batons – protected the volunteers from serious injuries. Still, fights raged across the city. A volunteer lost two teeth on the corner of Latrobe and Swanston Streets. Unionists caught up with one scab outside the Public Library, while another was knocked unconscious in Abbotsford Street, North Melbourne.

The wharfies had good reason for their anger. Working on the waterfront was – and remains – a difficult, dangerous business. A medical examination of wharfies in the 1940s (more than a decade after the strike) showed that one quarter of the workforce suffered from duodenal ulcers, and that many had inoperable hernias. These injuries were exacerbated by lax safety regulations and excessive hours – the new award allowed foremen to work teams for double-header shifts of twenty-four hours or more.

Unionists knew that without solidarity, they had no chance of alleviating their conditions. Simply put, scabbing meant a betrayal of the common interest for personal gain. Many years later, the veteran wharfie Tom Hills recalled:

> I wouldn't know of a scab that lived in Port Melbourne. It was like coming into the lion's den. It didn't matter if you was a wharfie or not. We never spoke to scabs. They weren't allowed to drink at the waterfront. No scab would dare go into one of those pubs . . . That's how bitter the struggle was. Wherever we met scabs they would be attacked.

The riot continued until early evening. Equally violent clashes flared over the next few days, as the registration of volunteers continued apace. Street militancy, however, was never going to be enough to win the dispute. The union leadership lacked the kind of resolve necessary for an extended industrial campaign capable of forcing the employers to back off.

By mid-October, the union leaders had surrendered. The men were ordered back to work. The unionists marched in disciplined ranks back into the Customs House on 19 October to apply for their licences.

There was, however, a sequel – and it proved even bloodier.

On 1 November, the special train commissioned to transport volunteers from Flinders Street to the wharves failed to arrive, and non-unionists were forced to travel alongside the unionists whose jobs they'd tried to take. Not surprisingly, fighting broke out during the journey. At Port Melbourne, a volunteer was thrown into the bay.

The following day, mounted police stood outside the entrance to Princes Pier and the employers refused access to any union members. The union men tried to clamber aboard the ships upon which the scabs were working. The police responded with baton charges. Then – without warning – they opened fire.

Four men were wounded. One, Alan Whitaker, later died of his injuries.

Nonetheless, the employers and their mouthpieces remained unrepentant. *The Argus* declared that 'the police concerned are worthy of the highest praise for their steadiness and courage in a critical situation'. *The Age* added: 'Those who demanded [firm action] should see that they do not suddenly become feminine and squeamish about it.'

These days, the Customs House holds the Immigration and Hellenic Antiquities Museums. The building has been beautifully restored, its opulence a testament to the importance of trade in early Melbourne. It seems as fitting a place as any to remember the struggles of the men upon whose labour the prosperity of the city so much depended.

# 8. Gaol and Stocks

## 455 Collins Street

Melbourne's first hospital once stood on the corner of Collins and William Streets. Here, in a dilapidated weatherboard building, the first surgical procedure in the new colony took place in 1838. The convict William Bone endured a penis amputation – without anaesthetic, of course – to cure his venereal disease.

Today, the spot – the windswept forecourt of the AXA building – is marked with a large statue of John Batman. Now we know that Batman – an individual often recognised as the founder of Melbourne – also suffered from VD. And while history does not chronicle the state of his penis, it does record that in 1834 Batman lost part of his nose to degenerative syphilis. One might be tempted, therefore, to conclude that this particular locale was chosen for a Batman statue to retrospectively immortalise the city pioneer's solidarity with the suffering undergone by the unfortunate William Bone – were it not for the fact that in the course of his career Batman showed no evidence of any particular empathy for the pain of others.

After all, prior to the expedition to Port Phillip, Batman's main notoriety stemmed from the leading role he played in the 'Black Wars', the campaign of extermination waged against the Aborigines of Tasmania. He embarked upon his pioneering expedition in 1835 motivated by nothing more noble than the desire for personal enrichment. The trip remained totally illegal, financed by private businessmen without the auspices of the colonial authorities, and the 'treaty' Batman claimed to have signed with local Aborigines was regarded by many even at the time as transparent cover for a gigantic land grab.

Batman, however, was not alone in the avarice with which he eyed Port Phillip. In 1835, John Pascoe Fawkner led another expedition into Victoria. The two parties almost immediately came into conflict, a struggle not fully resolved until the colonial authorities took control in 1836.

The enmity between Batman and Fawkner is well documented. Fawkner, for instance, described his rival as 'devoid of Intelligence, a mere bore who goes about with a short pipe in his mouth and always drunk when he can get the liquor and is very brutish in his address at those times – when sober he is a Specious Hypocrite'. The fact that a statue of Fawkner is displayed in the court-

*Police Court Melbourne 1841. Sailors sitting in stocks*

yard alongside the man he so despised is even more curious. What is there about this particular locale that unites early Melbourne's two bitter enemies?

In the 1830s, the forecourt formed half of the Western Market – the closest thing the new colony had to a city square. The official rationale for the statues stems from Melbourne's first land sale taking place near the spot in June 1837. But of equal significance is the fact that, as well as the hospital building, the land on which our city fathers are now commemorated once housed the city gaol.

This, in its own way, makes a kind of sense. As leading representatives of the Port Phillip colony, both Batman and Fawkner had an intense interest in establishing law and order. After all, in the 1830s, the indigenous inhabitants had not yet been fully dispossessed. The construction of a gaol house played an important role in bringing the full majesty of the law to bear on those Aborigines who refused to integrate into a modern capitalist economy. So, for instance, in the year 1840, eleven of the twenty-six people recorded as being in custody were Aborigines – the beginning of an extraordinary rate of indigenous incarceration that continues to the present day.

Furthermore, the colony needed prisons to discipline its convict workforce. Though the settlers of Port Phillip liked to think of themselves as free from 'the convict stain' which tainted other settlements, early Melbourne depended heavily on imported convict labour. By 1837, almost 130 convicts laboured clearing the scrub, cutting Melbourne's streets and erecting most of the settlement's early buildings. Not surprisingly, ensuring the docility of the convict workforce weighed heavily upon the early administrators – during the 1830s, floggings took place at least weekly.

Thirdly, and perhaps most importantly, the Melbourne gaol played the same role in the new colony as gaols played in the old world – keeping the masses in line. The 'free' population of Port Phillip remained tightly regulated. Working conditions depended on individual agreements between employers and employees, under the Masters and Servants Act. Working people could be gaoled for unsatisfactory conduct, 'absconscion' or a score of other offences.

The gaol on the Market Square was built in August 1839. Contemporary descriptions give it as a brick building, containing four apartments; two 20 feet long, 15 feet wide; one room 12 feet by 10; and one 12 feet by 13. Its original specifications list the structure as capable of holding sixty prisoners. By 1843, the number incarcerated had increased to ninety. One former inmate described it as 'a miserable hole' with 'a disgusting atmosphere' and 'filled with vermin of all descriptions'. He added: 'The most disgusting part is that there is not the convenience of a water closet on the whole premises.' But what the gaol lacked in toilets, it made up for with other, more important, pieces of equipment. For instance, Market Square boasted a set of stocks, set in front of the gaolhouse. The device – mostly used to punish drunkenness and other misdemeanours – was similar to the classic pillory of antiquity, except that it pinned the legs rather than the arms.

Garryowen noted:

> There was no guard to object to the passers-by having a yarn with the unfortunates, so that it often came to pass that their pals and other sympathisers would have a confab with the fellows in trouble and give them figs of tobacco, as modern philanthropists treat the monkeys to nuts at the Acclimatization Society's Gardens.

Allowance, of course, was made for the fairer sex:

> Three or four times an outrageous harridan of an abandoned woman was 'stocked', the concession being made in her favour that only one of her feet was shackled, and she could kick away as she liked with the other.

The use of the pillory was reserved for those of a certain class. Batman, who

*A supposed likeness of Fawkner, with Batman in the background.*

regularly remained drunk for days on end, never found his way there. But, when in August 1841, Timothy Clever pleaded guilty to a second offence of drunkenness, *The Port Phillip Herald* reported with a sneer:

> Having overdrawn his bank account, he was obliged to take a seat in the stocks for four hours.

In 1842, further refinements came to the gaol. The prison authorities noted with dismay that inclement weather made it impossible for prisoners sentenced to hard labour to work outside every day of their sentence. So the colony decided to outlay the not insubstantial sum of £280 to purchase a treadmill, a machine enabling the wardens to force sixteen prisoners at a time to march indoors without possibility of cessation. Garryowen noted with glee:

> If [the prisoner] let go his hold of the cross-bar only for an instant, he would be precipitated head foremost on to the mill, and a fractured skull or a broken limb or worse, would be the consequence. When once up, until the grinding stopped, there was no choice left but to stick on and dance away merrily or otherwise, pleased or displeased, until the signal to halt was given.

Unfortunately, when the manufacturers of this ingenious device installed it in the Collins Street gaol, they found the machine difficult to keep in working order:

> After a few weeks' working the concern broke down with a grand smash, under the prancing pedestrianism of ten lubberly scamps, and to the unmitigated delight of all the rascaldom in the Country.

With the construction of the large new prison in Russell Street (today's 'Old Melbourne Gaol'), the treadmill followed the inmates to their new home. The market gaol, like the hospital, has long since vanished from the landscape.

Today, the 1960s skyscraper looms above the forecourt. The plaques erected in 1979 alongside the Batman and Fawkner statues (both sculpted along heroic lines) give a carefully sanitised (not to say downright dishonest) account of the two pioneers. A third inscription proclaims, with astonishing insensitivity to Koories: 'This is your heritage'. In the authentic tone of Anglo-Australian chauvinism, the plaque continues: 'Preserve it and pay homage now'. It may as well add: 'Or else we'll throw you in the stocks'.

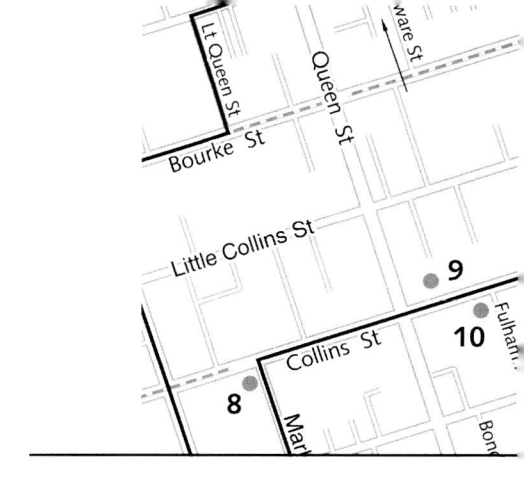

# 9. Stock Exchange

## 380 Collins Street

This ornate Gothic building is today part of the ANZ Banking Museum. But from 1891 to 1924, it housed the Stock Exchange, the nerve centre of Melbourne's business world.

The official history of the Exchange provides a detailed account of the doings of the various captains of finance who graced its floor. But it remains curiously silent about an extraordinary meeting that took place in 1908 when the representatives of big business confronted the spokesmen of international socialism.

In October that year, international events placed unemployment unexpectedly high on the political agenda. Agitation by the jobless of London had been widely reported in the Melbourne press, alongside the suspension from Westminster of the socialist parliamentarian Victor Grayson for lending support to the unemployed cause. Then, as now, Melbourne radicals drew succour from the struggles of their fellows overseas. The time seemed right for action to once more highlight the festering local unemployment problem.

Unfortunately, the Victorian Socialist Party's Tom Mann – who several years earlier had generated widespread publicity with a series of provocative unemployment marches – had recently moved to Broken Hill, leaving the VSP in the hands of the much younger (and considerably less well known) Percy Laidler.

Laidler had joined the VSP only two years earlier, after leaving a politically conservative rural background (his earliest enthusiasm had been for physical culture rather than politics, with the result that his small frame had been perfectly developed) to work in Carlton as a clerk. A simultaneous exposure to inner-city poverty and the oratory of Tom Mann transformed him into an ardent believer in the socialist cause. Within a year, he had become a regular VSP speaker; within two years, acting secretary of the party. Despite not having turned 24 (and looking much younger), Laidler's response to the opportunity created by the Grayson incident proved both prompt and decisive. He embarked upon a week of agitation for the right to work.

On Tuesday, 20 October, Laidler prevailed upon the left-wing MP George Prendergast to facilitate a meeting between Premier Tommy Bent and a deputation of the unemployed. He explained to Bent that the men were sober and

"I'LL BUY."

'Where the poor are never seen.' Outside the Stock Exchange at the turn of the century.

industrious, and had appealed through all the proper channels to the churches, the Labor leaders and the Prime Minister. But while 'they had been accorded plenty of sympathy, they had not been found any work'.

Bent pledged to supply work for some, but not all, of the men in difficulties. This was not good enough. Laidler resolved to take the case to Federal Parliament, sitting (in those pre-Canberra days) in Spring Street. He had been promised entry but the clerk, dismayed at the arrival of several hundred unemployed, closed the door to bar the men from the visitors' gallery. After a brief scuffle, Laidler retreated to the vestibule, where he conducted what *The Age* described as 'practically a public meeting within Parliament House':

> Mr Laidlaw (sic) . . . obviously in a state of mental excitement, set out the case for his friends. 'I know,' he said, 'of a man who is out of work in Carlton. He has a wife and three children, and his wife is expecting another. He cannot get work, and has not got enough money to pay 3/- rent, or get food for his little ones. Are you members in that condition, I ask? What can we think of you here when you let this sort of thing be unremedied. No wonder we attack you members! Who can be surprised when I say that if we were sensible men we would blow the damned place up. (Cheers, and hear, hear.) We will make you members sit up. You are a loafing lot of fellows, you members here today . . . We warn you that you will have to provide work for the unemployed (Frantic cheers). We will haunt you until you do find us work.'

Laidler, like many others in the VSP, had originally maintained hope that the ALP might be convinced to adopt more openly socialist policies. By this time, however, his illusions had been well and truly shattered. And, as the police escorted him from the building, he turned his attentions to the watching Labor members:

> We have made our attack, and we will leave the politicians to themselves. Leave the Labor party asleep on their benches. They will do no good for the unemployed. Good bye, you parasites of modern society.

The immediate response to the action was an increase in parliamentary security. Nonetheless, as *The Socialist* commented, 'the astounding fact remains that for more than an hour the Commonwealth Parliament was "stuck up" by a mob of their masters asking for – work.'

Over the next days, Laidler made good his promise to haunt respectable Melbourne. That Thursday, the unemployed met in Treasury Gardens. After some discussion, the crowd agreed that, Parliament having failed them, they would turn their attention to the real power in capitalist society – big business. Accordingly, a hundred or so of the jobless marched down towards the top end of town.

'Great sensation was caused in Collins Street,' wrote *The Socialist*, 'where the poor are never seen.'

But if the poor were never seen in Collins Street, they were never even *contemplated* within the Stock Exchange – at that time one of the grandest buildings in the city. Indeed, the rules of the Exchange permitted the public to enter its premises only insofar as they were 'respectable men and properly introduced'. The agitators with Laidler were neither. Nonetheless, they 'swarmed into the hall of the Exchange and settled down to stop till they got an answer.'

The effect of the appearance of a hundred impoverished workers proved everything that might have been anticipated:

> Great was the scurrying to and fro, but here, as elsewhere we were treated with the utmost politeness. The man in uniform at the doors appeared, and said we could send up four as a deputation to the chairman.

The dialogue that ensued between the chairman of the Exchange and the professional socialists of the VSP bordered on the surreal. Frank Hyett, a leading VSPer, put the case for a:

> man out of work whose furniture is to be seized under warrant of distress on Tuesday. If we can't get assistance in other ways we will defend that furniture by force. We are not going to let it go out of the house ... The assistance of the leading men in the financial world would have meant a lot of influence to us.

Mr Gilchrist, the chairman of the Exchange, countered by explaining that:

> at the present time many of our own members are unemployed, and others are experiencing anything but a profitable time. We don't think it part of our duty to dictate to the Government what they should do.

As if to underline the gulf between Hyett's jobless man about to lose his furniture and the Exchange members experiencing less than a 'profitable time', Gilchrist's associate Mr Boulter introduced a bizarre anecdote illustrative of his personal difficulties:

> I had a job for a man to do at Camberwell. It was to clear away a lot of rubbish and mend a fence and so on. I knew a carpenter, who had nothing to

The Stock Exchange, overshadowed by the massive modern buildings now surrounding it.

do, so I gave him the work. He said, 'That place at the back should have a coat of paint.' I said, 'All right, you can do it.' 'But I am not a painter,' he replied. 'You will get a painter to do that.'

Boulter left dangling the implication that the refusal of his carpenter to turn painter established unemployment as a matter of personal preference. Not surprisingly, the rest of the discussion became somewhat terse:

> Mr Percy Laidler: Is it possible to get the committee to vote a sum of money to be used in urgent cases of distress?
> 
> Mr Gilchrist: We are not a charitable institution, and we could not vote even £1 without the consent of the body of members.
> 
> Then your answer is that there is no hope for support for the unemployed from the Stock Exchange?
> 
> Not from the Stock Exchange as a body.

And with that, the meeting was over.

Though the men dispersed, Laidler's week of activity hadn't come to an end. Two days later, he led a march down Flinders Lane, stopping in front of all the large warehouses and sending in delegations to ask for work. In comparison with the raids on Parliament and the Exchange, the Friday procession might have seemed somewhat tame. It did, however, result in the arrest of Frederick Turner, for loitering – a charge that, as *The Socialist* put it, 'affords a pretext for running anyone in at any time and anywhere'.

In court the next day, Turner alleged that the policeman had described him as 'a loafer', mocking that he would not take work if he could get it. The magistrate flatly refused to accept Turner's version of events ('The bench considers that it is almost incredible that Constable Strickland called the young man a loafer') and levied a fine of ten shillings. But when Turner pleaded poor ('Well, I can't pay it. I have no money and there is nothing in the home. I suppose I will have to go to gaol'), the magistrate released him without imprisonment – a sign, perhaps, of the sympathy generated by Laidler's campaign.

It would be a long time before the government would consider anything approaching a genuine social security system, but the unemployed processions of 1908 did succeed in forcing both the churches and the state to come forward with some offers of limited aid for extreme cases. Perhaps more importantly, they helped establish a tradition of the unemployed as a potent force in radical politics – a tradition that would be revisited with more effect during the Great Depression some twenty years later.

# 10. Victorian Single Tax League

## 349 Collins Street

In March 1890, the American reformer Henry George came to Melbourne. *The Argus* sneered:

> Not many rich, not many mighty, not many well respected people went down to meet him, but certainly a marvellous assembly of 'kinks'... Members of Parliament, elected by chance, agitators who have acquired a certain notoriety by being 'agin everybody' and women who have laboured with much earnestness to 'emancipate' themselves from their sex, or at least from its ordinary sentiments and restraints.

Although today largely forgotten, during the late 1880s and early 1890s Henry George loomed as one of the most influential figures in Australian radical politics. He shot to fame with his 1883 book *Progress and Poverty*, which rapidly became the biggest selling work of political economy ever published in America. Much of its appeal lay in its relative simplicity. The correlation between the march of civilisation and the rise of urban poverty stemmed, according to George, from the monopoly a wealthy few enjoyed over land, the source of all wealth. Poverty, then, could be abolished by the trivial mechanism of replacing all taxation with a single tariff levelled on land values, thus unlocking vast tracts of the country for productive use and producing a boom to benefit country and city dwellers alike.

Australia, with its caste of wealthy squatters alongside growing urban destitution, proved just as receptive to George's message as the USA. His triumphant tour of Melbourne attracted crowds numbering perhaps three thousand to the Town Hall and the Exhibition Buildings, and left in its wake large numbers of would-be reformers determined to translate theory into practice. The most ardent formed themselves into the Victorian Single Tax League (VSTL), under the capable direction of Max Hirsch, a German-born economist who then dominated the Georgist movement for the next twenty years.

Most contemporary descriptions paint Hirsch as dry and somewhat earnest, an orator whose persuasive powers stemmed from carefully arrayed collections of statistics rather than rhetorical flights of fancy. He was undoubtedly intelligent;

**AN OLD RHYME IN A NEW DRESS.**

The Single Tax Cat took many forms. Here it battles its perennial foe, the Rat of Protectionism.

he was equally undoubtedly somewhat obsessed. The English Fabian Beatrice Webb encountered Hirsch some years later. She described him as 'a courtly and attractive German Jew' but noted 'he has one of those minds which seeks salvation in one principle, and one ideal, in faith in one line of development to the exclusion of all others.'

This went with the territory. To its adherents, the Single Tax meant more than any simple reform. After all, its introduction would – as one VSTL member put it – undo 'the hoary wrongs of civilisation'. Another supporter described the Tax as 'the logical outcome of Christ's teaching, [that] should ring from every pulpit in the country.' In a striking metaphor, single-taxers compared studying Henry George to staring at an optical illusion puzzle, where the viewer is invited to find the outline of a cat hidden amongst a tangle of leaves and grasses. Once the image of the animal comes into focus, it's difficult to credit that it hadn't always been visible. In a similar fashion:

> when a man has once had a clear view of our doctrines, wherever he goes, in town or country, at home or abroad, he sees the need for putting into practice the Single Tax. He has 'Seen the Cat'.

Max Hirsch saw the cat early and, from 1890 on, devoted himself to showing it to others.

His early campaigns centred around imbuing the labour movement with Georgist doctrine. VSTL members tended to be self-employed or skilled tradesmen rather than blue-collar workers, but the Single Taxers saw the Political Progressive League (the forerunner of the Labor Party) as a useful vehicle for propaganda. At first, the Georgists received a warm welcome as fellow travellers along the road of reform (as one unionist put it, the attitude seemed to be, 'You help us get socialism, and we'll help you get the Single Tax'). Hirsch became a regular columnist for *Commonweal*, the trade union paper, while other Single Taxers took leading roles in local PPL branches, managing ultimately to insert a reference to land value taxation into the League program.

Thus buoyed, the Single Tax League took rooms in the Mercantile Chambers in Collins Street, and set about producing its own magazine. The first issue of *The Beacon* (featuring the smirking Single Tax Cat as a recurring motif) hit the streets for May Day 1893. Indeed, the League took its place in the May Day parade, marching alongside the Knights of Labour, the Democratic Club and the unemployed. Hirsch later shared a platform on the Yarra Bank with the anarchist Chummy Fleming, and *The Beacon* reported that Fleming – representing the Knights of Labour – 'made a speech bristling with good sound sense'.

Yet in many ways the occasion represented the zenith of the League's radicalism, as the alliance with the labour movement came increasingly into conflict with the principles of Georgist political economy. The Single Taxers' desire to break up land monopolies could have come from any socialist platform. But Henry George also advocated the free market, defended 'honestly acquired' capital and remained at best ambivalent about unionism. In a Victorian labour movement dominated by protectionism, Hirsch's continued advocacy of free trade proved too much to stomach – particularly when he began meeting with employer organisations and extolling the wisdom of the Tory press. In early 1893, an anonymous correspondent to *Commonweal* declared:

> The Single taxers have at last come out in their true colors. By their company ye shall know them: Employers' Union, Patriotic League, *Argus*, etc.

Matters came to a head when Hirsch argued for free trade in a debate with PPL leader William Trenwith. *The Beacon* later claimed:

The old Single Tax League offices in Collins Street.

> The debate was marked by extreme discourtesy on the part of Mr Trenwith, who at times was positively insulting.

*Commonweal* responded in kind, expressing its disgust at 'the outflow of bile from the one central figure [Hirsch], who himself constitutes the League, his few admirers resembling limpets clinging to a rock'.

A satirical poem (credited only to 'Jason') laboured the point about Hirsch's dominance within the VSTL:

> *At the hour of eight, in his chair of state,*
> *Reclines His Majesty Max;*
> *A potentate he, of exalted degree,*
> *Lord High Boss of the Single Tax*
> *His henchmen around sit in silence profound*
> *Whilst he belabours the backs*
> *(Metaphorically speaking) of those who are seeking*
> *To discredit the dictum of Max.*

The Single Tax propaganda van spreading its message through Melbourne.

In the wake of this rebuff, the Single Taxers moved sharply to the right. Hirsch set about writing angry critiques of socialism and aligned his organisation with the Free Trade Democratic Association, a group dominated by conservative merchants. Yet the League's daily activities continued along patterns familiar to most of Melbourne's radical groups. Single Taxers attended the Mercantile Chambers for their 'Economic and Sociologic' classes. They embarked on furious letter writing campaigns. They conducted socials where recitations, recitals, songs, piano accordion and hornpipes were accompanied by tea and fruit punch (since many of the members also supported the Temperance movement).

Most of all, the Single Taxers attended meetings. The League held monthly assemblies in the Bourke Street coffee house, and regular open-air gatherings on the vacant block near the Town Hall in Bridge Road, Richmond. Hirsch personally took to a stage somewhere in the city most nights of the week, and *The Beacon* regularly appealed for other members to come forward as speakers. To proselytise outside the metropolis, the VSTL invested in a covered wagon and a stout draught horse (which they maliciously named 'Trenwith') to enable a 'Single Tax Red Van' to tour the countryside, acting as a kind of travelling meeting hall.

The Single Taxers moved from Mercantile Chambers in 1896, seeking 'more commodious premises' (which they found elsewhere in Collins Street). In many ways, though, their best days were behind them. With the economic crisis of the 1890s easing, they found fewer people interested in their doctrines. Alienated from the radical left and mistrusted by the mainstream right, the League never really lived up to the expectations generated by George's visit. Hirsch returned to private business shortly after Federation, dying during a commercial visit to Russia in 1909. Georgism continued, under different guises, regaining a certain degree of prominence during the Great Depression.

Today, a much reduced Henry George Club continues the struggle. The cat is still there, even if fewer people are interested in seeing it.

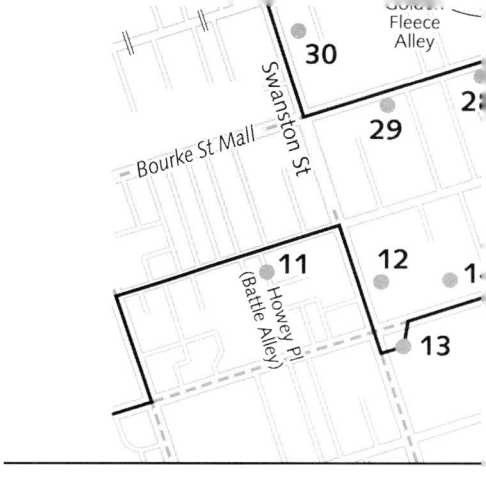

# 11. Cole's Book Arcade

## Howey Place

A summer evening in Bourke Street. Huge gas-fired letters flare in front of an enormous rainbow. Two tiny mechanical sailors, cranking furiously at a windlass. As they wind, a succession of metal plates flips down in front of you, each bearing a message.

The first says, simply, 'Read'.

Then, 'All Men are Brothers'.

The third, 'The Greatest Collection of Ornaments in the World'.

And the finale, 'One government, one language, one religion by 2000 AD'.

It's 1900. You are standing at the Bourke Street entrance to the famous Cole's Book Arcade.

Even now, few of today's megastores can compare with Cole's Arcade. At its height, in the early part of last century, it stretched for two blocks (from Bourke Street down past Little Collins to Collins Street) and stocked, so Cole claimed, some two million volumes. The Arcade's top storey (advertised as 'the prettiest sight in Australia') sold knick-knacks and ornaments. Its music department featured regular performances from a chamber orchestra. Scents wafting from Cole's perfumery competed with the more pungent odours emanating from his aviary and monkey house. Customers were permitted – indeed, encouraged – to sit and read, in chairs supplied for that purpose. If they had no interest in literature, they could choose instead to wander through the fernery, gape at the vestibule with its distorting mirrors, refresh themselves in the Tea Salon or perhaps insert a coin into the mechanical hen so that it cackled and laid an egg.

Not least amongst the Arcade's attractions was its proprietor, Edward William Cole. All of Melbourne (and much of the rest of the country) knew him as the man who had advertised (with a £20 reward) for a wife, an action derided as a publicity stunt until it succeeded in uniting him with one Eliza Jordan ('I have very carefully read your letter in *The Herald* and I think it a very sensible one'), to whom he remained married until his death. A shy, heavily bearded man, he delighted in jokes and puzzles. In 1879 he published *Cole's Funny Picture Book*, a collection of humorous drawings and doggerel reprinted numerous times since, and offered a hundred pounds to anyone who could prove it not the most amusing book in the world. In a subsequent edition, he added a pledge of a thousand pounds for someone willing to construct a flying machine and land it safely in Bourke Street (in front of the Arcade, naturally).

But there was another, more serious side, to the self-styled 'Fun Doctor'. Cole was a humanist, who entered the book trade originally in order to retail his own work. His commitment to social reform remained with him from the first pamphlet he produced (a plea for religious tolerance entitled *The Real Place in History of Jesus and Paul*) to the glory days of the Arcade, a building he inscribed with rhymed slogans espousing the need for a world federation. He chose the rainbow motif to adorn the Arcade to signify the improvement of humanity through education, while his monkey house testified to an interest in Darwinism and science.

Cole's abiding passion for comparative religion brought him into contact with the free thought movement. He acted as librarian for the Eclectic Association of Victoria – a secularist organisation, many of whose members were also active in Karl Marx's International Working Men's Association.

Though Cole struck tin medallions declaring that 'the money spent on intoxicating drink, drugs, sheer foolishness and war would feed, clothe and educate the whole human race', he himself was never a socialist, much less a Marxist. Nonetheless, the Arcade stocked a good selection of titles about free thought, sex education and religion, and included amongst its staff the free thinker William Pyke and the anarchist David Andrade. Cole himself maintained an

Opposite top: the Arcade at its height. Opposite bottom the view down Howey Lane. This page: Cole's original roof above Howey Lane today.

ongoing friendship with J.A. Syme, the rationalist and early leader of the Australian Secular Association.

Most notably, in an era in which the supposedly progressive journalist William Lane could write that he'd rather see his daughter 'dead in her coffin than kissing [a black man] on the mouth or nursing a little coffee-coloured brat that she was mother to', Cole maintained a steadfast opposition to racism. He brought out numerous pamphlets polemicising against the White Australia policy, pointing out that if one traced back far enough, everyone in the world bore a relation to everyone else. Quong Tart, a Chinese-born businessman, became a personal friend and, in 1903, the government of Japan invited Cole and his family to travel on a goodwill mission through its country.

Cole remained first and foremost a businessman, with a keen eye for the main chance. Nonetheless, some sense of the courage his stand against prejudice entailed can be obtained by considering that *The Herald* saw fit to review his pamphlet *What 40 Eminent Japanese Say of the White Australia Act* under the headline 'No Piebald Australia'.

The Arcade survived only another eleven years after Cole died in 1918, the majority of the astonishing edifice being demolished to make way for a department store. The Arcade's Bourke Street entrance is now a department store; a monstrous plaza has swallowed the Collins Street premises. The area has been so comprehensively developed that it's hard to feel much of Cole's presence.

However, the glass ceiling and wrought iron decorations Cole had constructed in the 1890s – in the lane extending between Collins and Little Collins Streets – still remain. The thoroughfare was once dubbed 'Battle Alley', since pedestrians had to fight their way through the collection of Indian hawkers that Cole had invited to trade there.

In 1901, the Arcade's printing department published the pamphlet *A White Australia Impossible*, which argued that Christian Australia's immigration policies were such that Jesus – a Jew and a coloured man – would not be permitted to settle. As you gaze up at what remains of Cole's ceiling, it is worth recalling that nearly a century later, a penniless Galilean making his way onto these shores would almost certainly face detention at Port Hedland until such time as our government could deport him back to Judea for crucifixion.

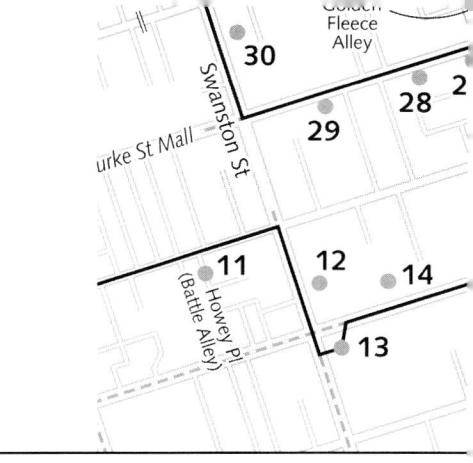

# 12. Town Hall

## Corner Collins and Swanston Streets

In early Melbourne, the corner of Collins and Swanston Streets belonged to the undertaker Samuel Crook. It was not until 1853 that the first Town Hall rose up on the ground where Mr Crook's funeral parlour once stood. The architect's plan called for a pleasing sandstone covering – an instruction ignored by a parsimonious council which produced an edifice universally acknowledged throughout the young city as a hideous monstrosity.

Fourteen years later, the gold rush had expanded council business to the extent that the Town Hall needed to be demolished to make way for larger premises. Conveniently, Samuel Amess, the town mayor, doubled as the city's largest building contractor. When finished in 1870, the new building proved hugely expensive. Amess celebrated its completion with a magnificent concert and a feast of positively Roman proportions. Reporting the occasion, *The Argus* noted:

> Not only the Governor, but almost every gentleman of rank and station in the metropolis gladly joined in aiding the celebration.

However, it reassured its readers:

> The [police] were judiciously stationed around the Town hall and courteously but firmly prevented ordinary passengers from interfering with or getting in the way of the ladies and gentlemen attending the concert.

Not surprisingly, a building thus conceived and constructed as a display of municipal power subsequently proved handy on occasions when the authorities required an imposing symbol of authority around which to rally their forces. The Town Hall served to recruit young men to the slaughter of two world wars. It acted as a labour bureau for scab workers in a number of important industrial disputes. And, on at least two occasions, it provided a drill hall for 'special constables' – baton-carrying civilians, sworn in to protect the rights of property.

The 1890 maritime dispute was the first of the great strikes that helped spur the formation of the ALP. The conflict began in August when shipowners refused maritime officers the right to affiliate to the Melbourne Trades Hall – a decision seen by both sides of politics as a calculated assault on the principle of

Above: beds of flowers where specials once marched – the Town Hall today. Below: The *Bulletin*'s view of specials during the Maritime dispute.

trade unionism. Within a few weeks, *The Herald* described Melbourne as being 'on the brink of a great struggle which at this period is expected to uphold or destroy the supremacy of Trades Unionism', while *The Argus* declared that 'the eyes of the civilised world are upon Australia . . . In these colonies is being waged what the Germans would call a world battle'.

As the strike wave spread, both labour and capital prepared for a major confrontation. The unions organised a massive rally on the Yarra Bank, attended by up to a hundred thousand people.

While the unions could organise people, the authorities could organise violence. The Cabinet called out two hundred of the Mounted Rifles, the Victorian Rangers and all the available cavalry to protect the Mint, Customs House, General Post Office, Public Library, National Museum and various railway stations. Troops took position just down from the union rally, with orders to shoot to kill if necessary, while the mayor bolstered police resources with a force of hastily enlisted 'special constables'.

That day, the Town Hall saw two hundred men sign on as specials. *The Argus* maintained little pretence that volunteers were required for anything more than strong-arm work, noting with admiration that 'those who were sworn in are very likely-looking men, most of them being young and of good physique, and have received useful training'. Yet they were no down-town toughs – as *The Age* commented, 'most of those sworn in yesterday are not of the working class, but are men engaged in Flinders Lane and other city houses'.

In essence, then, the Town Hall muster represented, in more-or-less naked form, the members of one class arming to

*The Special Constabulary Force parades, November 1923.*

suppress another. The fascistic aspects of the procedure came to prominence the next day, when more volunteers joined.

*The Argus* of 1 September reported:

> muster was held in the courtyard on the basement of the Town Hall which was dimly lit with kerosene lamps, and the whole scene was a most extraordinary one. Shortly after 8 o'clock the men were marshalled into six companies, according to pre-arrangement and each company elected its own lieutenant by vote . . . Glancing down the lines one saw many well known faces. The law had quite a number of representatives, both solicitors and barristers. A frequent practitioner at the City Court was there, ready to substitute the convincing argument of the baton for the more tedious procedure of legal formalities, and a rising young barrister stood near him, apparently by no means displeased at the prospect of laying down his brief for the prosecution in the Premier Permanent cases in order to take his place in the ranks of the special constables.

In the event, the specials found no occasion to put the 'convincing argument of the baton' to the test. The Trades Hall Council capitulated, the maritime officers' officials signed a shoddy compromise, and the strike collapsed in disarray, leaving the union movement crippled and rudderless. The gentlemen from Flinders Lane were able to safely return to the business of making money.

Nonetheless, for the Melbourne council, the dispute provided some valuable experience. Thirty years later – when the police force walked out on strike – the Town Hall again became a drill hall for 'specials'.

Six hundred police abandoned their posts in 1923 in a dispute over pay, pensions, conditions and – most of all – the supervision of beat constables by plain-clothes 'spooks'. On the Friday night of the spring racing carnival weekend, the authorities found themselves with almost no police willing to patrol the city.

The police used a section of the Town Hall to house their traffic division and – even though almost all of the traffic police joined the strike – the building became a rallying point for loyalist officers. That Friday, an angry crowd abused the constables who ignored the strike call, and forced them to retreat to the Town Hall. A vocal mob surrounded the building, taunting the loyalist police as 'scabs', 'blacklegs' and 'curs', and daring them to come out.

*The Argus* recorded:

> Efforts were made by the crowd to break down the main door, and a smaller door, but the demonstrators were lacking in spirit, and the attempt soon ceased. For a time there was a period of comparative inactivity, then bottles and eggs were hurled at any person who evinced sympathy for the loyal policemen. Ten minutes later, the doors of the Town Hall swung open, and the force of police, numbering about 30, with the sub inspectors at the head, charged the crowd with batons and handcuffs flying.

The baton charges were repeated over the course of the evening, so that the Town Hall's courtyard (hastily converted into a first-aid station) filled with injured civilians. The police inside also used the building's high pressure hoses to clear the crowd sufficiently to allow a number of loyalist constables to scurry inside from Little Collins Street.

The next day, the authorities realised drastic measures were necessary. According to *The Herald*:

> There was an exodus from Melbourne and suburban picture theatres on Saturday night when the management flashed upon the screen –
>
> > *The ministry ask all returned soldiers to rally around General ('Pompey') Elliott at the Melbourne Town Hall to enrol as special constables and assist in preventing further looting in the city.*
>
> A splendid response followed. From 8 o'clock Saturday night until midnight last night the Town Hall was a scene of activity. It was reminiscent of the early days of the Great War when recruiting was in progress. Young, old and middle-aged men enrolled as special constables. Officials found it difficult to cope with the rush . . .
>
> Among the volunteers were leading commercial and professional men. Several Victorian and interstate graziers who were visiting Melbourne for the Melbourne Cup also took the oath and marched out with the squads.

Saturday night saw widespread looting of major city shops. But by the following day, over fifteen hundred specials had been enrolled. Indeed, such was the enthusiasm with which Melbourne's professional classes responded to the call that organisers found they had a problem – they lacked sufficient batons! Fortunately, the caretaker of the building recalled the truncheons that had served during the maritime dispute. These were hastily recovered from the storeroom and, *The Argus* noted, 'although [the batons had been] laid by for 32 years, [they] proved serviceable in disposing of the unruly mobs that had gathered in the streets'.

By the end of the weekend, the squads of freshly enrolled special constables had succeeded in putting an end to the pillaging of department stores – but at a cost. Hospitals treated some two hundred people, most of them injured around the head. Indeed, such was the specials' enthusiasm for their work that even the largely supportive press dubbed them the 'brethren of the baton', while their commanding officer found himself forced to advise his troops to refrain from whirling their clubs around their heads when driving through crowds on patrol. Unsurprisingly, the Special Constabulary Force (SCF) remained widely hated – specials found it difficult (and dangerous) to venture into working class suburbs, where they were regularly stoned, bashed and even shot at.

But perhaps the biggest irony about those who signed on to replace striking police is that within three weeks they themselves had held a stop work meeting to complain about their conditions. By 17 November, the government wanted to move the SCF out of the Town Hall (where they had been fed free of charge) to make way for a newly recreated, regular police force. A group of specials convened a protest meeting in their new quarters in the Alexandra Avenue drill hall to complain about the new arrangements, before the terrified authorities managed to smooth over the discontent.

When a more regular force took over policing, many specials found it difficult to rejoin their former employment. One volunteer was told by other employees in the firm for which he'd worked for twenty years that staff would strike if he returned. Others found themselves publicly apologising to co-workers for joining the SCF.

Nonetheless, some specials retained a taste for military-style organisation, with former SCF members playing leading roles in the paramilitary fascist organisations of the 1930s (the White Guard, the League of National Security and others).

The Town Hall today seems a genteel and pleasant building. Nonetheless, it's difficult not to wonder whether there are still a few batons kept in storage in a dusty cupboard somewhere, just in case.

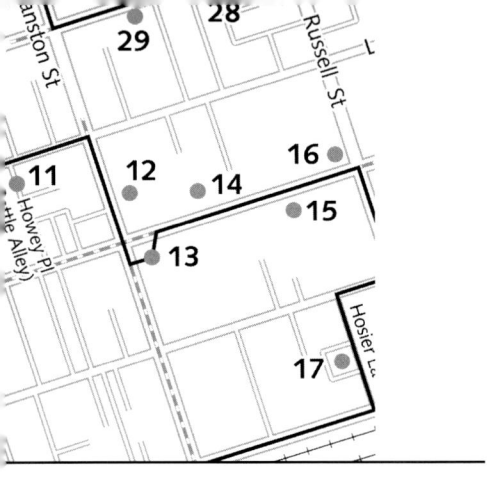

## 13. Burke and Wills Statue

### Corner Collins and Swanston Streets

In 1860, the Royal Society commissioned an expedition to make a sea-to-sea crossing of Australia. The mission lacked any scientific rationale whatsoever (after all, why begin exploring Australia's north from *Melbourne*?), having been planned mostly to scoop a similar expedition setting off from Adelaide. The Society – consisting mostly of wealthy gentlemen, a few of whom had an interest in scientific endeavours – chose Robert O'Hara Burke as leader.

Why Burke? Well, while Burke had garnered a reputation for losing his way on his short trips around Beechworth during his years as a police officer, he *did* belong to the Melbourne Club and he *had* been born in a country manor house in Ireland. Besides, when policing in Castlemaine, he had enthusiastically smashed up union picket-lines for the engineering magnate John Vans Agney Bruce, a man who wielded decisive influence upon the expedition's selection panel.

Today, a cairn near the intersection of Macarthur Road and The Avenue marks the spot where Burke and his men left from Royal Park in 1860, initially heading to a camp on the south edge of Brunswick. By the time they reached Menindie on the Darling River, Burke had already fallen out with three members of his party, including its sole bushman.

The team continued on to Coopers Creek, a place inhabited by Aborigines who lived off fish, game and edible grasses. Burke sent one member of his team back to Menindie for stores, left another building a stockade as protection against the blacks, and pressed on to the Gulf with William Wills, John King and Charles Gray. Later when, during an inquiry into the failure of the expedition, the camp superintendent was asked if Burke had left any instructions on dealing with Aborigines, he replied: 'Yes: at the time he left he seemed to think that they would be very troublesome, and he told me if they annoyed me at all to shoot them at once.'

Likewise, Wills wrote in his journal: 'A large tribe of blacks came pestering us to go to their camp and have a dance, which we declined. They were very troublesome, and nothing but the threat to shoot them will keep them away . . .'

The pathological reluctance to accept native help ensured that the expedition battled constantly against malnutrition. The men could eat only what they had

*The base of the Burke and Wills monument transported through Melbourne.*

brought – rice, flour, salt pork and a special type of expedition biscuit made out of pulverised meat and wheat flour. They didn't know which plants or roots were edible, or how to hunt for animals; as one of the men stated later, 'there were plenty of fish, but none of us understood how to catch them'.

Burke, determined to be the first to cross the continent, suddenly decided to dash the 1600 kilometres to the Gulf of Carpentaria, with only three men and little food.

Charles Gray died in the Stony Desert on the return trip – not long after Burke thrashed him for taking extra rations. The surviving three arrived at the base camp at Coopers Creek, only to find their supply party had left the same day.

It began to dawn upon Wills that survival depended on Aboriginal assistance. Burke, however, knocked fish nets out of the blacks' hands as they approached – a policy he explained to King as necessary to ensure the natives would not hang around.

By the end of the month, starvation loomed once more, and Burke and King went searching for the blacks they had spurned. Wills remained behind, dying shortly afterwards. Burke made it another nine miles before he too succumbed. King survived, solely because the deaths of his putative leaders enabled him to join the Aborigines, who cared for him until a rescue party arrived.

At this point, the story is simply one of racism and incompetence – two themes which extend throughout Australian history like mould through blue cheese. But the fate of the expedition caused a sensation throughout the colony, and when the sole survivor John King arrived at North Melbourne station on 25 November, he found himself swamped by crowds. So the powers-that-be decided to use the

65

The Burke and Wills monument today.

story as a salutary example of the moral superiority of the haves over the have-nots.

*The Argus* – a paper always conscious of the niceties of class – published an article which argued that 'no immoderate transports should be indulged in' over King, who, unlike Wills and Burke had not been born a gentleman. While professing its 'admiration of the zeal and fidelity with which he served the leader of the Expedition', it insisted that he shouldn't be made 'the theme of hyperbolical praise, and the subject of the same ovation which we should have awarded to Burke and Wills, if, haply, they had survived'. After all, there was, it said, a broad distinction between 'moral heroism' and mere 'physical endurance'. King owed his preservation to:

> that tenacity of life which characterises some constitutions, and which is not a moral quality, but a physical accident. On the other hand, it is not improbable that the death of Burke and Wills was accelerated by the activity of their minds, by the incessant play of their emotions.

When the bodies of Burke and Wills (but not Gray) were retrieved by a special expedition, the Exploration Committee once more disgraced itself. Dr John Macadam, the scientist entrusted with the key to the box of bones, arrived late and reeking of alcohol. This was not the kind of spectacle *The Argus* had anticipated:

> The weeping Doctor, overcome by emotions which he had imbibed, staggering over the bones of poor Burke and slobbering drunken kisses upon those sacred remains . . . reduced the sublime to the ridiculous.

News had already arrived that the South Australian John Stuart had successfully completed the sea-to-sea crossing. Nonetheless, Burke and Wills were accorded an enormous state funeral. Around the city, anonymous placards appeared demanding: 'Where is poor Gray?' But the authorities plunged ahead with a competition for a sculpture to commemorate Burke and Wills.

The eventual results were less than inspiring. *The Herald* described one of the entrants as featuring:

two relatives of the immortal [Dickens' character] Chadband leering at an old woman with several nugget bags, and surrounded by bales of wool in impossible positions, and many monsters bearing distant resemblances to lions, emus, camel-leopards, abnormal kangaroos and peculiar sheep. Nor was this very striking work eclipsed by another in what may be termed the packing case school of art, wherein a digger, a farmer, a squatter and a maker of colonial wine, were standing severally at the four corners of a box of cuboid proportions, the box being surmounted by two individuals whose avocation was at the least uncertain.

The successful proposal submitted by Charles Summers omitted all members of the expedition other than Burke and Wills. It then rendered both men entirely unrecognisable, transforming their frail physiques and chinless features into proportions more appropriate for heroes (as well as outfitting them in what appear to be European stage costumes).

The original design for the monument included Aboriginal figures in Greek-style costumes.

    The sculpture's patrons were, naturally, well pleased.

    Unveiled in 1865 before a crowd of ten thousand, the statue went on to undertake a journey to rival the travels of the explorers it depicts. Displaced from its original location at the intersection of Collins and Russell Streets by the introduction of cable trams, the monument was re-established near Parliament House. It then migrated to the Carlton Gardens when the underground station was constructed. In 1979, it was moved to Collins Street, before finding a final resting place at the corner of Swanston and Collins Streets.

    It remains there today, a permanent reminder of the Melbourne Club's two favourite bunglers. There's still no memorial to poor Charley Gray. And there's most certainly nothing commemorating the Aborigines to whom the expedition's sole survivor owed his life.

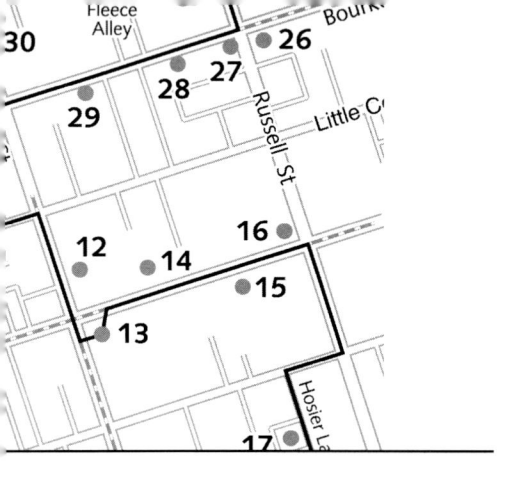

# 14. Mechanics Institute

## 188 Collins Street

Most know the Athenaeum today as a theatre, a beautiful old building on Collins Street. But it began as something quite different – one of the centres of adult working class education known as Mechanics Institutes.

In the early nineteenth century, the British ruling class generally regarded popular education with some suspicion, best expressed in the reactionary aristocrat Lord Eildon's declaration that 'The March of Intellect . . . is a tune to which one day or the other a hundred thousand tall fellows with clubs and pikes will march against Whitehall'. As industrialisation brought more and more of the population in contact with new technology, the enforcement of the feudal ignorance Eildon espoused proved no longer viable. Instead, a new, more sophisticated strategy evolved, in which authorities promoted a selective and intensely ideological education to reconcile the poor to their lot. The Mechanics Institutes – where 'respectable' craftsmen studied a syllabus from which any mention of politics or religion had been carefully excised – exemplified the new approach, and so were assiduously boosted throughout the length and breadth of the British Isles.

In Melbourne, however, the powers-that-be went one step further than simply monitoring the curriculum offered to their inferiors. The demand for an Institute had originated in 1839 with a group of master builders (who presumably felt that the new colony offered working men greater scope for self-improvement or advancement). After the initial meeting, respectable Melbourne managed to hijack the project more or less in its entirety. The 'preparatory committee' appointed to supervise the construction of the Institute consisted primarily of establishment figures, while the list of the first elected officials read, according to historian Michael Cannon, like 'a roll call of the emerging bourgeoisie'.

In practice, that meant the Institute abandoned any attempt to educate workers in the science behind their trade, deciding instead to provide a platform from which local worthies could spout on about more or less whatever they wanted. For instance, the series of lectures scheduled in 1840 as a means of generating enthusiasm for the Institute featured the rising lawyer Redmond Barry (who later presided as judge over the trial of Ned Kelly) discoursing on agriculture – at first blush an eminently suitable topic. Yet as a contemporary noted:

> It would be absurd to fancy that anyone could have been enlightened by a lecture of which six pages of its printed form are devoted to speculations on the agriculture carried on in the garden of Eden, a subject throwing so very little light on the conversion of gum tree forests into cornfields; of which the next eighteen pages only serve to carry the reader through an erudite but purposeless series of quotations from Strabo, Virgil and a hundred writers of antiquity who have incidentally alluded to agriculture; and to the very end of which there is nothing said about the agriculture of modern times.

The Athenaeum.

Unsurprisingly, workers departed, uninspired by such effusions. So, although the construction of the Mechanics Institute (a two storey red brick edifice containing offices, library and reading room, and a hall that served as a meeting room for the town council for many years) came to completion late in 1842, by the end of the decade the Mechanics Institute could claim only one member in twenty as performing any kind of manual work. The refurbishments of 1853 – when the committee embellished the original plain stone in imitation of a Greek temple – reinforced the resolutely respectable aspirations of Melbourne's first public institution.

If respectable Melbourne had hijacked the Institute, on one memorable occasion in 1854, ordinary people returned the favour. In December of that year, government soldiers killed thirty miners who had formed an armed camp to protest against licensing fees at the diggings – the famous battle at the Eureka Stockade. As rumours spread that thousands of armed diggers were preparing to march, the authorities swore in fifteen hundred special constables to protect Melbourne. They then announced a special public meeting at the Mechanics Institute to bolster support for the government's handling of the crisis.

The overwhelming response (more than three thousand attended) necessitated a move onto the street, where the meeting took place amidst general confusion. The recently founded *Age* (then advertising itself as a journal of liberal politics) reported:

> throughout the entire proceedings a very hostile feeling was displayed towards the government, which was chiefly manifest in those confused and sometimes almost indistinguishable exclamations in which excited multitudes give expression to their feelings, and of which it is difficult to give an adequate idea in a newspaper report.

The official speakers tried to pass motions supporting the maintenance of law and order, but often had to struggle to make themselves heard. Then, as the radical sentiment of the crowd became clear, a Mr Fox from the Bendigo diggings stepped forward. According to *The Age*, he complained that:

MONSTRE MEETING IN SWANSTON-STREET, MELBOURNE.

Melburnians rally behind the Eureka uprising.

in the resolution, they had been called upon to keep order but the first thing they had got to do was enquire whence the disorder had arisen (cheers) and then to adopt the best means to repress the riots now in the Colony. There were different ways of putting down things which were wrong, as shown once by Oliver Cromwell. He had seen that from the creation of the earth, the only way to preserve peace was to right those things which were wrong; he did not want them to use a rifle or bowie knife or a sword which were unnecessary for this purpose. This was the only way to establish order – to get rid of those who caused the disorder. (Great cheering)

Rather than bolstering the government, the meeting clearly showed that public sentiment had swung behind the rebellion (a fact confirmed by the enormous attendance at a demonstration outside St Paul's Cathedral a few days later). When the survivors of the stockade came to trial for treason the next year, the government found it impossible to win a conviction.

In 1872, the Mechanics Institute chose to bring its name more in line with reality, and so re-opened as the more respectable-sounding 'Athenaeum' (taking its name from the statue of the Greek goddess of wisdom that featured on its refurbished facade). Its library and reading room still exist, albeit in somewhat reduced circumstances.

As for working people, from 1859, the newly constructed Trades Hall offered them classes of their own – in recognition of the role of 'education' as one of the fundamental pillars of the labour movement.

# 15. Anti-Fascist Protest

## 167 Collins Street

Melburnians first experienced the wonder of cinematic sound at 167 Collins Street, a concert hall built in 1913 with seating for two thousand and then converted into a cinema. On the evening of 2 February 1929, movie-goers packed it out for the debut of the talkies.

For the most part, the new movies were well received. Footage of the singer Beatrice Lillie caused many to exclaim at how well her voice had been rendered, while the comedy number 'The Family Picnic' generated suitable hilarity. Unfortunately, history does not record the reaction to a main feature 'The Red Dance' – a drama about the 1905 revolution in Russia, featuring 'songs of the Petrograd cabarets in the days of the Czar, and the choruses of the turbulent Reds'.

The real drama of the evening, however, didn't take place on screen. It manifested itself in the reaction to the cinema's decision to show a short film of the Italian fascist dictator Mussolini addressing the American public.

By 1929, Mussolini had been in power for seven years. During that time, he had murdered opposition leaders, gaoled communists and union leaders, and burnt down the offices of dissident newspapers. Prior to Mussolini's seizure of power in 1922, only eight thousand Italians lived in Australia. By 1930, some twenty-five thousand people fled Italy for Australia. These migrants congregated in boarding houses and socialised at Italian clubs, which often became centres of anti-fascist agitation.

The first branch of the Fascist Party opened in Melbourne in the mid-1920s. Its support came largely from wealthy expatriates, skilled tradesmen and professionals, bitterly opposed to the more working class migrants who formed the backbone of the Italian anti-fascist organisations.

Italians weren't the only people attracted to fascism in the 1920s. Much of the Australian establishment also regarded *Il Duce* with admiration, whilst the working class movement noted with alarm the growth of sinister local paramilitary formations.

In the circumstances, the decision to use a short film about Mussolini to demonstrate cinema sound might be thought rather provocative. Members of the Matteotti Club (named after the Italian parliamentarian murdered by Mus-

The Auditorium advertises the screening.

solini, and made up of Australian-Italians, many of whom were anti-fascists or anarchists) certainly thought so. On the night of the operning, Matteotti Club members had gathered in the audience, ready to make their protest heard.

According to *The Argus* reporter, the Mussolini film began with a speech by the United States Ambassador in Rome. Then:

> the Italian 'Dictator' was shown stepping from the verandah of his residence. A voice in the dress circle cried 'Viva Il Duce'. Immediately an angry murmur arose and appeared to travel rapidly around the theatre. It was almost impossible to follow the first part of Signor Mussolini's speech, which was a message in English to the American nation; and when the Italian language was used for the second part of the message, the sound of their native tongue aroused the anti-Fascist element to a greater outburst.

The newspaper's use of inverted commas around the word dictator leaves the reader in little doubt as to where its sympathies lay. Nonetheless, it did record the:

> shouts in broken English of 'Traitor!' 'Who killed half our countrymen?' and other excited remarks, accompanied by jeers, groans, and the blowing of squeakers.

That evening in 1929 – unlike many other clashes between fascists and their opponents – did not culminate in violence, although the commotion entirely drowned out the rest of the movie. *The Argus* records that the majority of the audience 'accepted the incident philosophically' and that shortly afterwards 'a talking film of King George opening the Tyne Bridge was loudly cheered'.

In the decades to come, the Italians who had most strenuously campaigned against fascism were interned as dangerous subversives, while the establishment figures guilty of initially championing Hitler and Mussolini went on to lead the war effort.

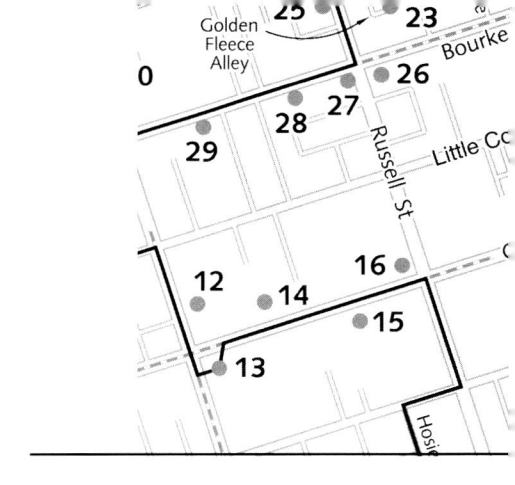

# 16. Unemployed Demonstration

## 140 Collins Street

The Scots Church is a homely building, nestled on the Collins Street hill, and more suited in scale to a small provincial town (as indeed Melbourne was when the church was built). It's difficult to believe that here, in June 1906, *The Age* witnessed:

> a mild example of what this earth would be under the regime of Anarchy . . . Nothing like it has ever before been seen in Melbourne.

What *The Age* editorialist had encountered was in fact the culmination of a campaign by the jobless to draw attention to the problem of unemployment. Without any government social security net, lack of work presented families with a grim choice – they could either appeal to middle class charity organisations (which would usually assist only after finding the appellant suitably 'deserving') or face absolute destitution. A slow economy rendered jobs increasingly difficult to obtain, yet most politicians flatly denied the very existence of unemployment (other than as a result of individual shiftlessness).

In 1905, a group of Melbourne radicals formed the Social Questions Committee (in imitation of similar campaigns conducted by the Fabian Society in Britain) to provide indisputable proof of the jobless situation through a detailed survey of the working class suburbs. The results proved so disturbing (and the indifference of the authorities so palpable) that, by early 1906, the group had evolved from an investigative committee to an agitational political organisation – the Socialist Party (later, the Victorian Socialist Party).

Tom Mann, the driving force behind the party, had already developed into something of a legend (that year, the radical paper *Tocsin* advertised its Trades Union Tailoring Depot with the slogan: 'Worker! Be a Mann!'), both for leading the British Dock Strike in 1889 and for organising for the Labor Party in Australia. If respectable Melbourne wouldn't go to the unemployed, Mann reasoned, well, the unemployed would go to them. And what better time to confront the well-to-do than on Sunday, when they gathered at church?

Accordingly, on 4 June 1906, a crowd of several hundred unemployed assembled on a vacant block on Swanston Street. Beside Mann, at the head of the

Opposite: *Melbourne Punch*'s vision of the Scots Church invasion. Dr Marshall stands in the pulpit; Tom Mann is on the left; Chummy Fleming is on the right. The figure in-between is presumably an invention of the artist.

march, stood the anarchist John William 'Chummy' Fleming, an activist whose history in unemployed struggles stretching back to the mid-1880s had once provoked a conservative politician to declare that 'agitators of the Fleming type should be exterminated like rabbits'. Though personally a gentle, slight individual, Fleming remained indefatigable in defence of liberty, and his presence at the march must have caused the police more than a little concern.

Having previously warned Archbishop Clarke of its intentions, the crowd set off to the corner of Flinders Street, behind twenty women singing 'Hold Up the Red Flag'. When they arrived at St Paul's Cathedral, the Archbishop directed them to specially allocated seats, before preaching a sermon on the text: 'Now if any man have not the spirit of Christ he is none of His'. In the course of his oration, he confessed himself deeply distressed to learn that there were men unable to find work:

> How was that so when the country was wonderfully successful? Everywhere around building was going on. Something must be wrong.
> A voice – We have too many Parliaments.
> Archbishop Clarke – That was a political matter. It was a good thing for a man to save a little money. (Derisive laughter)

Despite the interjections, the service ended amicably with the Archbishop expressing his hope that the church might do more for the genuine unemployed. The protesters left before communion, announcing to those outside their intention to hold a meeting on the Yarra Bank that afternoon.

Over the next weeks, events followed a similar course. Advertisements in *The Age* proclaimed: 'Unemployed Church Parade Sunday morning. Swanston Street. "God Save the People". Meanwhile let us save ourselves.'

Visits to the Australian and Baptist Churches proved successful. Both ministers expressed some sympathy, with the Reverend Charles Strong of the Australian Church offering to personally visit twelve 'respectable' unemployed, 'with the earnest desire to help those who really are in trouble' (although his enthusiasm fell somewhat when Mann replied that Melbourne contained, not twelve, but five thousand men without work).

On 17 June, the protesters decided to take their campaign to the Presbyterian Scots Church. After alerting the church's Dr Marshall of their intentions, about two hundred unemployed proceeded along Collins Street carrying a red flag. According to *The Argus*, two church officers met them at the door, confiscating the flag, and informing Mann that special seats had been reserved:

> 'Oh, have they?' he said. 'We are not going to be stuck at the back.' Raising his voice, he called, 'Come up to the front, comrades,' and to the front they went, as far as they could get.

In contrast to the other clergy, Dr Marshall presented a stern, unsympathetic figure. The VSP's paper *The Socialist* described:

## DIVINE WORSHIP (?)

(And Satan finds some mischief still for idle hands to do.)

*THE CLERGYMAN.*—"My Father's house is a house of prayer, and ye have made it a den of agitators."

> When the preacher began his sermon, his tone was cold, austere, harsh and emphatic, with profound and dramatic shakings of the head, like a burlesque figure of Jupiter set nodding. He discoursed upon immortality, and had not one word of kindly sympathy or the slightest manifestation of brotherly regard for those in distress.

But let us return to *The Argus*, which provides perhaps the fullest account of the morning's events:

> The first part of the service was conducted without any disturbance, except that there was a little groaning when the Rev. Dr Marshall prayed, 'Bless the rich, O Lord, and make them poor in spirit.' ...
>
> First sign of disorder was a sudden and loud cry of 'Hear, hear' from Mr J.W. Fleming when Dr Marshall was declaring that if there were no life after death there would be a contempt of all authority.
>
> This was the signal for a general outburst from the 'unemployed'. 'What's the good of talking about after death?' shouted one.
>
> Several of the unemployed called, 'Order, order,' and Dr Marshall attempted to proceed. He was assailed by cries of 'Rot'.
>
> This epithet was eagerly repeated by a great number of the 'unemployed' and cries of 'rot, rot,' were mingled with appeals of 'Order' from the less turbulent spirits.
>
>> Dr Marshall – Do away with the fear or the hope of immortality (cries of 'Rot' and 'Order') and convince men (interruption) that there is nothing after death –
>> A voice – Tell us how to keep alive (Disorder).
>> Dr Marshall – And you ring the death knell of principle.

With proceedings becoming more and more unruly, Chummy Fleming rose to his feet to loudly remind the well-heeled congregation of Jesus' commandment to sell their possessions and give the proceeds to the poor, a declaration greeted with cheers by his comrades.

Less than enamoured of the prospect of debating scripture with a notorious anarchist, Marshall responded with a threat to end the service unless the noise abated. The response did not prove gratifying (one man loudly replied, 'You crucify Christ all the time'; another cried, 'Give us Christ's true history and we will sit still') and so, after a hurried benediction, he retreated behind the vestry.

With Marshall gone, the worshippers filed out (to the jeers of the protesters). As the church emptied, Chummy called for 'Three cheers for the new social revolution'. Meanwhile, Tom Mann demanded of the church officers that Dr Marshall reappear to explain himself. When they refused, he tried to slip past them into the vestry:

> He was repeatedly gripped and pushed back by one of the officers. A few of the unemployed closed round, and one of them, turning forward to the

crowd, beckoned them to come forward. For a moment matters assumed a serious aspect, when Mr Fleming, seeming unaware of the struggle at the end of the aisle, opportunely created a diversion by again calling for cheers for new social revolution. These were lustily given.

A final push from one of the officers sent Mr Mann back several paces. Mr Fleming cried, with a loud voice, 'It is written, "My house is a house of prayer, but ye have made of it a den of thieves",' Cheers followed the quotation and many voices took up the cry, 'A den of thieves; a den of thieves.'

When it became clear Marshall would not reappear, the unemployed departed, loudly remarking on the wealth of the church officers as they walked out ('These people are representatives of Christ – nice representatives they are, wearing gold watch chains'). Outside on the street, Tom Mann gave a brief speech, and called for 'Three groans for the anti-Christians'. Later on, at an afternoon meeting on the Yarra Bank, he mocked Dr Marshall's claim not to know of the existence of the unemployed:

The Scots Church caught in a rare sliver of sunlight.

> What kind of a gospel could he have been preaching
> if he did not know the distressful conditions existing in the city?

The precise nature of Marshall's gospel became clearer when the good reverend explained to the press: 'I have every sympathy with the unemployed and I would have closed the service in the same way no matter who had made a disturbance – rich or poor', an argument distinctly reminiscent of Anatole France's observation that wealthy and destitute men have an equal right to sleep under bridges.

Over the next week, the fury of respectable Melbourne mounted. *The Age* declaimed against 'an unmannerly little mob of insulting rowdies, led by a Socialist and an Anarchist', and suggested that churches make preparations to defend themselves against further marches. *The Argus* conducted a discussion as to which charges might best be laid against the protesters, while the official Labor Party weighed in, not to support the jobless, but to declare:

> The people who were most prominent in the disturbance, although a few
> are members of our branches, are really not acting in the interest of the Labor
> Party, but are injuring it more than our greatest enemies can.

*The Socialist* took the furore as evidence of the campaign's success. At long last, the authorities had been forced to acknowledge the existence of unemployment:

> The two capitalist morning papers devoted columns to the subject, chiefly to
> try and bolster up the plutocracy in their selfish disregard of the suffering

*The Bulletin* illustrates a suggestion to defend the churches.

"Each Church should form a defence brigade strong enough to refuse entrance to any organized disorderly procession (Age)

Chucker-out:— In the name of the Lord, out you go on your ear!"

around them – but they have to discuss it all the same. Their hands were forced, and that which a fortnight before they refused to notice, now *The Age* and *The Argus* devote leading articles to, and open their columns for letters thereon, providing the letters defend the 'proputty, proputty, proputty' crowd sitting tight.

Despite the endeavours of *The Argus*, no charges were laid over the church invasions. The VSP moved on to other activities; Dr Marshall returned to preaching his doctrines of immortality.

Today, the Scots Church remains just as it was in 1906, on a day when two very different worlds collided.

# 17. Communist Party Office

## 3 Hosier Lane

But behold a new spectacle! A long line of uniformed men marching down Swanston Street! At their head a banner bearing the words: 'The People's Army. To Protect Socialism and the Brotherhood of Peoples'. They sang as they marched. People hurried from all sides to see them pass, and cheered them loudly as they would cheer heroes or friends. They showed a real love and respect for their comrades in the ranks.

The text is from *Socialist Melbourne*, a 1939 Communist Party pamphlet in which the party intellectual Ralph Gibson walks the reader through the geography of the workers' paradise to come. His Melbourne of the future includes an industrial plant seen by the employees more as a club than a factory, a Parliament House where a Soviet Congress sits in session, and a planned economy managed from the Collins Street Commonwealth Bank buildings, which are adorned with the hammer and sickle, 'the emblem of . . . the toilers of the town and the country'.

The real city of the late 1930s was not quite ready to cheer communists as heroes (let alone love them as friends). But the party had certainly grown. In 1935, its headquarters moved to 116 Little Bourke Street in the heart of Chinatown, from whence issued *The Workers Voice*, the official paper of the Victorian party.

A year later the party again moved, into 3 Hosier Lane. With close to nine hundred members in Melbourne, the communists maintained a city office, a bookshop, a whole spectrum of regular publications, and a series of branches throughout the city and rural Victoria. Under the auspices of its youth wing, the Young Democrats, it organised an astonishing program of activities ranging from classes in political economy and public speaking to camps in Daylesford and Cowes (with as many as two thousand people attending) to cookery and sports (under the slogan: 'To win in the class struggle, we have to keep fit').

By the mid-1930s, Stalin had directed the international communist movement to proclaim popular fronts – broad alliances between the proletariat, farmers and the middle class, in which distinctively Marxist demands were quietly

Hosier Lane. The CP rented the dark building.

shelved. The relative political moderation that ensued encouraged an impressive array of writers, academics and other intellectuals to participate in organisations like the Writers League and the New Theatre. With these middle class elements in mind, *The Workers Voice* invited applications for party membership in 1936 on the basis that:

> To join the Communist Party does not mean that you will be over-burdened with work.
> To join the Communist Party does not mean that you will be driven to do things you don't want to do.
> To join the Communist Party means that you will be better equipped to draw your workmates and friends into the class struggle.
> To join the Communist Party means that you will learn what you can do best and how to do it in the fight for a Soviet Australia.

The frantic schedule recorded in the memoirs of communist activists suggests that the promise of a leisurely pace was not always honoured, as the example of Gibson himself illustrates. His father, Boyce, had been Professor of Philosophy at the University of Melbourne and Ralph also seemed destined for an academic career until, appalled by the Depression, he left his comfortable life to throw his lot in with the communists.

Small, thin and self-effacing, Gibson made an unlikely revolutionary. But by the time the party had moved to Hosier Lane, he had established himself as a senior party official. His dedication and capacity for self-sacrifice remained a by-word in party circles. Len Fox, a colleague from the Movement Against War and Fascism, remarked that Gibson possessed the ability to perform the organising work of two men, while another, Arthur Howells, described him as a 'human tornado':

> He despised lifts. When the MAWF office was in Bourke House (Russell Street), and later Law Court Chambers, it was always deemed to be safer to go down in the lift rather than risk walking down when there was a possibility of meeting Ralph dashing up.

Not all members possessed Gibson's energy. But the dire world political situation of the late 1930s certainly provided new recruits with plenty to become active about. When fascist Italy invaded Abyssinia, CP members marched in protest. When Japan invaded China, the party led the wharfies of Port Kembla out in protest against the provision of iron to Japan. It campaigned against local anti-Semitism following Prime Minister Lyons' decision to limit the number of Jewish refugees from the Nazi Kristallnacht pogrom allowed into Australia.

But the Spanish Civil War – the Vietnam of the 1930s – probably generated the most passion. The Australian government officially maintained a position of neutrality about the conflict between a Republican government (in which communists played a leading role) and Franco's fascists. But wide sections of the Australian establishment made it clear they wanted to see the Republicans defeated. For instance, in a 1938 May Day procession, a marcher who shouted 'Down with Fascism! Spain today – Australia tomorrow!' found himself fined two pounds for behaviour offensive to the police.

Defence of the Republic thus became a major communist campaign. For some activists, this meant actual combat as part of the International Brigade, a unit formed from volunteers from around the world. A handful of Australians gave their lives in Spain. The death of Ted Dickinson (a long-time leftist, and a popular Yarra Bank speaker) achieved the most publicity. Dickinson perished in front of a fascist firing squad, reportedly telling his executioners:

> If we had ten thousand Australian bushmen here, we'd have pushed you bastards into the sea.

Back in Melbourne, the CP prompted the Victorian Council Against War and Fascism and the Spanish Relief Committee to organise aid and resources for the beleaguered Republicans. As well as producing innumerable pamphlets explaining the war, communists regularly challenged fascist supporters (usually Catholic activists) to public debates. On one memorable occasion in 1937, something like a thousand people assembled in the Public Lecture Theatre at Melbourne University to listen to a pro-fascist team led by B.A. Santamaria take on a Republican side featuring two members of the Communist Party. *The Catholic Worker* approvingly recorded, 'The debate developed into chaos . . . the fascist supporters made so much noise that it was impossible to hear the negative side'.

On occasion, the communists displayed considerable verve in getting the anti-fascist message across. In February 1937, some eighty thousand people attended the MCG to watch the fifth of the tests in the series between England and Australia. During the lunch break, a communist scrambled down the roof of the new stand, trailing a banner that read: 'Aid for Spain'. As he reached the ground, more banners appeared on the balconies, a placard-carrying runner sprinted across the ground, and twenty thousand leaflets scattered down over the stands. The text read:

The CP paper, with Ralph Gibson on the cover. The cartoon depicts the British Labour Party and the ALP in a toadying competition.

> What is Bodyline compared with this?
> Hundreds of women and children killed and maimed by Nazi bombs over Madrid.
> Thousands of defenceless civilians slaughtered by German aeroplanes.
> It is the first stage of the second world war.
> Outlaw Bodyline in world affairs.
> Help Spain!

On the back was a cricket score sheet with the message: 'Write your score and help the Spanish people settle theirs.'

Ultimately, the Spanish people did not prove able to settle any scores. Madrid fell to Franco's fascists – a disaster stemming at least in part from the Spanish Communist Party's inability to capitalise on the revolutionary opportunities presented to it. Indeed, the communists added their own contribution to the tragedy of Spain by massacring thousands of their opponents on the left.

How did the CP respond? The party leadership in Melbourne enthusiastically endorsed the purges – just as, on the eve of the notorious Moscow show trial of Bukharin and other old Bolshevik leaders, *The Worker's Voice* had boasted that 'the world will hear the story of the guilt of these mad monsters from their own lips'.

Similar apologetics for the crimes of the Russian dictatorship continued throughout subsequent CP history, warping and deforming its traditions and ideas. Yet it remains both possible and necessary to separate the struggles led by the communists of the 1930s from the canker of Stalinism within their party.

Ultimately, the majority of people joining the CP did not do so to glorify oppression. Instead, as the anti-fascist activist Len Fox later argued in his memoirs, they:

> wanted to find an organisation in which they could join with other men and women in doing something about the evils of depression, fascism and war ... Some of the Labor Party groups, and some Church groups, were covertly or openly pro-fascist. It was not strange that the Communist Party, whatever its weaknesses and limitations, appealed to many people as a body in which they could work.

On a dark night, Hosier Lane – with its cobbled pavement sloping down to Flinders Street – can still look much as it must have done in the 1930s. However, the CP's old building – vacated in late 1939 – is today occupied by a frighteningly chic bar with funky 1960s-style decor. If you stand outside in the lane and peer through the barred windows as the fashionable sip their drinks, Gibson's socialist Melbourne seems a long way away. But if that city is ever to be built, the process will require from future generations the same energy and dedication shown by the communists of the 1930s.

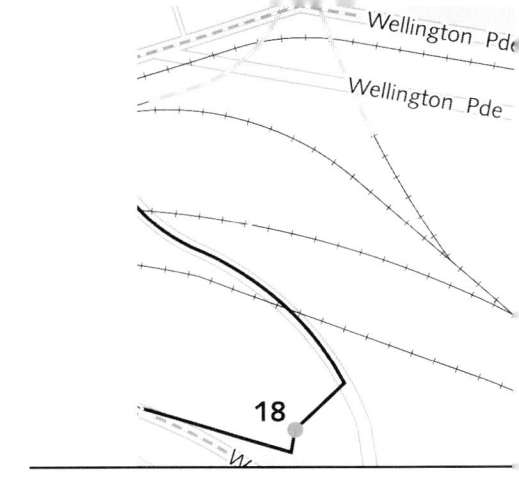

# 18. Speakers Forum

## Yarra Bank

From the metropolitan streets, laid in symmetrical grids to prevent twists or turns where the poor might fester, to the privately owned hotel erected upon what was once a city square, political control in Melbourne has invariably involved struggles over public space.

In the earliest days of the colony, dissenters turned to open air meetings to express their views. Street oratory, after all, requires no capital or resources, other than a few sympathisers for moral (and, on occasion, physical) support and a makeshift platform from which to declaim.

So by the depression of the 1890s, a series of regular Sunday forums had sprung up around the city. Radical speakers dodged the police to hold forth at the Eastern Market (facing Exhibition Street, between Little Collins and Bourke Streets), at Queens Wharf, outside Trades Hall, at Studley Park (down from the boatshed) and at an open area above the Merri Creek, near St George's Road.

Detective Wardley, one of the many police assigned by Victoria's rulers to quell such dangerous eruptions of free speech, recorded orators speaking on 'Socialism, Anarchy, Democracy, Capitalism, Dynamite, One-Man-One-Vote and other social reforms'. He noted with some alarm that 'Her Majesty the Queen and members of the Royal Family, governments . . . landlords, capitalists and clergymen' all came in 'for a great deal of abuse'.

But Melbourne's most successful stump – and certainly the longest lasting – proved to be that on the Yarra Bank.

During the 1890s, radicals realised that large meetings could be held on the flat ground near the boatsheds on the south side of the Yarra, just down from Princes Bridge. This was the first forum, neatly intersecting with the route of the traditional promenade down from Flinders Street.

Not surprisingly, the authorities proved less than enamoured of a motley collection of agitators delivering their harangues a stone's throw away from the CBD. After years of harassment, the forum was moved to the north side of the river, a barren patch of mud in line with Exhibition Street. In 1925, the city council – no doubt hoping to keep the whole business safely tucked away behind the railway yards – granted a degree of official sanction, with earthen

Above: Tom Mann speaking at the Yarra Bank, May Day 1906.

Below: anti-conscription rally at the Bank in 1916.

mounds for speakers and freshly planted trees to shade spectators. The plain-clothes policemen, however, remained.

Over the next forty years, the Sunday forum grew into an institution.

The most regular Yarra Bankers – the Communist Party, religious groups, a number of determined individuals – maintained permanent stands from which they would speak each week. But anyone could join in, either mounting one of the ten or more stumps, or simply holding forth from where they stood. At the forum's height, it was not unknown for twenty or thirty meetings to proceed simultaneously, each speaker conducting a passionate, unamplified declamation, often punctuated by interjections and jeers. Hecklers didn't always restrain themselves to verbal interruptions – during the campaign against conscription it became common practice for anti-conscriptionists to remove their shoelaces before taking the stump, in the expectation that they would soon need their feet free to swim.

Most of the time, in a wowserish city in which most amusements closed on Sundays, the Yarra Bank simply provided a form of free entertainment. For those interested in ideas, though, the forum offered what Labor Prime Minister John Curtin (himself no slouch on the stump) rightly described as Melbourne's 'university of the working class'.

The centrality of the Bank – as well as the relative freedom accorded to those who met there – made it a popular location for demonstrations. Perhaps the Bank's most dramatic assembly came during the monster rally that crowned the 1890 maritime dispute. At its height, the strike (a complicated struggle where sailors, shearers and wharfies combined to defend the right to be unionists) virtually paralysed the city. An eerie darkness hung over Melbourne (the gas stokers were on strike) and, throughout the country, some fifty thousand people were thrown out of work.

*The remaining corner of the speakers forum.*

On 31 August, the unions called a mass rally for the Bank. As *The Argus* described:

> From the city proper, South Yarra, Jolimont, East Melbourne, and Richmond, continuous crowds of pedestrians made their way to one common centre. The suburban trains and trams coming into Melbourne found their way by vehicle or foot to the park. The Botanical Gardens and Jolimont Bridges presented a curious sight, being continuously occupied by a moving mass of humanity, and hundreds of people took a straight course over the railway lines choosing their opportunity between the passing of the trains.

This vast throng – perhaps a hundred thousand people, from a city of four hundred thousand – confirmed for many that revolution was at hand.

But the authorities had made their own preparations. The Chief Commissioner of Police had already brought reinforcements to Melbourne from the country districts, and stocked a large cache of rifles and carbines in stations in Bourke Street and Russell Street. A thousand 'special constables' had been sworn in to service in the basement of the Town Hall and presented with a baton, a badge and a sheet of instructions.

On the day of the rally, mounted horsemen hid in the old morgue building near the corner of Batman and Swanston Streets. Hundreds more waited in the Victoria Barracks, where an impromptu army camp had been assembled.

Preparing for the union march, the commander of the Mounted Rifles, Colonel Tom Price, addressed his men:

> One of your obligations imposes upon you the duty of resisting invasion by a foreign enemy; but you are also called upon to assist in preserving law and order in the colony . . . You will each be supplied with forty rounds of ammunition – leaden bullets – and if the order is given to fire don't let me see one rifle pointed up in the air. Fire low and lay them out – lay the disturbers of law and order out so that the duty will not have to be again performed. Let it be a lesson to them.

In the event, the meeting passed uneventfully. The Social Democrats established a platform a hundred yards from the main stage, decorated with what *The Age* described as 'a hideous daub representing the dawn of socialism in appropriate shades of red and yellow as the background to a number of allegorical figures . . . precisely like those familiar announcements which invite the unwary public to "walk up and see the wild beasts".' But the official speeches were stolid and uninspired, and the rally as a whole remained remarkably well behaved.

The strike itself dragged on for another two months, before most of the unionists were forced back on the employers' terms. But Tom Price's speech still resonates today, as a warning that in Australia, as elsewhere, the final recourse of the powers-that-be is always naked violence.

The Bank provided a venue for major rallies on many other issues, from the fight against conscription (during which *The Argus* managed to describe a mass anti-war stop work as being both 'futile and ridiculous' *and* 'dangerous and sinister') to the struggle against fascism. Its more customary role, though, was as the locus for that most durable of working class festivities, the annual May Day procession.

The first May Day in 1893 was more than a celebration. Several hundred workers tramped down from the Burke and Wills statue to the south side of the Yarra Bank (opposite Government House) in a consciously radical alternative to the somewhat staid Eight-Hour Day march. Once assembled, they heard addresses from a slate of well-known militants, including the anarchist Chummy Fleming, who had earlier shocked union officials by leading an unemployed rally behind the banner: 'Feed on our flesh and blood you capitalist hyenas: It is your funeral feast'.

The course of Fleming's political career is worth noting, for it coincides neatly with the rise and fall of the Yarra Bank as an institution. As May Day's founder, Chummy insisted on taking pride of place in the march, waving his anarchist flag defiantly. In the 1930s, when the less-than-sympathetic Communist Party dominated proceedings, he maintained his position, starting a block ahead of the other marchers, and proceeding so slowly that the rest of the procession gradually caught up to him.

Each Sunday, Chummy gave voice to his anarchist principles from his private stump on the Bank. Unless ill or in gaol (he was a constant target of police harassment), he could be relied upon for a weekly defence of libertarianism from the 1890s until his death in 1950. On occasions, his lectures attracted sizeable crowds. More often, he stood with a flag proclaiming 'No Gods, No Masters', facing an audience that was small and sometimes hostile. It was not unknown for him to be physically attacked.

When Fleming died, his friends (in accordance with his wishes) took his ashes (augmented to make a respectable pile with some char from a fireplace) to scatter on the Yarra Bank.

In the mid-1970s the veteran Communist Party orator Jim Coull recalled the event:

> We'd arranged to hold a meeting, had a lorry there, where they have the May Day platform . . . There were different meetings and groups on the Bank, and I was to blow a whistle and all meetings would stop, and the people would gather round the Party platform. There was a big crowd. Ralph [Gibson] spoke first then myself. I said that we were there to remember Chummy Fleming, say a few words about his activities, and his loyalty to the working class which was never, ever in doubt.
>
> Then I called on Neville Preston, who was a personal friend of Chummy's to say a few words and distribute the ashes. Naturally I thought that he'd have a little box like a snuff box or a matchbox and he'd blow them away as we'd usually seen it done. But another man hands him up a Groves and McVities Biscuit tin. And this tin is filled with sand and what looked like powder. And it was funny . . . it was a very windy day, really blowing . . .
>
> So the man said, 'I will now cast the ashes of my dear departed comrade to the winds', and he dived his hand into the biscuit tin, and heaves forth these ashes. And he didn't use just one hand, but he went on with three or four and more. And the people are staggering back. It was blowing in their faces. And they'd had Chummy – didn't care what happened to him.

Much later, Coull was recorded as declaring: 'I still after all these years can't get the taste of Chummy Fleming out of my mouth'.

As a forum, the Yarra Bank outlived Chummy but not by long. The social ferment of the 1960s and 1970s did not prevent its gradual decline. The universities provided sites for discussions on the Vietnam war; the streets themselves the venue for protests. The forum became the property of a diminishing group of diehards, and eventually collapsed altogether.

Today, the area around the speakers' mounds has been sliced into by the Tennis Centre, a huge extension of Exhibition Street and, most recently, ornamental ponds. It's now a shady triangle of about an acre, at the south-eastern corner of Birrarang Marr. The developers have attempted to compensate for obscuring the site by installing some historical plaques, additions that serve only to more clearly identify the forum as a museum exhibit rather than part of a living culture.

However, in a new century, the problem that motivated Chummy Fleming and his comrades to take to the Bank has reasserted itself with a vengeance. In the new Melbourne of casinos and giant outdoor television screens, there are almost no places in which people can congregate. The inadequate space outside the State Library has become the focus for every rally and demonstration, simply because nowhere else exists.

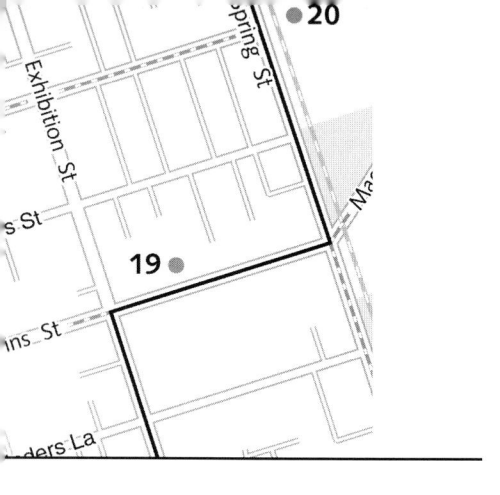

# 19. Melbourne Club

## 36 Collins Street

According to Garryowen, the idea of an exclusive club in Melbourne was first conceived during a cricket match in 1838 by squatters who had become fabulously rich by seizing vast tracts of Victorian land. They decided that a clubhouse (which they located first in a succession of hotels and then later in a permanent building at the top end of Collins Street) would 'afford a comfortable method of meeting Gentlemen' while removing the need to put up with 'dirty and disorderly' inns when they visited Melbourne.

Yet the Melbourne Club offered more than separation from the unwashed masses. In a very new colony, thousands of miles away from England, many of the social niceties that distinguished the classes seemed to have collapsed. One wealthy pastoralist from New South Wales, for instance, described the founders of the Melbourne Club:

> as rough, and uncouth looking men as I ever met. Many of them were dressed like ploughmen. One in particular seemed to disregard attention to personal appearance so much that he actually walked about with such a rent in his trowsers as displayed to the wondering gaze of the multitude the ample fullness of his brawny buttocks.

A private gentlemen's club, then, provided members of the developing ruling class with the opportunity to develop the manners and habits befitting those born to rule.

Or that, at least, was the theory. In practice, the Club distinguished itself in its early years primarily by its oafishness. Most of Melbourne's early duels – and not a few of its brawls – involved the Melbourne Club, where rivers of alcohol flowed between quarrels, fist fights, nose pullings and the occasional horsewhipping.

For instance, in 1839, 'hot words at dinner' between Peter Snodgrass and William Ryrie provoked a duel on the western slope of Batman's Hill. Yet the resulting contest resembled less an affair of honour than a low burlesque:

> The distance was measured, the pistols primed, and the men placed; but just as the fatal signal was about to be given, Snodgrass, who was always a victim to over-impatience, or ultra excitement on such occasions, so mis-

*Melbourne Club members, 1861.*

managed his hair-trigger, that it went off too soon, so, instead of slaying his antagonist, he wounded himself in the toe.

The duel forgotten, the inebriated spectators cast around for some other amusement until:

> one drunken humourist hiccuped something in effect that as the captain's ammunition was nearly all there, they could not do better than back Dr Thomas against a tree as a mark for some pistol practice. Thomas, who had a slight impediment in articulation, grew alarmed, and stuttered out a vehement objection. Though a great joker himself, he had no liking to be turned into an Aunt Sally of this kind and experimented on with bullets instead of sticks. A compromise was finally effected by Thomas consenting to allow a new bell-topper he wore to do proxy for himself, and upon this corpus nailed to a gum-tree they operated in rotation with the two hair-triggers, until the Smithian cartridges were exhausted, and the medico's head-gear well riddled.

Rather than improving the behaviour of the city's cloddish squatters, the early Club seemed rather to have encouraged their degeneration. Garryowen marvelled at:

> the duels initiated, the practical jokes perpetrated, the nocturnal 'wild oats' scattered about the town, in which no mad freak seemed impossible, from the mobbing of a parson to pummelling a policeman, besieging a theatre or unbelling a church, demolishing a corporation bridge, or a wholesale abduction of signboards.

Naturally, while Club members enjoyed virtual legal immunity for their pranks, the same licence did not extend to their social inferiors. Snodgrass and Ryrie might fire loaded pistols in the city streets without penalty, but a servant employed in the Club had received a seven-year sentence for stealing matches.

The disparity emphasises how, if the Melbourne Club did not prove able to teach the rich and powerful some culture, it did succeed in cohering them into a conscious ruling class. Before very long, it had become a place where members could not only enjoy the first water closets in the city but could band together to ensure that the privileges of landowners were upheld.

The Eureka Stockade in 1854 – in which Ballarat gold miners rebelled against a hated licence – demonstrated just how far the tentacles of the Melbourne Club had stretched. While most ordinary people – both on and off the goldfields – supported the Eureka rebels and the associated democratic movement, the central figures involved in crushing the uprising all belonged to the Club. The Commissioner of the Ballarat goldfields, Robert Rede, who ordered the assault on the stockade and who wrote of wanting to 'crush the democratic agitation in one blow' was a member, while Charles Hotham, the Governor of Victoria who pushed for treason charges against the rebels, received an invitation to join just two days after his arrival in Melbourne. Other members included John Leslie Fitzgerald Foster, the Colonial Secretary (eventually forced to resign), Captain Charles Pasley (the commander of the troops that attacked the stockade) and John D'Ewes, the Ballarat Police Magistrate whose actions precipitated the burning of the Eureka Hotel by diggers. The former secretary of the Club, Redmond Barry, presided over the trials of most of the rebels (another Club man Justice William à Beckett judged the rest), while the former Club president William Stawell led the prosecution.

Still a bastion of privilege, as luxurious and secretive as ever.

Not surprisingly, the Melbourne Club quickly became a focus of resentment amongst Victorian workers. A couple of years later, when a reform group known as the Land Convention organised a monster demonstration to march to Parliament (with a brass band playing the Marseillaise, and banners proclaiming 'When justice is denied, allegiance ceases to be duty!'), the procession paused to give 'three groans for squatters' as it passed the Melbourne Club.

The Club still sits on the top end of Collins Street. A thick wooden door enables those inside (a roll call of luminaries from the upper echelons of big business and the Liberal Party) to discuss the affairs of the state free from interference from the hoi polloi.

Today's Melbourne Club presents itself as the embodiment of tradition, elegance and old-moneyed sophistication. Yet, as anyone who has been unfortunate enough to encounter establishment Melbourne at play knows, all that separates Club members now from their oafish forefathers is a hundred and sixty years and more stoutly tailored trousers.

# 20. Parliament House

## Spring Street

Just below the level of the roof of Victoria's Parliament nestle two horizontal slits. These are gun lofts. They are intended to allow riflemen a clear field of fire to shoot at demonstrators marching along Bourke Street. They remain as a shocking reminder that, from Victoria's earliest days, our parliamentarians have never been terribly keen on those they represent coming too close to the House of the People.

In the early days, the elites did not bother to keep their feelings hidden. To hold a seat in the upper house of the early Parliament, you had to possess at least £2000 worth of land. The right to vote depended upon owning £50 worth of land or belonging to a respectable profession (like medicine or law). The franchise thus excluded Aborigines, women, immigrants and the entire urban working class.

The armed insurrection at the Eureka Stockade changed all that. By 1857, Victorians enjoyed both universal manhood suffrage (in voting for the Legislative Assembly) and the secret ballot, as a terrified ruling class gave ground before a radicalised citizenry. And just as popular protest moulded the institutions of Victorian democracy, it also shaped the physical environs of the Parliament building.

After the colony of Port Phillip officially separated from New South Wales in 1851, the first meetings of the Legislative Council took place in St Patrick's Hall, Bourke Street West – the site of today's Law Institute of Victoria. But the building soon proved too cramped (and insufficiently ostentatious) to serve as a Parliament. In 1853, the Council decided upon the high ground at Bourke Street as a site, in part to present the new building to best advantage and in part (as Surveyor-General Robert Hoddle recognised) for the purely sectarian purpose of obscuring St Patrick's Catholic cathedral.

Initially, they staged a competition to uncover promising designs. Then, when none of the entrants proved up to scratch, the task passed to Captain Charles Pasley. Unfortunately, the good Captain rendered himself ineligible in the eyes of the public by volunteering to lead the attack on the miners of Eureka. The baton passed instead to the designer John Knight and the architect Peter Kerr.

The site with which they were presented did not appear altogether prepossessing. Kerr described (apparently without irony) the grounds between Bourke

DESIGN FOR THE HOUSES OF PARLIAMENT.

Melbourne as the new Rome. The original grand design for Parliament.

Street and the old St Peter's School, where the building needed to be erected, as:

> Unformed, full of holes and dirt, stagnant water, refuse, etc. and it was in addition a harbour for undesirable characters.

Undaunted, he drew up plans for a grand, classical design, complete with huge dome and a stone facade surrounding the entire building. Then came the crunch. While Hoddle growled that the building would be 'well adequate for a State Prison or a lunatic asylum', the government proved quite happy with its colossal size. It wasn't, however, too keen on a bill of corresponding scale. So the structure we see today is only a shadow of the original, heroic design.

Further difficulties arose. Bluestone specialist W.C. Cornish accepted the contract for the basic stone work. But he immediately came into conflict with union agitation for shorter working hours. When Cornish flatly refused to concede an eight-hour day, stonemasons working at Melbourne University walked off the job. They marched down to call out the men labouring on the Parliament site, and then joined with them in a parade through the city. It's likely that the pressure on Cornish to complete his building ready for its opening in November 1856 played a role in the union's historic win.

In the aftermath of the dispute, Charles Jardine Don, one of the stonemasons involved in the struggle, stood for the seat of Collingwood. His victory rendered him the first worker elected to any legislature anywhere in the British Empire.

At the time, politicians received no salary (the assumption being that they possessed independent means), and so Don continued to work on the further construction of the building during the day, while sitting in it as a legislator in the evening. Described by one journalist as 'a cross between a poet and a pirate', Don remained proud of his origins, at one stage declaring:

> Look at yonder city, illuminated by its magic lamps, its windows glittering with wealth, a city with palaces worthy of kings and temples worthy of gods, which labour has placed there in the short space of a quarter of a century . . . and by whom has the change been effected? By the rich, the wealthy, the kid gloved, fine handed gentry? No, by the horny handed sons of the soil . . .

Yet like so many subsequent parliamentary representatives of labour, he eventually came to neglect the interests of those he served and lost his seat in 1864.

The Parliament building unveiled in 1856 reflected many of the prevailing attitudes about how governmental business should be conducted. It contained, for instance, a dungeon, into which anyone found in contempt of Parliament could immediately be transferred. Parliament's powers of discipline were put to the test a number of times in the nineteenth century – mostly after members had thrown punches at each other. Today, the underground chamber – complete with bolted doors and barred windows – serves more sedately as a cleaners' tea room.

After the Council and Assembly Chambers, the rest of the building was assembled in a number of discrete stages – the library in 1860, the vestibule and Great Hall in 1879, and the west facade and entrance steps in 1892. From 1901, the Commonwealth Parliament took over the Spring Street building. When it moved to Canberra in 1927, Victoria received £50,000 appreciation, which – in the last major addition to the structure – built new parliamentary refreshment rooms.

Early in the construction process, Kerr advised the government to buy the land on the corners of Bourke and Spring Streets to create a forecourt enabling the Parliament Building to be properly displayed. This (on the face of it, eminently sensible) suggestion was rebuffed, as was a similar proposal in 1929.

Why? The authorities feared the resulting public square would provide a site capable of holding demonstrations.

Square or no square, demonstrations have taken place outside Parliament almost from the day it was completed. The building provided an obvious focus for the Land Convention, a body that met weekly at the Eastern Market (on the corner of Bourke and Exhibition Streets) in 1860 to demand that some of the vast acres of land seized by squatters be made available to ordinary people. The

One of the parliamentary gun slits.

Convention reached a crescendo in August that year, with a mass demonstration outside Parliament House.

*The Argus* described how:

> As the time arrived for the re-assembling of the House, the crowd, now transformed into a mob, came rolling up Bourke Street in a disorderly and defiant manner, and entering the reserve, began throwing stones at the police and the walls of the House.

The police eventually dispersed the crowd with a baton charge, 'sweeping back the baffled disorderlies like so many sheep'. The next day, Parliament enacted a law making it a crime punishable by six months' hard labour for more than fifty people to meet in the area immediately in front of the building. Variants of that law have remained in force ever since. The Unlawful Assemblies and Processions Act – still theoretically in operation today – allows police to disperse, kill, injure or maim any person in a group of fifty or more illegally assembled in the vicinity of Parliament.

During the depression of the 1890s, the Parliament became a popular target for radicalised workers. For instance, in May 1892, a delegation of unemployed marching on the building were repelled by police, allowing *The Age* to report that 'the amateurish efforts of a few incipient anarchists were promptly nipped in the bud'.

Such incidents disturbed the authorities more than *The Age*'s rhetoric would suggest. The tumult of the decade – during which, after the maritime and shearers' strikes, many mainstream commentators spoke openly of the approaching revolution – is indelibly recorded in the stone of the west facade, completed in 1892. When, ninety years later, NSW parliamentarians visited the building as part of an investigation into parliamentary privileges, they reported that, alongside the gun slits, the building held other surprises:

> the ornate doors are riot proof, with concealed trap doors to enable special attention in an enclosed area behind them [and] a secret passage runs from the basement of the building to an innocent looking picnic shelter in the midst of the grounds.

There's no record of the parliamentary escape hatch being put to use, but it's not difficult to imagine occasions during which certain politicians must have found it a tempting prospect.

During the First World War, for instance, anti-war activists led numerous processions to the Parliament House site, which at the time housed the Federal Parliament. In August 1917, for instance, the Women's Peace League (a group associated with the Victorian Socialist Party) held a demonstration against the high food prices brought on by the war. Headed by Adela Pankhurst – an English suffragette who had joined Australia's feminist movement, and then shifted rapidly in a socialist direction – they gathered in the Treasury Gardens and then marched on Parliament House. When police fortified the building, Pankhurst

# The Strange Story of the Missing Mace

ON THE NIGHT OF 9 October 1891, the Clerk of the Parliamentary Assembly was horrified to find the Speaker's Mace – the archaic symbol of Westminster democracy – missing.

Less than a fortnight later, *Melbourne Punch* claimed that 'there is reason to believe that [the mace] was taken from its place by a member of Parliament in a drunken freak'. A year later, the Sydney *Bulletin* reported that the mace resided in 'a bagnio in Lonsdale Street, Melbourne' and that detectives had been ordered to let it stay.

Now, Melbourne in the 1890s was awash with prostitution – some two thousand women in a city of 283,000 regularly selling themselves. The major hotels all maintained 'saddling paddocks', rooms where prostitutes waited for customers.

By coincidence, though, the most notorious red-light areas operated in close proximity to Parliament. Streetwalkers congregated in Little Lonsdale Street, while Stephen Street became so notorious that, after the International Exhibition in 1878, the council decreed it would henceforth be known as Exhibition Street. But Lonsdale Street housed the city's most infamous brothels, where bawds such as Scotch Maude, Biddy O'Connor and Annie Wilson plied their trade.

The morals campaigner Reverend Dr Bevan cemented the link between the Parliament complex and the nearby houses of ill repute in 1892, when he noted with dismay that Madame Brussels' expensive bordello had recently been connected to one of the city's first telephones. The scarcely veiled insinuation was that the authorities wanted a phone to reach parliamentarians needed for a division.

On 12 November 1892, the respectable *Ballarat Courier* returned to the mace scandal:

> It is said that the mace was abstracted from Parliament House by some courtesans who had been entertained by public men, and that the abstraction was viewed at the time as a joke, equal to anything in 'Boccaccio'.

The final phrase constituted a none-too-subtle wink to sophisticates, who were sure to recognise 'Boccaccio' as the name of an establishment operated by one of Madame Brussels' rivals. The story was thus well and truly out. Even though, when summonsed to Parliament, Madame Brussels denied all knowledge, the tale of the mace in the brothel haunted the Parliamentary Speaker (and later Premier) Thomas Bent to the end of his days.

In his pamphlet investigating the incident, Raymond Wright argues that no solid evidence connecting the mace with the Lonsdale Street brothels ever existed. He suggests instead that it was stolen either by a parliamentary staffer or in a simple burglary.

In many ways, however, that's not really the point. What's interesting is the way the public so speedily drew the connection. When Tommy Bent eventually resigned after a land scandal, it seemed to most people perfectly evident that he probably had something to do with the missing mace. After all, as the magazine *Table Talk* said in its article on the affair: 'The present government is notorious for discovering reasons very obvious to themselves why the public should not be informed of their doings.'

A brief verse from the Sydney *Truth* serves to summarise an incident that, if not strictly true, certainly should be:

> *Nellie the harlot thinks it's no disgrace*
> *To house the politician and the mace.*
> *Sir Thomas, fresh from legislative duties,*
> *Relaxes in the smiles of Nellie's beauties.*

led the crowd down to the Town Hall where they denounced scabs enlisting to break a dock strike before making their way back to Parliament. *The Age* noted, with the bitterness of a butcher watching bullocks escape the paddock, that the men singing 'The Red Flag' seemed 'robust, healthy looking and, apparently, eligible [for war service]':

> At the steps of Parliament, the police seized Pankhurst, and led her off to be charged.
>
> Roused to fury by this development, several women acted in a most disgraceful manner and umbrellas and fists were used against the police.
>
> Though unsuccessful in rescuing their leader, the protesters were not deterred. Orators declared Prime Minister Hughes afraid to meet with them and announced their intention to continue the campaign.

Their subsequent protest the next month produced an even more violent clash. On 20 September, *The Argus* described how:

> half a dozen shrill-voiced girls, who carried a red flag [led] a mob of men and women . . . through city streets last night, singing songs of revolt and smashing windows out of pure wantonness.

Again, the demonstration aimed to march to Parliament; again, a cordon of police along Spring Street halted its progress. This time the protesters simply moved through the city, smashing the glass of newspaper offices and big stores before marching off to join a group of striking workers.

The agitation around food prices only came to an end when the authorities invoked the Riot Act, prohibited all public gatherings at the Yarra Bank, Flinders Park and other forums, enrolled special constables and arrested most of the main leaders (including Adela Pankhurst).

The unemployed struggle of the Great Depression also proved particularly violent. A demonstration on 26 February 1930 gives a sense of the times. Five hundred unemployed men marched down from Trades Hall. The ushers hastily closed the gates of Parliament. Police arrested three of the men for trying to break them down. A melee developed, and the crowd was dispersed – but not before the police confiscated all their banners.

There's no record of the parliamentary gun rises ever being used. The response, however, to the various demonstrations that have assembled outside the building leaves one in little doubt that those inside would have no compunction in putting them to use, should the need arise.

# 21. Melbourne Anarchist Club

## Her Majesty's Theatre

In May 1886, a proclamation greeted the Melbourne public:

> The Melbourne Anarchists' Club extends its greetings to the liberty loving citizens of these young colonies and appeals to them to assist its members in their efforts to remove those public sentiments and public institutions, which have been transplanted here from the northern hemispheres, retard social progress and happiness; and to substitute in their place the enabling principles of Liberty, Equality and Fraternity!

That prospectus – first read aloud to about fifty people a fortnight after the formation of the Melbourne Anarchist Club – can be found today in the State Library of Victoria. The headquarters of this extraordinary organisation can, over a century later, be viewed simply by strolling down Exhibition Street to Her Majesty's Theatre.

That is, although the original Alexandra Theatre was revamped several times – and almost totally destroyed by fire in 1929 – the facade of Her Majesty's today remains substantially the same as in 1886. The best way to view it is to stand on the median strip of Exhibition Street, looking at the Little Bourke Street side. In the 1880s and 1890s, the street level consisted of shop fronts. The second and third floors, however, look much as they must have been in the nineteenth century. Here, in a room above one of the shops (probably the third window along), the Melbourne Anarchist Club assembled.

What kind of organisation was this? The circular advertising its first meeting noted that: 'Anarchists, Communists, State Socialists, Republicans, Democrats, Conservatives, liberals, Radicals, nihilists and Royalists, all warmly welcomed'.

Such an appeal – which today seems almost perversely inclusive – should be read in the context of the tradition of radical self-education, in which dedicated autodidacts grappled with an astonishingly diverse array of subjects. While it's doubtful that the anarchists (including refugees from German social democracy, American industrial struggles and the English Chartist movement) genuinely expected an influx of conservatives or royalists, a quick glance through their publication establishes the seriousness of their commitment to eclecticism.

RADICAL MELBOURNE

Above: Alexandra Theatre in the 1890s. The anarchists probably met at the third window from the left above the fruit barrow. Top: the same building today. Opposite: J.A. Andrews

After all, the Anarchist Club newspaper – which the members wrote, printed and sold themselves – took its name not from Proudhon or Kropotkin or other such libertarian theorists but from a Shakespearian passage that appeared on its masthead:

> There is no terror, Cassius, in your threats for I am arm'd so strong in
> Honesty, that they pass by me as the idle wind, which I respect not.

The pages of *Honesty* are then littered with epigrams from Thomas Jefferson, Shelley, Dickens, Zola and Victor Hugo. The Anarchist Club's lectures manifest the same spirit. Each Sunday at 7.30 p.m., the anarchists hosted a meeting and debate, on topics that today seem quite mystifying. For instance, on 19 June 1887, the Melbourne Anarchist Club sat down to 'Optimism and other Popular

Anti-Progressive Theories'. Two weeks later, they followed with the more forthright 'A Colony of Lunatics'. Other topics included 'Prostitution, and how it may be Ameliorated', 'Modern Slavery' and 'Money: a study of the Currency Question, especially in its relation to Equity, Utility and Liberty'.

Who were the anarchists? David Andrade, a shopkeeper with a penchant for political theory, served as the Club's secretary, having formed the organisation with his brother William 'for the purpose of meeting to exchange our thoughts and make them known to others'. Alongside Andrade, John Arthur Andrews, a journalist and poet of some note, claimed the role of chief theoretician. The frail and ascetic Andrews generally dressed in rags and wore his hair long; some said he was 'given to the use of Eastern narcotics'.

Chummy Fleming also attended meetings regularly. A bootmaker by trade, Fleming had been warned by a magistrate to 'stick to his last' after his first arrest – advice that he spent the next fifty years ignoring. Other members included Larry Petrie (described by a contemporary as a 'super class' rebel) and Monty Miller, a fiery agitator who at 18 had fought at the Eureka Stockade.

While predominantly male, the Melbourne Anarchist Club maintained remarkably advanced attitudes to women. Its meetings regularly debated the question of female emancipation while *Honesty* pointed out and decried instances of ill-treatment of women. In one issue, the paper argues for free divorce for women, declaring that marriage 'should rest entirely with the contracting parties to make or break as they desire'.

As a small and beleaguered organisation in isolated Australia, the Melbourne anarchists avidly followed events around the world. They bundled copies of *Honesty* to political groups overseas, and then printed the resulting foreign correspondence in subsequent editions. French anarchists declared: 'We have been much pleased in receiving the first copy of your Anarchist paper, and we are glad to see that there are Anarchists in all parts of the earth-ball', while *El Socialismo* responded: 'We have had the pleasure of seeing, for the first time at this office, our beloved Australian colleague *Honesty* . . . we wish this new soldier of the revolution every success, and recommend it to the comrades who read English'.

The anarchists were avowedly internationalist, declaring:

> *Honesty* will espouse the cause of the Laborer, whether local or foreign, whether religionist or scientist, whether popular or unpopular. It will contend for the right of labor to the full fruits of labor, and it will show the laborers how to co-operate in order to return that product.

They regularly argued against anti-Chinese sentiment, pointing out that 'while the white workers are quarrelling with their yellow-skinned fellow workers, the monopolists whom they both support are grinning in their sleeves at their stupidity'.

The Melbourne Anarchist Club dissolved in the early 1890s as a result of internal political differences – and lack of public support. But many of its leading members continued to play an important role in Australian radicalism. Chummy Fleming remained a thorn in the authorities' side for the next half century. David and William Andrade both opened radical bookshops, while Monty Miller joined the Industrial Workers of the World (IWW), copping a sentence of six months' hard labour for sedition at the age of 84. Larry Petrie moved to Sydney and became an organiser for the Australian Workers Union. A contemporary described him thus:

> He had only one arm, having lost the other through fighting a big 'scab' in one of the shearing sheds. On the slightest – or no – provocation, Petrie with flashing eyes and bristling black moustache, would sing 'The Marseillaise' then the workers' one revolutionary song. When he came to the chorus 'To arms, to arms!', he wildly waved his arm, to the delight of the cynical crowd.

Petrie later travelled to join a utopian communist experiment in Paraguay. Returning, somewhat disillusioned, to Australia, he died in an accident at work.

As for J.A. Andrews, he, too, left Melbourne after the collapse of the MAC, carrying a bag of oatmeal, a rusty rat trap to catch game and a swag of revolutionary leaflets. A description survives of his activities in Sydney:

> Clothed in an overcoat to cover his sometimes shirtless body and tattered clothes, Andrews would proceed to the Domain. Tying a long pole with a small black flag attached to an overhead tree, he would deliver a two or three hours' exposition of the tenets of philosophic anarchy, to the proverbial crowd of two men and a dog.

Somehow, Andrews made a living from radical journalism, although he faced gaol many times. He eventually made his way back to Melbourne to edit the socialist magazine *Tocsin*, but died of tuberculosis not long after.

Given the anarchists' strongly expressed views as to royalty, it's a nice irony that the only physical reminder of their club should be Her Majesty's Theatre. Next time you pass, the appropriate memorial is to raise your fist and declare, in suitably impassioned tones: 'Liberty, Equality and Fraternity!'

# 22. Secret Society Riot

## Corner Market Lane and Little Bourke Street

On 13 February 1904, *The Age* reported:

> considerable excitement in Little Bourke Street last night, [as] the bulk of the population of China Town . . . congregated in front of premises situated at the corner of Market Lane, the interior of which was filled with turbulent Chinese. They seemed to be all arguing the point at once, and the noise that they made in the process gradually increased in volume till it developed into an indistinguishable babel of sound . . . The doors were opened, and about 30 agitated Chinese were ejected one by one on to the sidewalk by an organised force concealed within.

The journalist had stumbled across a long-brewing conflict between the two secret societies that dominated Melbourne's Chinatown. The older of the two, the Yee Hing, originally formed in China as an underground revolutionary organisation, a secret band aiming to overthrow the tyrannical Manchu dynasty. When the Manchus put down the Taiping rebellion in 1864, the ensuing repression forced thousands of dissidents to flee. Chinese emigrés in Australia established local branches of the Yee Hing, both as a means of ensuring the continuance of their resistance and, more immediately, as a kind of mutual assistance society for refugees thousands of miles away from home. The society wrapped a basic message of brotherhood and solidarity in mystical trappings and – in the absence of a social security system – helped its members find jobs, resolved disputes and occasionally lent money.

But as the years wore on – and the struggle in China remained at a low ebb – the emphasis on members' day-to-day problems came to predominate over any political idealism. The secrecy of the society – once necessary to evade the Manchu authorities – developed into a screen for less honourable activities, up to and including small-scale racketeering. As *The Age* commented:

> The original ambitious purposes of the Yee Hing appear to have become submerged in a sea of petty local affairs, and it usually has so much trouble on hand quarelling with members of rival organisations that the Manchu dynasty need have no immediate cause for alarm.

Young men in Chinatown in the 1890s.

In reaction, non-Yee Hing Chinese formed a society known as the Bo Leong. Its name meant 'to protect the weak and decent people', and it had the avowed purpose of safeguarding its members from Yee Hing harassment. Like the early Yee Hing, the early Bo Leong espoused philanthropic aims, lending assistance to distressed, aged or poverty-stricken Chinese, and using its resources to assist with the long and expensive passage home to China.

The three-storey shopfront on the corner of Little Bourke Street and Market Lane provided a meeting hall and offices used as a cultural centre within the Chinese community, resources that both groups coveted. The Bo Leong initially took the offensive, massing its supporters to eject the Yee Hing from the hall. Yee Hing supporters rallied, and then returned in force. After a brief fight, the Yee Hing succeeded in retaking the building, which they then barricaded before applying for police protection.

Seven months later, the struggle erupted again. The Bo Leong had – despite its puritanical rhetoric – begun following the same shady path as its rival. When police charged some of its members for selling sly grog and opium, the society blamed Yee Hing informers. The white press described the resultant violence with typical racism:

Between 8 and 9 pm shots rang out in a fan-tan and cook shop on the south side of Little Bourke St, about twenty doors down from Russell St, which bears over its portals a Chinese legend which, interpreted, means 'The Abode of the Righteous', or something of that sort. The shots were followed by sounds as of all the animals of a menagerie being let loose together and a horde of yelling Chinese seethed through burst doors and fell upon one another indiscriminately in the street. Plain Clothes constables Kelly and Hawkins, who were in the street at the time, rushed among the frenzied Orientals and by dint of sheer muscular force and the aid of steel handcuffs upended a dozen or so of the most turbulent of the mob. The constables, however, could not cope effectually with the whole yelling gang, who were tilting at each other with long poles, whacking with clubs and stabbing with knives. A young man named Hussey, who was engaged in some private detective work in the street, after having been rolled over by the first rush of the uncontrollable mob, took the tidings to Russell Street. Inspector Cawsey and Sub-Inspector Cahill at once directed a force of men to the locality to assist Constables Hawkins and Kelly, who were growing somewhat tired of the monotonous work of 'knocking 'em down' and a dozen stalwart constables with clubs, amongst whom the impressive figure of Constable Barber, armed with a fence post, loomed largely, soon scattered the struggling crowd.

The nonchalant brutality of the police – and the satisfaction with which *The Age* reports this litany of bashings – allows one to appreciate the attraction provided by the societies as an alternative source of authority within Chinatown. When the law is personified by Constable Barber and his fence post, an all-Chinese association, with its own rules and regulations, must have seemed an absolute necessity.

Nevertheless, the Chinese community made known its disapproval of the Bo Leong's violence, and the organisation dissolved in 1912.

The re-emergence of an oppositional movement in China gave the Yee Hing society a new focus. One estimate claimed that in 1911 its members numbered about three thousand in Victoria, out of a total Chinese population of just under six thousand. Increasingly involved with Sun Yat Sen's republican movement, the Yee Hing changed its name to the Melbourne Chinese Masonic Society, and in 1920 built an extensive headquarters in Little Lonsdale Street (since demolished).

That same year, the first Chinese Nationalist Party Convention was held in Sydney, attended by delegates from trades hall – including Jock Garden, soon to become leader of the Communist Party. To host the second convention in 1921, the Nationalists commissioned famed architect Walter Burley Griffin to renovate the facade of the Market Lane building, which subsequently provided a centre for the Chinese Nationalist Party in the period between the two world wars.

Today, the Chinese Masonic Society is much like any western Masonic group, providing a social club for its (mostly ageing) membership. It now meets at 7 Waratah Lane, a slightly disreputable lane running between Lonsdale and Little Bourke Streets, housing a curious mixture of sex shops, rubbish bins and fashionable restaurants.

But though the days of whacking with clubs and stabbing with knives are long over, the current – less than salubrious – address lends the society a whiff of the intrigue that it possessed in the distant past.

The Market Lane building, the decaying Burley Griffin renovations still obvious alongside the otherwise identical building to the left.

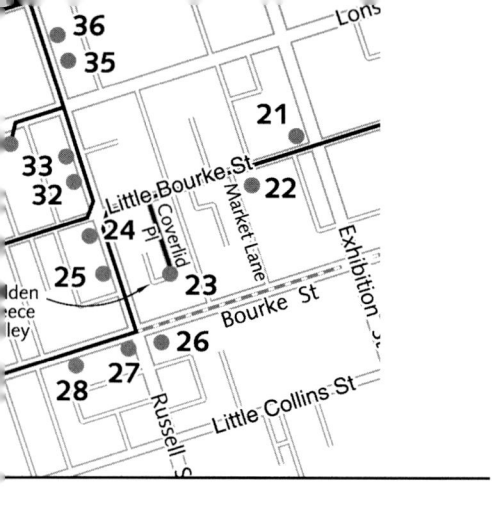

# 23. Golden Fleece Hotel

## Coverlid Place

Strolling along Little Bourke Street, you pass any number of little lanes, many of which are today home to fashionable bars and nightspots. But there's nothing chic about Coverlid Place. On the far side of Russell Street, it's an unprepossessing alley, littered with bins, cardboard boxes and graffiti. Anyone venturing down it of an evening is likely to be frequenting the seedy pool hall on the left side of the alley, slinking into the adult cinema on the right, or shooting heroin in the shadows at the end.

But there is another reason to explore. At the end of the lane, the old street sign bears the name 'Golden Fleece Alley'. The alley branches to the right, extends a few more metres and then, on the right, leads to the back of an ugly carpark. This was once the Golden Fleece Hotel.

In 1889, a small band of men came together in the Golden Fleece to form the Melbourne branch of the Australian Socialist League, a radical – but heterogeneous – organisation established in Sydney earlier that year. Many of the Melbourne founders also attended the Melbourne Anarchist Club; it was the well-known anarchist Chummy Fleming who kick-started the January meeting by informing a 'very attentive audience of between 30 and 40 people' that the objects of the League should be 'to expose the misery produced by the capitalist system and educate the workers in the principles of socialism'. He then proceeded to read aloud Kropotkin's 'Appeal to the Young', which was favourably received and inspired 'an excellent discussion'.

Excellent it may have been, but to anyone new to socialism the breadth of terrain over which it ranged must have seemed rather overwhelming. A Mr Krick responded to Chummy by urging 'the absolute necessity of thorough organisation to prepare for the coming of the Socialist Revolution', while John Fraser advocated 'a closer study of social economy by the workers', and Mr McNaught sketched 'the evolution of society from slavery to the hoped freedom'. It was left to Larry Petrie to elegantly endorse 'the communistic views of Prince Kropotkin', and Sam Rosa to point out (rather obscurely) that 'not only did the rich rob the poor of the fruits of their labor, but of their love also; of the most beautiful, amiable and intelligent of their daughters'.

Though fourteen people signed up on the spot, the question as to the precise nature of the organisation remained somewhat vexed. When, a few days later, the same band convened in the Golden Fleece's upstairs hall, it quickly became apparent that individual comrades held very different views on what had been decided. One member later explained that 'Petrie and I had first thought of establishing a Communist-Anarchist group. Comrade Fleming had thought of a Melbourne branch of the Anarchist Club . . . Comrade Rosa was contemplating a Social-Democratic Federation'.

After a lengthy discussion, those assembled decided that it was as yet impossible to agree sufficiently as to enable general propaganda to be distributed. Nonetheless, they emphatically concurred that, at such time as it was found that they could agree on something to be done, they would immediately do it.

The discussion as to the election of officers in such a libertarian body also created controversy, and harmony was restored only when an 'officer' was carefully defined as entailing 'someone who agrees to do, and is simply authorised to do, what any member can do, but which if left to any may be attended to by none'.

Golden Fleece Lane.

In essence, the ASL was a radical discussion group in which an extraordinary variety of philosophies could be canvassed. What held it together for its brief lifespan was a strongly held belief – shared with other radicals of the time – in the imminence of socialism. The ASL's greatest asset lay in its core membership – charismatic figures, absolutely devoted to their cause, and prepared to spend hours clarifying their ideas in meetings and articles.

As well as the Golden Fleece meetings, the ASL members took on what they referred to as 'wharf work'. On any Sunday, Comrades Fleming, Rosa, Petrie and other dedicated ASL-ers would make their way down to Queens Wharf (the forerunner to the Yarra Bank) to deliver long speeches to a crowd that was invariably lively and only occasionally sympathetic.

The police responded with threats and the occasional arrest. One ASL report noted that 'the police took part in the wharf meeting in a way, by repeatedly telling Fleming he had said enough and had better go home or he would soon be arrested', and by informing another who had declared his atheism that 'he ought to be chucked in the river'. Another recounted that the officers, in between moving supporters on, often stood around listening to the speakers, sometimes discussing the merits of their case with the onlookers. 'Probably', the writer continued optimistically, 'one or two of them will end by becoming converts to the social movement.'

Political events overseas provided a constant source of inspiration to isolated Australian enthusiasts. In 1871, French workers had taken over Paris for a month and run the city along collective lines, before the authorities regained control and massacred the insurgents. In March 1889, the Melbourne Anarchist Club, the Verein Vorwärts (a German socialist group) and the Communist-Anarchists (a grouping within the Melbourne Anarchist Club) joined the ASL in celebrating the anniversary of the first revolutionary workers' state. They decorated the meeting hall at the Golden Fleece Hotel with a red flag, and advertised the celebration in the press. Amongst the many who attended were a number of Frenchmen, 'of whom there would have been more but for the fact that some doubts had obtained as to whether the announcement might not be a capitalistic hoax'. After speeches in English and French, the group 'then sang the Marseillaise in French, all joining in the chorus, and rising to sing the last verse all together . . . After this, amidst enthusiastic shouts of "Vive La Commune, Vive La Revolution Sociale", the meeting dispersed'.

By mid-1889, the differences of political opinion within the ASL had brought about the collapse of the organisation, and many of its members dispersed to pursue other radical projects. Sam Rosa and Larry Petrie joined with Dr William Maloney – whose preferred wardrobe of cream silk suit, red bow tie, panama hat, waxed moustache and goatee beard made him a somewhat unlikely radical – to form the Social Democratic League, a less anarchistic group that met in Trades Hall or (when that had been denied to them) the Golden Fleece.

The creation of the SDL coincided with the onset of a savage depression and Rosa and co. set to work organising the swelling numbers of jobless. For some two months, the unemployed – sometimes numbering up to a thousand – met daily outside the Working Men's College (today's RMIT). Delegations demanding relief work visited the Premier and James Patterson, the Minister for Public Works, who provoked especial resentment through his helpful suggestion for those without work 'to show some British pluck'.

The SDL decided to adopt a more militant tack. At the next meeting, Rosa stood before the crowd to announce that, if no assistance were to be provided, the unemployed had a moral right to loot shops (although he advised them to remember that 'raids should only be on the shops of rich men, and not on those of the poor').

The scandalised authorities promptly set guards on jewellers' stores in Collins Street, and seriously contemplated arming all the police in the city. Rosa himself became a figure of infamy. A report in *The Bulletin* played on his notoriety by describing him as 'a piratical looking cuss' boasting 'a big Punch looking nose, with terrific red hanging mustachios, like the late King of Sardinia, matching his

**A NEW INDUSTRY.**

*In view of the constantly increasing demand for effigies, doubtless their manufacture will soon become a regular business. Who will be the first to profit by our idea and open a shop?*

The unemployed protests did not go unnoticed. The faces are those of politicians of the day.

shock of red hair . . . always grinding his teeth, like boar tusks' (though it signalled the joke by adding 'another account to hand says he is a very quiet looking, pale, inoffensive, little young man').

In subsequent rallies, the unemployed continued to send delegations to see VIPs, but began refusing to announce which distinguished personage they intended to visit until after their rally had set off through the city, thus forcing the police to guess the probable destination. In this way, throughout the winter of 1890, Rosa led his followers to greet the Governor, the Premier, the Anglican Bishop, the Catholic Archbishop, the mayor, the President of the Chamber of Commerce, the President of the Chamber of Manufacturers and the Minister for Public Works.

Patterson responded with a denunciation of the unemployed as 'a lot of blasphemous, atheistical, socialistical, communistical, nihilistical men, who went upon the wharf Sunday after Sunday to denounce everything that was good and decent and virtuous'. Rosa rejoined that 'the fact that the scum always rises to the top is probably the reason why Patterson is Minister of Public Works'.

The following Sunday, about six thousand people gathered on the wharf to hear speeches by Rosa, Petrie and Chummy Fleming (who, despite his differences with the new group, had also thrown himself into the campaign). Fleming then carried an effigy of Patterson adorned with the label 'cattle-duffer' (Patterson had previously been a butcher) up Flinders Street to the Yarra Bank, with a crowd following, singing 'We'll hang Jimmy Patterson on a sour apple tree'.

When they arrived at the Bank:

> the 'effigy' of Mr Patterson – old trousers, coat ditto, stuffed with straw, and surmounted with a 'belltopper' – was 'decapitated' amidst groans and

general execrations, set alight, and thrown to the bottom of the embankment, the remark being made that if Mr Patterson were there in the flesh he would be similarly served.

The next Sunday, the agitators displayed an effigy of the Premier to an even larger crowd, though a police baton charge and the subsequent arrest of several participants saved the dummy from the fire. The following week, the unemployed managed successfully to decapitate Alfred Deakin.

That proved the climax of the agitation. Rosa and the SDL abruptly abandoned the campaign, perhaps fearing that events were getting out of hand. After a brief attempt to participate in the Great Maritime Dispute that year (where, according to *The Argus*, SDL speakers 'found fault with both the Trades Hall and employers of labour in connection with the crisis which has taken place'), the Social Democrats became involved in attempts to form a labour party. Some time in the early 1890s, they collapsed as a distinct organisation.

The lane leading to where the Golden Fleece stood is today a less than salubrious location; its proximity to Melbourne's heroin trade and the piles of refuse building up there don't encourage you to linger. Indeed, one can only imagine that any propensity to loiter would be regarded with acute suspicion by the police who are never far away from this section of town. Over a century ago, though, it would have been the police doing the loitering – watching with misgiving the comings and goings of some of Melbourne's earliest revolutionaries.

# 24. IWW Office

## 171 Little Bourke Street

On the corner of Little Bourke and Russell Streets stands a three-storey, red-brick, Victorian building with a chemist at street level and the Da Hu Chinese restaurant above. You'll find the entrance to Da Hu a few metres down Little Bourke Street. Climb the stairs, sit down at a table, and order the Da Hu's speciality – little pancakes of Peking duck.

Now imagine that it's 1916. Instead of round tables covered in starched white, the room is ornamented only by cheap worn chairs. The clientele is different, too – there are labourers, wharfies, unemployed men of all nationalities, and a handful of working class women. Rather than dining with friends, you're spending Saturday night listening to a fiery orator denouncing the evils of capitalism and declaring his opposition to the war raging in Europe.

That is, the Da Hu restaurant was once the headquarters of the famous Industrial Workers of the World – referred to with sympathy as 'the Wobblies' or, by the bosses, as the 'I Won't Work brigade'.

The IWW originated in the United States in the early years of the twentieth century. Its founders had wanted an alternative to the cautious, bureaucratic union federation of the States, and their preamble encapsulated the bold mood of those involved:

> The working class and the employing class have nothing in common. There can be no peace as long as hunger and want are found among millions of working people and the few, who make up the employing class, have all the good things of life. Between these two classes, a struggle must go on until the toilers come together on the political as well as on the industrial field.

When the organisation split in two a few years later, it was not because members backed away from any of these sentiments. If anything, it was sparked because some in the IWW believed that the preamble did not go far enough; at a conference in 1908, a motion was moved to change the last line of this paragraph to read:

> Between these two classes, a struggle must go on until all the workers of the world organise as a class, take possession of the earth and the machinery of production, and abolish the wage system.

On the ground floor, a chemist shop; above, the old headquarters of the Wobblies.

The division which resulted from the following debate was over the question of whether political action had any useful role to play in the revolutionary process or whether – as the more radical IWW organisation insisted – the action of workers seizing control at the industrial level was the one and only revolutionary strategy.

By 1907, IWW-ism had arrived in Australia – bringing with it radical ideas about union organisation. The IWW aimed to organise workers into a single union for each major industry – rather than the existing small 'craft' unions. According to this schema, the industrial unions would link up into One Big Union, and this OBU – as it was known – would then eventually take over the factories and begin running society collectively.

Sounds unlikely? Maybe. But then, Australian working conditions at the beginning of last century were shocking. After a series of heavy defeats during the 1890s, the union movement had rejected militancy in favour of arbitration, parliamentary action and the establishment of the Labor Party – which, once formed, almost immediately abandoned any vestiges of radicalism.

The IWW – with its calls for aggressive industrial unionism – offered a stark alternative. The Wobblies' approach showed through in the little stickers which they plastered all over town with messages such as: 'Fast Workers die young. Someone has to be last – let it be you', and: 'The hours are long, the pay is small – so take your time and buck 'em all.'

Both flavours of the IWW had been established in Australia, but it was the militant, direct-actionist IWW which flourished. The Melbourne branch of this IWW was not founded until 1915. It had initial difficulties in setting up headquarters, since its first landlord voided the lease after discovering he housed the infamous Wobblies. The group moved briefly to a new building in William Street where they were able to have both a library and reading room, and by August 1916 had settled in 197 Russell Street (a large room above a pawnshop on the corner of Little Bourke Street), where they remained until their organisation was banned.

Here, more nights than not, Melbourne IWW members could be found climbing the stairs to attend a lecture or meeting, or occasionally a dance or a social. On Monday night, the local held a business meeting, Wednesday a speaker's class, Thursday night an educational class on topics such as 'Working Class Economics', and Saturday, a public lecture.

Although constantly harassed by police, the Melbourne Wobblies didn't hide themselves away. On the contrary, they would take their meetings to street corners. In days before TV and cinemas, street meetings formed an important part of popular entertainment. The IWW came into its own – its members being humorous as well as fiery speakers – and Friday nights would see them down at the South Melbourne Market or in Brunswick, at the corner of Sydney Road and Victoria Street.

Often their performances would turn into a battle of wits with the local police, who tried to break up radical meetings. The IWW came up with unorthodox methods of continuing proceedings, occasionally shimmying up trees to finish their speeches from the branches. In Townsville, when police attempted to break up a gathering on the beach, the speakers simply moved the meeting into the ocean, addressing the crowd of several hundred from the sea.

It was the IWW's theatrical bent, as well as their militancy, which won the Wobblies popularity amongst workers. Music was always a part of their activities, and even when the Sydney local was on the verge of bankruptcy and its assets little more than a printing press and a large stock of literature, it still managed to retain a piano. As well as publishing a book of radical tunes titled 'Songs to fan the fires of discontent', the IWW invented a colourful vernacular where workers who scabbed or sucked up to employers were known as 'Blocks' while a capitalist was invariably 'Mr Fat'. The Salvation Army became the 'Starvation Army', clergymen 'blackcoated vultures', the ALP the 'Hard Labor Party' and the New South Wales Parliament the 'Macquarie Street Gas House'.

Tom Barker, editor of the Wobbly paper *Direct Action*, gives a sense of the organisation's spirit when he recalls the time that the police came looking for the IWW editor, advertised in *Direct Action* as A. Block. According to Barker, the members had:

> got a block of wood with a dingy old top hat on it and kept it behind the door in the editorial room. When the detectives came round they got very annoyed when they were introduced to the editor.

The IWW vociferously opposed the racism of White Australia, arguing that joblessness should be tackled not by discrimination but by active unionism – fighting for shorter hours so that more people could have jobs. They sought to organise Chinese workers in Melbourne, translated literature into other languages, and encouraged white Australians to identify with foreign-born workers by publicising accounts of strikes organised by groups of Italian, Spanish or Chinese workers. In Queensland, one IWW local was composed entirely of Russian immigrants, and members said that they knew only one foreigner – the Boss!

As *Direct Action* explained, the question for workers should be:

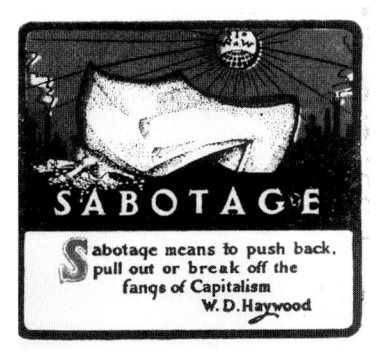

'What are you – worker or parasite?' rather than the inane cry of 'Where do you come from?'

This internationalism also led the IWW to trenchantly oppose the First World War (within days of its outbreak, they had organised an anti-war demonstration in Sydney). By 1916, Australians were debating conscription – with the campaign being accompanied by mass demonstrations and strikes. Before long, Prime Minister Hughes had identified the IWW as the leaders of the anti-war and anti-conscription movements, and launched a vicious campaign against them.

At first, this only served to help the IWW. They grew rapidly, their membership peaking at around four thousand. They managed, however, to have an influence far outweighing their actual membership numbers, with IWW speakers often addressing crowds of tens of thousands at anti-conscription rallies. Indeed, until the emergence of the Communist Party, the Wobblies represented the most serious revolutionary organisation in Australia's history.

In response, the government and the police stepped up their campaign against them. As the referendum on the question of conscription approached, the police cracked down on the IWW, raiding their clubrooms around Australia and arresting members. The worst of the police harassment was levied against the Sydney local where police framed twelve of the leading members for 'conspiracy to commit arson and sedition'. By July 1917, the IWW was banned and its members raided, arrested, gaoled – and even deported.

The Melbourne branch, despite being one of the weakest sections with a reputation for conservatism, came under fire along with the Sydney local. Undercover police regularly frequented meetings; on at least one occasion, a Detective Coonan secretly attended a meeting and had determined that 'most seemed of the poor working class' before members of the audience, becoming aware of his presence, rose to denounce 'spies and pimps and their treachery to the working class'.

Despite its bravado – and genuine bravery – the IWW could not withstand the assault from the state. The Melbourne IWW attempted a few manoeuvres to avoid police harassment – including changing its name – but by August 1917 had dissolved itself. The IWW as a whole was not to last much longer than the war. By 1920, the organisation had collapsed – but by this time, the newly formed Communist Party was ready to take on where the IWW had left off.

# 25. Victorian Socialists League

## 177 Russell Street

The building at 177 Russell Street – today, the middle of three combined into a bleak and noisy video arcade – boasts the distinction of having housed no less than three separate far-left organisations within the space of one tumultuous decade. From 1898, this building (handily, just across the road from where Temperance Hall, the main left-wing meeting place, once stood) served as an office for the Victorian Socialists League, then the Social Democratic Party, and finally, the Industrial Workers of the World Club, in a process neatly embodying a pre-war generation's political swing to the left.

Although the Victorian Socialists League was formed only a few years before 1900, its politics owed more to the utopian traditions of pre-Marxist socialism than to the militant atheism associated with twentieth-century communism. When, for instance, the VSL's Comrade Willmott addressed a meeting in Richmond:

> he asked his hearers to dispel from their minds the erroneous idea that socialists believe in no religion. It was an absurdity. The Socialist Party preached the Fatherhood of God and the Brotherhood of Man. He went on to say that through want of knowledge there is a section of the community who is very prejudiced. They have an idea that Socialists intend to use force. He assured his hearers that they do not intend any such thing.

The VSL rented rooms in 177 Russell Street in mid-1900. The building served as a hall for a meeting every Wednesday or Thursday – a half-hour discussion of VSL business followed by a lecture, with guest speakers ranging from anarchists to Fabians. The party provided a theoretical class each Sunday ('any young man or young woman interested and wishing to join will be given a hearty welcome') led by the poet Bernard O'Dowd, a man well suited to the role of guru. The painter Norman Lindsay described O'Dowd around this time as 'making a staggering presentation of the conventional Jesus, with his pale, peaked face, his ginger beard and a lot of long meek red hair combed back from his pallid forehead, and dripping over his coat collar'.

177 Russell Street.

Yet the real centre of the VSL came not from the economics class but from the wide array of social activities the group offered its adherents. The Quadrille Club convened regularly in Russell Street, while Sunday night mass meetings invariably incorporated a musical performance, often provided by the party's own Socialist Band. 'Monster Socialist Picnics' (including a trip scheduled immediately after the election of 1900 – to enable members 'to bless our cup of cheer or drown our youthful sorrow') gave inner-city workers a chance to enjoy the great outdoors, while regular 'Grand Social Evenings' offered them dancing, dominoes, cards and chess.

This schedule of dancing and board games renders it difficult to believe that, in its day, 'the Socialist Party was looked at as a very dangerous body' (as a certain Comrade Hannah once complained during a Richmond meeting).

Yet when the English Fabians Sidney and Beatrice Webb (the acme of genteel, middle class reformism) visited Melbourne in 1898, Beatrice's notes of an encounter with the VSL provide an extraordinary insight into just how the respectable world viewed the Victorian Socialists and their League:

> In an out of the way, dirty and badly ventilated place we met our 'poor relations', the believers in socialist shibboleths: a nondescript body of no particular class, and with a strong infusion of foreigners; a Polish jew as secretary and various other nationalities (among them a Black) being scattered among the audience. The chairman was the usual SDF [Social Democratic Federation – the main British socialist organisation] young man, with narrow forehead, bristling hair, retreating chin and dirty coat, and the inevitable red tie. 'Comrade', 'revolution', 'trade unionism played out', 'capitalist press', 'class war' and all the rest of the Socialist well-meaning cant was showered over us, and we responded by a douche of cold water both as to practice and theory . . . Sidney in a wily address tried to explain the Fabian policy of permeation [that is, allowing gradual reforms to be slowly accepted by the population], with the result that the Chairman in his concluding remarks recommended the meeting to adopt, 'Mr Webb's suggestion of taking the capitalist down a back street and then knocking him on the head'!

The black whose presence the Webbs found so offensive was almost certainly Chris Casimir, a key VSL organiser, who could indeed be numbered among the ranks of the Victorian Socialists' genuine radicals. Casimir – who worked as a private schoolteacher, until the parents of some of his pupils encountered him in the midst of a fiery harangue on the Yarra Bank – inherited his dark skin from a Mauritian mother and (his contemporaries claimed) his gift of oratory from a French father. According to the socialist Ernie Lane, during visits to the Lane household, Casimir would ask:

> 'Mrs Lane, do you mind if I stand on a chair? I can speak so much better when I have room to talk.' We would laughingly agree, and it was a sight for the gods to see and hear Casimir throwing his thunderbolts at the capitalist system and prophesying the early triumph of the workers.

By 1902, several leading Victorian socialists had grown tired of the VSL's well-meaning but woolly eclecticism. The visit of the famous British radical Tom Mann provided impetus for change, with a majority of VSL members accepting his suggestion of a merger with another smaller group to form what one of them subsequently described as 'a real party founded upon a sound Democratic basis'.

This new organisation christened itself the Social Democratic Party, the name by which the Marxist parties across Europe were known. After a frustrating attempt to find office space, the SDP reverted to 177 Russell Street, as both a meeting place and a reading room where supporters were reassured that the 'party exercises discretion in the choice of its literature', and warned 'trashy stuff, dished up as "socialistic" . . . can be kept out of the Australian movement by developing a taste for scientific socialism'.

A taste for scientific socialism did not prevent the SDP from inheriting the VSL's pleasure in good wholesome fun. The report of a SDP mass meeting in Queens Hall on February 1903 included a description of the evening's (typical) entertainment – 'a piano solo, two capital recitations by Mr Mayne and a strong bass song excellently rendered'.

Such evenings proved popular – by 1904, the Social Democrats could boast some six hundred members, the majority of them unionists. But although the SDP had been formed with the mission of creating a 'straight out socialist party', its political program depended upon a naive faith in the ALP's evolution into a genuine representative of the working class. By 1905, the conservatism of mainstream Labor leaders made such a transformation seem increasingly unlikely.

Bernard O'Dowd.

Again, Tom Mann took the lead, with a call for a new organisation – one which aimed to actually fight to convert Labor to socialism. With the rank and file of the SDP in tow, Mann founded the Victorian Socialist Party.

Yet while the VSP quickly became the dominant force on the state's far-left, it did not have the field entirely to itself. The Industrial Workers of the World – the third organisation to use 177 Russell Street – represented one of the many alternatives.

IWWism developed initially in the United States, where radicals counterposed industrial unionism (involving the unity of all workers in a particular industry) to the traditionally cliquish organisation of the conservative union leaders.

The Melbourne IWW Club formed in 1908. Where the VSP aimed to reform Labor from within, the IWW Club condemned the ALP lock, stock and barrel – a position nicely expressed in a song written by a Melbourne member, Bill Casey, in which a Labor politician boasts:

> *Some very wealthy friends I know*
> *Declare I am most clever,*
> *While some may talk for an hour or so*
> *Why, I can talk for ever*

before bursting into a chorus of:

> *Bump me into Parliament,*
> *Bounce me any way,*
> *Bang me into Parliament,*
> *On next election day.*

It was a critique which many found convincing. Much of the IWW Club's initial membership of fifty came from defectors from existing socialist organisations, distressed at their party's organisational or political ties to the ALP. Indeed, Tom Mann himself, before leaving for England in 1910, confessed to finding the IWW creed appealing.

As its inaugural secretary, the Club appointed Montaigne O'Dowd – the less hairy son of the VSL's economics tutor, Bernard. Leah Jarvis, a Collins Street physiotherapist, became one of the first women to join. She had been imprisoned two years earlier for her part in the fight for free speech in Prahran. The post of chairman went to Monty Miller, an ex-member of the Melbourne Anarchist Club and the SDP, a veteran of the Eureka Stockade, who – at 76 – remained sufficiently lively to earn the title of the 'darling of the ladies of the club'.

In its early years, the Club concentrated on addressing union branches about the principles of industrial unionism, as well as holding its own regular open air meetings. When the American fleet visited Melbourne in 1908, the IWW Club demonstrated its solidarity with its persecuted comrades in the US by plastering the city with red stickers explaining:

> Armed Force Keeps Union Men in America's Gaols.

An IWW pamphlet hammered home the attack, complaining:

> the officers of the fleet and the gold-bugs of Australia are feasting on the choicest food, swilling champagne and having a luxurious time generally. A lot of talk is indulged in about our fine cities and our splendid country, and all the time the robbery of the workers continues.

Ironically, though, the new radicalism that helped spur the formation of the IWW very quickly returned to cause it difficulties. For all that the Club lambasted the ALP, it didn't condemn participation in Parliament altogether – a point that quickly became a bone of contention. As early as 1908, Monty Miller had stormed out in protest against Club members' insistence on discussing the possibility of 'political' action (that is, standing candidates in elections). That same year, the American IWW split over the question of the desirability of parliamentary activity in addition to industrial action, and, from 1911, the more radical IWW 'locals' began to appear in Australia. Their orientation to direct action captured the imagination of the most radical workers.

Before long the locals were established as the 'real' IWW, leaving the IWW Clubs isolated stagnant discussion groups. By 1915, the Melbourne IWW Club had been reduced to writing to *The Age*, plaintively claiming the mantle of authentic IWWism, and denouncing the 'extreme' tactics of its rivals. Shortly thereafter, the Club abandoned the field by changing its name altogether.

Today, the inability of the Australian Labor Party to provide genuine social change continues to disenfranchise many from the political process – the youths in 177 Russell Street are not alone in their preference for pinball over politics. The struggle to build an alternative to Labor's betrayals remains as important today as when first debated here inside the VSL.

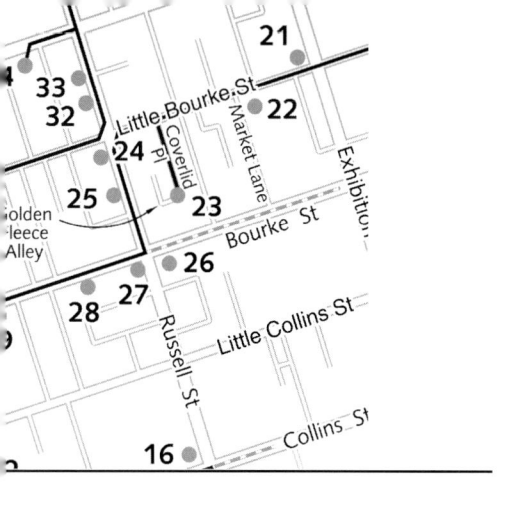

## 26. Workers Art Club

### 175 Bourke Street

The Workers Art Club lasted scarcely more than a year. But between 1932 and 1933 it represented a genuine (if not always successful) attempt to involve working people in art, and art in working class struggle.

The core of the WAC came from a small but determined coterie of (mostly) young men, as passionate about politics as literature, theatre and painting. A few belonged to the Communist Party; others were in the process of joining. Their inspiration came from the *Proletkult* movement of the Soviet Union in the 1920s, which proclaimed that the working class would develop its own artistic forms in a complete break with a bourgeois culture from which it had nothing to learn.

However specious this might have been, *Proletkult* provided the WAC with the self-confidence ('Art', ran its slogan, 'is a weapon') necessary to establish rooms in a city not noted for its appreciation of artistic experimentation. The Club's first public event consisted of a 1932 exhibition of watercolours and drawings by Jack Maughan, a waterfront clerk whose paintings expressed the abiding hatred for war he'd learnt on the beaches of Gallipoli.

In her 1945 novel *Ride on Stranger*, Kylie Tennant describes a body known as the Proletarian Club, clearly modelled on the Melbourne WAC and that first exhibition:

> The special series of pictures designed to uplift and cheer the opening of the Proletarian Club were black and white sketches; battlefields with figures in the foreground, usually with a string of entrails proceeding from them, skulls in helmets, mutilated and blinded and unpleasantly distorted corpses in all shapes and sizes.
>
> The guests gave these decorations the admiration they deserved, and exclamations of: 'Superb stuff, you know. What I like is their strength and vigour' were accompanied by a critical appraisal with the head on one side and the eyes half shut . . .

Certainly, the catalogue notes for the Maughan exhibition ('The 27 exhibits of this young artist speak for themselves – and not in a whisper!') suggest that the

# ART IS A WEAPON

WAC members took their event rather seriously. Nonetheless, Maughan's images *are* remarkably powerful, and the show received surprisingly favourable notices in both The Age and The Herald (where the reviewer described the Club as 'a little difficult to find' but the pictures 'well worth a visit').

Thus encouraged, the WAC hosted a collective exhibition of paintings before relocating (according to Tennant, in the original rooms, 'there was no ventilation, a little matter the committee had overlooked in its joy at the cheap rental') to 14 Royal Lane (near the Tivoli Theatre). The attic, rented for a pittance from a sympathetic old anarchist cobbler, provided a studio for the young artist Noel Counihan.

In early 1932, Counihan – increasingly drawn to politics – had agitated for higher pay in the hosiery company where he worked and had been abruptly dismissed for his pains. When his disgusted father burned his collection of left-wing literature, Counihan stormed out of home, and began dossing down in the WAC rooms, where he and the caretaker Taffy Morgan slept on wooden benches and dined on two upturned boxes above a concrete floor.

At around the same time, the Club became involved in a more immediate political campaign. In May 1932, right-wing students attacked members of the Melbourne University Labour Club, a Marxist group with links to the Communist Party.

Above: the Workers Art Club met on the top floor, now luxury apartments.
Top: Workers Art Club logo.

119

Conservative students force Labour Club members to sing 'God Save the King'.

A crowd of three hundred broke down the doors to the *Farrago* office, seized Labour Club member (and WAC supporter) Sam White – who had supposedly made 'disloyal' remarks during a meeting of the Historical Society the previous week – and threw him into the university lake. Two other Labour students who tried to defend White were also hurled into the pond, where the mob forced them to salute the King and sing the National Anthem.

The incident attracted considerable newspaper attention, with the bulk of it openly applauding the attack upon White. The WAC rushed into print with a pamphlet entitled *The University Riots: A Presentation of the Facts*, which argued that the episode presaged a more general confrontation between fascism and democracy.

In August 1932, the Club returned to art, with a theatrical performance of Ernst Toller's *Masses and Man*. A thousand people attended the Temperance Hall, where the evening's program explained:

> Booze, sex-suppression and money grubbing are the main themes about which the capitalist futilities of bourgeois art resolve . . . While Capitalism in

> its last dying hours gurgles forth a last hymn of frustration, the growing vitality of proletarian or workers' art manifests itself.

A reviewer noted that 'many of the ladies in the audience wore red blouses and the men's neckties and the programmes were of the same sanguine colour. An atmosphere of intense seriousness pervaded the house'. At the conclusion of the evening, the audience showed its approval by singing the revolutionary anthem, the 'Internationale', as the last curtain fell.

Towards the end of 1932, the Club moved to Little Bourke Street, where it launched its own journal. The first issue of the optimistically titled *Masses* implored its readers: 'We want news from the Class Struggle. Send Us Contributions: Stories, sketches, reviews, poems, cartoons, etc. Anything real!'

Evidently, little real was forthcoming, for *Masses* didn't run to another edition. The WAC dissolved itself in 1933, its hard-line rhetoric no longer in accord with the Communist Party's new orientation to broad alliances with the middle class. Many of the Club's supporters remained involved in the arts. Jack Maughan, for instance, joined the New Theatre, where he worked as actor and director, while Counihan became a major figure in Australian painting.

Years later, a reviewer in *Smith's Weekly* recalled the Workers Art Club as having 'little or nothing to do with workers of any kind, but includ[ing] in its membership a collection of young men and women of pink political views and somewhat bohemian manners'. Perhaps more surprisingly, this assessment seems to have been largely shared by the Communist Party – Tom Le Huray, a communist leader, described the members as 'a pack of petit-bourgeois degenerates'. The CP had no objection to putting such degenerates to work – the May Day procession of 1932 saw communists marching behind banners adorned with Counihan sketches of Marx, Engels, Lenin and Stalin – but otherwise found it difficult to shake off a nagging suspicion of artists and their works.

The later WAC rooms (in Royal Lane, and Little Bourke Street) have vanished. But above Florsheim's shoe shop on the corner of Bourke and Russell Streets, you can still make out the floor where the Maughan exhibition must have taken place.

## 27. Movement Against War and Fascism

### 145 Russell Street

In 1938, Robert Menzies – founder of the modern Liberal Party – returned from a visit to Nazi Germany to declare: 'There's today a really spiritual quality in the willingness of Germans to devote themselves to the service of the well-being of the state'.

Menzies' enthusiasm for the Hitler regime confirmed the left's long-standing suspicion that establishment politicians worried more about fighting radicalism than the dictators in Germany or Italy. The Victorian Council Against War and Fascism – once housed in the 1920s building on the corner of Russell and Bourke Streets – provided perhaps the most vocal opposition to appeasement both at home and abroad.

Originally known as the Movement Against War, the organisation came into being in 1933 through the efforts of the Communist Party and its fellow travellers. It held meetings, collected signatures and distributed anti-war literature – activities which brought it into constant conflict with a respectable Australia for whom any critique of militarism smelled suspiciously of treason. When activists laid a wreath at the Shrine to pledge to the dead of the last war a determination to fight against future conflicts, their flowers were removed and mainstream papers thundered against the desecration of the 'spirit of Anzac'!

Today, the question posed in the title of the movement's journal *War! What For?* sounds insipid, almost inane. But in the 1930s, it proved sufficient for Attorney-General Menzies to slap a ban on the magazine, in a wave of censorship that meant by 1936 over a hundred left-wing publications could not legally be transmitted by post. At the same time, Menzies specifically rejected calls to outlaw Hitler's *Mein Kampf*.

In 1934, a police agent reported an attempt by 'apparently well-to-do foreigners, students of the Methodist Ladies College, Ministers of Religion, Communists and unemployed revolutionists' to invite a mysterious 'Ewart Risch' to attend an Anti-War Congress. When the spy managed to straighten his notes 'Ewart Risch' turned out to be Egon Kisch, a noted left-wing journalist and refugee from Nazi Germany. But while Kisch's hard-hitting brand of literary journalism had brought him great acclaim throughout Europe (where he had earned the sobriquet of the 'rampaging reporter from Prague'), his identification with the communist movement put his tour squarely in Menzies' sights. The Australian government promptly announced that neither Kisch, nor the New Zealand delegate Gerald Griffin, would be permitted to land.

Accordingly, when Kisch's boat arrived in Fremantle, customs officials boarded and prevented the reporter from disembarking. Kisch thwarted them by leaping from the ship onto the wharf in Port Melbourne, breaking his leg in several places but touching down on Australian soil, and thus complicating the government's legal action.

Menzies then tried a different tack. Australia's racist Immigration Act allowed police to examine the fluency of undesirables in a European language. Since Kisch was famously multilingual, the authorities administered his test in Scottish Gaelic, a language which they safely assumed he would not know. His failure saw him sentenced to gaol.

Outrage swelled around the country, and a court eventually upheld Kisch's appeal on the basis that Gaelic did *not* constitute a European language – much to the dismay of Australia's Scottish nationalists!

Bourke House.

Prior to the tour, Kisch had been largely unknown in Australia (at one meeting, a well-meaning chairman filled locals in on Kisch's biography by reading from an entry in the Czech Encyclopedia, which informed guests of their visitor's reputation as a connoisseur of Prague night life, intimately familiar with prostitutes and criminals). Menzies' ham-fisted attempt to silence him turned Kisch into a bona fide celebrity.

In Sydney, he attended a meeting of some twenty thousand on the Domain, at which the 80-year-old Reverend Arthur Rivett delivered a fiery anti-Nazi speech and then collapsed and died of a heart attack. When Kisch took the stand, he paid tribute to Rivett and then declared, 'My English is broken, my leg is broken, but my heart is not broken; for the task, which I was given to do by the anti-fascists of Europe is fulfilled when I speak to you, the anti-fascist people of Australia.'

Gerald Griffin had entered the country in disguise. He spoke at a huge meeting at West Melbourne stadium. At the evening's conclusion, the waiting police were tricked into arresting an impersonator, while the real Griffin slipped out to continue his agitation.

In Melbourne, Kisch and Griffin together led a torchlight anti-war protest through the city streets. A crowd estimated at thirty thousand watched a procession that included scores of different European language groups and an Aboriginal gumleaf band playing 'The Red Flag' wending its way from Trades Hall

**LEADING THE TORCHLIGHT PROCESSION from the Trades Hall to Yarra Bank last night.—Mr. Gerald Griffin (left) and Herr Egon Kisch headed the demonstration.**

to the Yarra Bank. Kisch departed shortly thereafter, his tour a success beyond anyone's imagination.

The Kisch incident marked the high-point of the anti-fascist agitation. As the decade wore on, the VCAWF's links to the Stalinised communist movement became more and more of a hindrance. The perspectives of official communism were more determined by Stalin's foreign policy than by the interests of the international working class, and the resulting zig-zags made it difficult for the campaign to attract large numbers of ordinary people.

But though the VCAWF left Bourke House in 1936, the building still has a few points of interest today. If you sneak past the elaborate security system, you won't find much remaining on the fourth floor, which was where the anti-fascists once had their rooms. But two floors lower, you'll discover a dusty old nameplate advertising an outfit calling itself the Heritage Bookshop.

Unless you're at the head of an angry demonstration, we don't advise a visit. The Heritage Bookshop is in fact the distribution arm of the Australian League of Rights, the group described in a 1991 government report as 'undoubtedly the most influential and effective, as well as the best organised and most substantially financed racist organisation in Australia'.

Egon Kisch, it's time to come back!

# 28. Andrade's Bookshop

## 201 Bourke Street

Today, 201 Bourke Street is a KFC outlet. It sells chicken – whole or in pieces, with or without fries. It doesn't sell socialist papers. It doesn't sell condoms. And it most definitely does not sell ventriloquists' dummies. Things have changed in the last hundred years.

Will Andrade, the younger brother of David, helped found the Melbourne Anarchist Club in the 1880s. Perhaps not as dynamic as his brother, he appears to have kept more in the background. Sent to represent the Anarchists at the Australasian Freethought Conference in Sydney in 1886, he subsequently stayed on in that city as a bookseller. After a number of other ventures, he returned to Melbourne in 1898 and then took a loan from a relative to launch the shop in 201 Bourke Street.

The socialist paper *Tocsin* reported the event as follows:

> The opening of a new bookshop in Melbourne is always a matter of interest to the few people in this benighted city who may be described as thinkers, but when that shop boldly displays radical literature in the window, it calls for special notice.

But Andrade's books weren't the only part of the shop calling for special notice. As with surprisingly many of the free thinkers, Andrade's interest in exposing mysticism led him to an appreciation of sleight-of-hand and carnival magic. On the second floor of the long, narrow building, he displayed theatrical and conjuring supplies – make-up, plays, elocution pieces, masks, wigs and ventriloquists' dolls. Under the counter, he sold contraceptives (usually euphemistically described as 'medical aids'). May Francis, a contemporary of Andrade, recorded her discovery of his sideline:

> I had no inkling . . . until I was told the story of a 'new girl' who enclosed the leaflet advertising [contraceptives] when sending out the new play catalogue to customers, including convent schools. The whole shop, about five employees, seemed to enjoy the thought of the nuns getting a shock.

Since his Anarchist Club days, Andrade had retreated somewhat from active politics (as early as 1891, he'd complained of how the average Melburnian 'preferred to waste his time . . . going to the races and soaking his brains at public houses rather than attending to the emancipation of the working class'). But he still maintained a desire to participate as little as possible in the rat race of capitalist competition. He and his family lived frugally on the third floor of the shop – as long as the business provided enough for them to eat, he cared little for profit. So he hired his staff mostly on the basis of their need for employment rather than any particular propensity for work. As Francis noted, 'You got on a payroll at Andrade's, and work was comfortable and almost incidental in the day's routine'.

On occasion, this policy was exploited – as, for instance, when one of the staff was caught stealing from the stock. To soften the blow of her dismissal, Andrade offered to sign whatever reference she wrote about herself. She produced a glowing testimonial, not neglecting to make specific mention of her honesty and trustworthiness!

In 1911, Andrade employed the veteran socialist Percy Laidler as his bookshop manager. The presence of Laidler – described by *Melbourne Punch* as 'about the best mob orator that has struck Melbourne for many years' – alongside the sundry other radicals who found their way into Andrade's helped establish the shop as a centre for radical debate and discussion. At the time, fashionable Melbourne was given to promenading around the Collins Street Block on a Friday night. Working people did the same up and down Bourke Street – and outside Andrade's there was always a crowd.

Laidler's daughter Bertha Walker describes how: 'Twenty to thirty men and a few women, representing all shades of political opinion . . . would thrash out rival policies, finally splitting up into two, three or four groups as the arguments grew more heated'.

Opposite top: Andrade's Bookshop, now an outpost of American imperialism. Below: a sketch of the bookshop. Above: Percy Laidler looking remarkably serious while demonstrating a trick in the shop

For the same reason, interstate or international radicals passing through Melbourne would head up to Andrade's, confident of finding someone there able to explain the complexities of the local political situation.

During the police crackdown on the left in the aftermath of the First World War, the shop naturally became a target. But the special squad matched its enthusiasm for combating subversion with a complete incomprehension of the doctrines it intended to suppress. So detectives removed from the shelves every volume whose label suggested disloyalty – regardless of the actual contents. Racy but apolitical novels like *Red Passion* and *Flaming Youth* were snatched; revolutionary texts with more sedate titles like *The Materialist Conception of History* remained undisturbed.

But the authorities *did* have genuine reason to worry. For as well as selling literature, Andrade's had begun publishing it. In the aftermath of 1917, very little was known in Australia about the Russian revolution – one local paper had so misread the international cables that it polemicised against the activities of a nefarious individual known as General Bolshevik. So Laidler went to work publishing (from the shop) the writings of Lenin, Trotsky and Bukharin, as well as commentaries and descriptions of the revolution. *The Proletarian Review*, Australia's first communist magazine, was put together in the shop, while Laidler went on to chair the foundation meeting of the Communist Party in Melbourne.

In 1922, Andrade sold the bookshop part of the business. Its new owner was himself apolitical, but maintained the radical focus on a purely commercial basis. Andrade's retained the top two floors, with Laidler living on the premises and (since he, too, was now a skilled amateur illusionist) managing the magic shop.

In 1929, it seemed that the lease would not be renewed, and Andrade rented a new property in Swanston Street. When the owner of the Bourke Street building relented, Andrade had already made up his mind to move. At the last moment, though, Laidler informed him that he had decided to retain the staff and take on the Bourke Street lease in his own name, thus leaving Andrade in a new building devoid of both employees and a manager.

More than one observer thought this something of a shabby trick. Nonetheless, both enterprises flourished into the postwar period. Andrade's new shop sold some socialist literature, but mostly continued his interest in the theatrical side of the business.

Andrade himself eventually moved to Sydney. He died surfing in 1939 at the age of 76, when a freak wave dumped him heavily on the beach. Despite its new name, and several different owners, the premises at 201 Bourke Street continued to operate until 1960, always known popularly as Andrade's. Since then, it has been a shoe shop and now a KFC restaurant.

Today, KFC combines what was once Andrade's with the building next to it. The bookshop area is now the serving counter. Walk up the stairs to the second floor, where the theatrical goods were kept. It's a good place to sit and remember the part played by magic in the foundation of Australian communism.

# 29. Tivoli Theatre

## Tivoli Arcade

You can discern the history of the Tivoli Arcade from its name. This was the site of the famous Tivoli Theatre, before fire destroyed it in 1968. In fact, there have been theatres on this site since the days of the Gold Rush when diggers down from the Ballarat and Bendigo fields came to the Varieties Music Hall. In later years, Melburnians watched the first moving pictures at what by then was the Prince of Wales Opera House.

In 1928 – with jazz providing the soundtrack to what seemed like imminent prosperity – the Tivoli Theatre announced a series of performances by a new American jazz band called Sonny Clay's Colored Idea, a tour involving a troupe of thirty-five singers, musicians and dancers.

By this time, Australia boasted over a hundred years of racial intolerance. Fear and hatred of Aborigines, the Chinese and more or less anyone else not white and European fuelled the racist diatribes of the respectable newspapers of the day. The one force that might have challenged such racism – the organised labour movement – had, with a few honourable exceptions, capitulated to White Australia.

Into such a scene arrived The Colored Idea, an all-black band under black bandleader Sonny Clay. While performances by blacks in Australia were not unknown, they had tended to involve shows that portrayed the artists in a disparaging light (such as 'minstrel' cabarets). By contrast, The Colored Idea was confident, exuberant and accomplished – and on the cutting edge of the jazz movement.

In the eyes of the establishment, however, jazz remained inherently suspect. It owed nothing to European traditions but was new, American and popular with the young. From jazz, the authorities reasoned, it was a short step to drugs, communism – and dancing. So, as soon as Sonny Clay's Colored Idea left America, the Commonwealth Investigative Branch – Australia's secret police – dogged its steps, determined to prevent the musicians 'consorting with white women'.

Unbeknown to the band, someone else was hanging around – a reporter from *Truth* newspaper. The Melbourne-based *Truth* could best be described as a nasty little rag, whose very name was a lie. It specialised in sexual tittle-tattle and snide innuendo, with headlines like 'Detective Describes Embrace which Lasted Ten Minutes' and 'Amazing Confessions of Illicit Love'.

It was presumably with such a story in mind that *Truth*'s reporters presented themselves at the Colored Idea gig. They, however, described their motives somewhat differently to their readers: 'An early visit to the stage door of the Tivoli just after [the musicians] had commenced their season satisfied *Truth* that they required watching.'

The Colored Idea continued to play to crowds at the Tivoli, occasionally hanging out in a jazz cafe around the corner in Swanston Street after their performance, or throwing parties at the flats they rented. Yet, even outside these apartments, police and reporters were stationed day and night. A tree (as they later admitted in court) partially obscured their view, leaving their imaginations free to conjure up more and more prurient versions of what was taking place within.

At 3.00 a.m., the police raided the flat, to discover six jazz musicians and six Australian women holding a party. *Truth* painted the gathering in lurid colours:

> For hours [the police] had watched abandoned dancing and shocking happenings before the windows of the flat, and, on making their raid, discovered a worse condition within. Empty glasses, half-dressed girls, and an atmosphere poisonous with cigarette smoke and fumes from the liqueur – and, lounging about the flat, six negroes.

Some of Sonny Clay's Colored Idea Company throwing a hoof on the steamer which brought them to Australia.

Unfortunately, the conclusion of the raid presented the police with something of a problem. Despite *Truth*'s outrage, no laws prevented black men entertaining white women – even if sexual contact had occurred.

The police turned on the women. They were charged with vagrancy, a statute commonly employed when no other laws had been broken. Unfortunately for the police, the women all proved to be in steady employment.

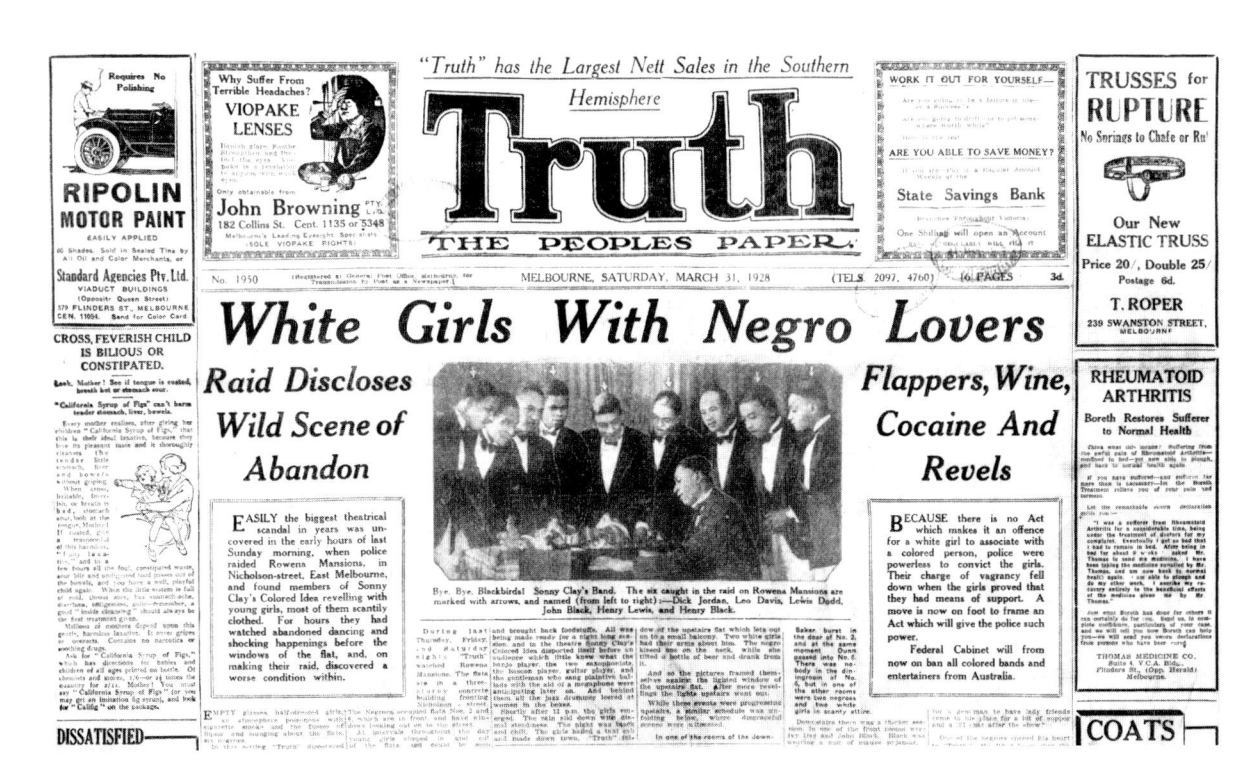

Though no charges could be made to stick, the affair dragged on. A sustained media campaign (involving supposedly respectable papers like *The Age*) led to the matter being raised in federal Parliament. The Honourable Mr Jackson treated the chamber to headlines such as 'Nude Girls in Melbourne Flat Orgy' and 'Raid Discloses Wild Scene of Abandon; Flappers, Wine, Cocaine and Revels' and asked, 'Does the Minister not think that in the interests of a White Australia and moral decency, permits to such persons should be refused?'

The Minister did think so – and the band members were forced to leave on the next ship. All up, six of the band were deported. The other five left of their own accord – unsurprisingly, given that the Tivoli had cravenly cancelled their contracts.

But worse followed. The Musicians Union – which had been campaigning for protection from foreign bands and musicians for years – used the incident to achieve a ban on black musicians. While individual black musicians could play (and black bands with white front men), no all-black bands were to be allowed into the country. It was not until 1954 that another American band led by a black performed in Australia – a ban that substantially retarded the development of Australian jazz.

Standing on the somewhat sordid Bourke Street today and looking at the concrete in Tivoli Arcade, it's very difficult to imagine a swinging theatre with red-hot jazz and a crowd dancing to a syncopated beat. It remains, however, depressingly easy to imagine Australian newspapers whipping themselves into the kind of frenzy that led to the persecution of The Colored Idea.

Opposite top: the only sign the theatre once stood here is the name of the Tivoli. Opposite below: The Colored Idea in action. Above: *Truth* whipping up racism.

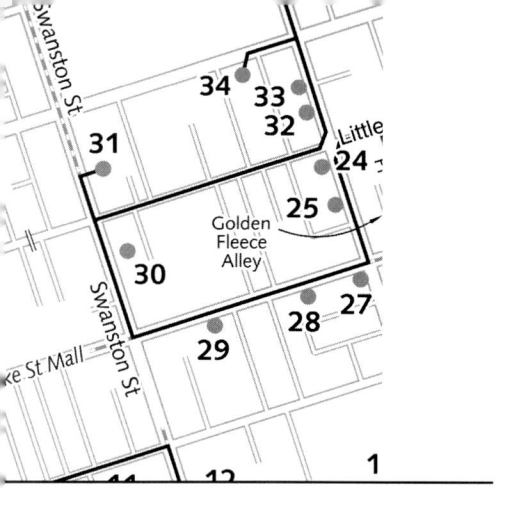

## 30. Communist Party Office

### 224 Swanston Street

Today, the building at 224 Swanston Street sells bicycles. Eighty years ago, it provided the first headquarters for the Communist Party of Australia, the most important left-wing organisation of the century.

The Russian revolution of 1917 generated tremendous enthusiasm throughout Australia, with red flags flying on union halls around the nation. The NSW Labor Council declared that it 'rejoiced' in the revolution, while the Federal Conference of the ALP extended its congratulations to the Russian people. The Australian Workers Union, the biggest working class organisation in the country, editorialised:

> History will tell our children that the world has known no greater messengers of freedom . . . now accomplishing the liberation of millions of souls who today draw their first breath as free citizens and human beings . . . Lenin and Russia have brought joy and hope to a world writhing in pain, bloodshed and misery.

But while more respectable elements of the labour movement applauded the revolution for removing a foreign dictator, those on the left drew far more radical conclusions. If workers could take power in backward Russia, well, why couldn't they do the same in an advanced country like Australia?

The obvious first step for would-be Bolsheviks lay in the formation of a Leninist party. Accordingly, a meeting in Sydney in late 1920 brought together a motley collection of radicals (former IWWers, followers of the doctrinaire Australian Socialist Party and assorted ALP militants) to announce the existence of the Communist Party of Australia. A Melbourne branch followed quickly, with a meeting on Christmas Eve in the Theatrical Employees rooms (now the Apokalypsi Nightclub) in 189 Lonsdale Street.

Declaring a party was one thing, working together quite another. The Melbourne organisation had barely established itself when word arrived from Sydney of a split, each of the two resulting factions claiming the mantle of communist orthodoxy. The first party consisted largely of followers of the Australian Socialist Party; the second of supporters of the trade union official Jock Garden

*A group of young Victorian Socialist Party members at a picnic. Many later joined the CP.*

and William Earsman, prominent in the Amalgamated Engineering Union.

The Melbourne branch chose to remain with the Garden–Earsman party. In January 1921, the paper of the new organisation, *The Communist*, assured its readers that 'in spite of difficulties, comrades in Melbourne are doing good work'.

Despite Lenin's instructions to communists to build 'parties of a new type', the 'good work' of his Melbourne followers proved remarkably reminiscent of the traditional activities of Australian socialists. Members engaged the building at 224 Swanston Street as an office and hall (with the party leader Carl Baker and his family living on site), and then embarked on a hectic timetable of meetings, rallies and paper selling.

By mid-1921, they had settled into a regular weekly schedule. Every second Monday, all the members assembled for a general meeting. On Tuesdays, the branch committee met to allocate organisational tasks. Wednesdays were given over to public lectures in the hall, on Thursdays senior members conducted study classes, while on Fridays the branch held an open meeting in the South Melbourne market. Saturday evening saw another public discussion in the hall, Sunday afternoon a lively session of spruiking on the Yarra Bank, and the week ended with a Sunday evening lecture.

Despite this punishing program, the first CP branch maintained a remarkably eclectic internal life. *The Communist* recorded discussions ranging from Marxist theory (Guido Baracchi's study group on the state) to philosophy ('economic education and the will') to current affairs (the communist response to the

The 1921 Communist Party headquarters today.

Washington Conference). Adela Pankhurst – one of several female members – spoke on the relevance of Marxism to women, while several meetings were devoted to rebutting the latest scare campaigns about conditions in Russia. The party even invited the prominent anarchist Chummy Fleming to outline his theories to the branch – something that would have been unthinkable in the Stalinised monolith the CP later became.

Nonetheless, the Melbourne comrades quickly ran into problems. The departure of two leading members (Carl Baker moved to Sydney to edit the paper; Guido Baracchi, a notorious philanderer, fled to New Zealand to avoid a romantic entanglement) left the group bereft of cadres. Abandoning the expensive Swanston Street premises, they re-established the branch in the less prepossessing Theatrical Employees rooms in 189 Lonsdale Street.

The move did nothing to alleviate growing internal tension. By late 1921, the bulk of the Melbourne membership had become increasingly critical of the Sydney leadership for spending too much time in factional manoeuvres – to the point where the branch flatly refused to distribute issues of the magazine that engaged in unnecessary slander of the other (ASP) communist group.

In January 1922, *The Communist* struck a hopeful note:

> The Melbourne branch of the party look forward to real work in the new year.
> On 1 January, the lecture was delivered by Comrade Earsman, who created a pleasant surprise by walking in unexpectedly, many not having seen him since his return from Russia.
> Comrade Earsman spoke for two hours dealing with Russia from an economic, political and historical point of view to an audience who are agreed that the lecture was the best ever heard in Melbourne for some time.

This report was, to say the least, disingenuous. By 1922, few of the Melbourne members believed Garden and Earsman to be other than a pair of unscrupulous intriguers. Indeed, rather than providing a pleasant surprise, Earsman's unexpected visit sealed the fate of the branch, when his open relish in the accidental death of an ASP rival proved too much for his comrades to stomach.

May Francis, one of the foundation members, later recalled:

> There was no question of us remaining in the Earsman party, although this group had received Comintern recognition. The membership were divided as to whether to transfer to the Reardon Party or to disband. It was subsequently decided to disband [the Melbourne branch].

Jock Garden subsequently led the party from Sydney until 1926, when he decided that a man of his talents might be better served within the ALP. He went on to become a close ally of NSW Labor Premier Jack Lang. As for Earsman, he moved to the Soviet Union, and dropped out of the life of the Australian party. A new leadership built the CP into a major force – and provided the basis on which a Melbourne branch could be re-formed.

Today, the only revolutions discussed at 224 Swanston Street are those powered by pedal. The upstairs hall – once able to hold two hundred proletarians – now stores bicycle parts. Nonetheless, the building occupied by Fitzroy Cycles remains largely intact – a permanent reminder of communism's first, brief toehold in Melbourne.

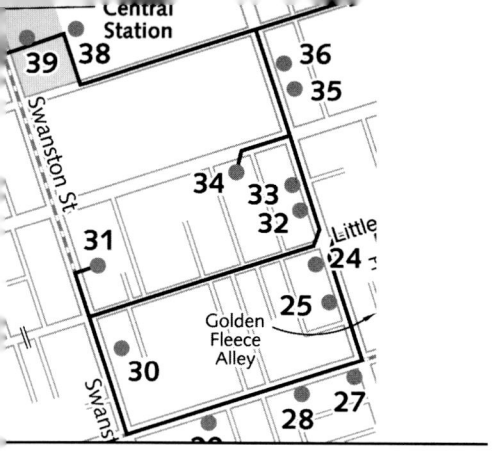

# 31. Communist Party Office

## 252 Swanston Street

> Commonwealth and State police are given free access at all times, by the use of force if necessary, to any premises in which it is suspected there are books, documents or papers relating to a body declared unlawful . . .
>
> The regulations prohibit the publication in any way or the broadcasting of anything advocating unlawful doctrines, the holding of meetings to advocate unlawful doctrines or the collection of money for the promotion of unlawful doctrines.
>
> In a prosecution for these offences averment by the prosecution has been made prima facie evidence of the offence and the onus will be on the person charged to establish his innocence.

Thus did *The Age* approvingly expound the state of freedom existent in Australia in June 1940, shortly after the Communist Party of Australia had been declared illegal, and its premises in Swanston Street raided by a hundred detectives from the political squad.

Today, with the history of the Second World War obscured by the fog of *Saving Private Ryan*-style nostalgia about the 'Good War', the extent of the Menzies government's clampdown on civil liberties is not often recalled. But in 1939, many working Australians remained deeply suspicious about the conflict looming in Europe. Even the ACTU (and the ALP) declared its intention to boycott a register of labour, fearing it marked an attempt to introduce conscription. For a while, it seemed as if an anti-war campaign might be mounted – with the Communist Party of Australia at its head.

The Communist Party's position on the war stemmed less from a serious Marxist analysis of imperialism than from an unthinking loyalty to the Soviet Union. Throughout the 1930s, communists had crusaded against fascism, both at home and abroad. Yet in August 1939, the Russian dictator Stalin signed a cynical non-aggression pact with Hitler. Thus when the European war broke out a few months later, the USSR declared it to be an unjust contest which no communist could support, since the Allied nations were more interested in territorial claims than opposing fascism.

But while this assessment of Western motives may have been broadly correct, the task of defending an anti-war position became much more difficult for Australian communists when Stalin revealed his own imperialist ambitions through a brutal invasion of eastern Poland. Nonetheless, the CP did its best, tapping into still-vivid recollections of the slaughter of the First World War and of the mass campaign against conscription. In its publications, meetings and forums, it reminded workers that until recently Prime Minister Menzies had openly expressed his admiration of both Hitler and Mussolini.

The "New Spirit," displayed on the notice board, expresses much of the work of the Young Democrats. At this buffet, tea and biscuits are served for threepence. The waitress is a voluntary worker, who will be relieved by others.

Above and overleaf: photographs from *Pix* magazine's 1939 feature on the Young Democrats.

Just as in the First World War, those agitating against the slaughter found themselves a frequent target for loyalist mobs, which operated with the tacit support of the police. So throughout 1939 and 1940, party stumps in Footscray, Collingwood (on the corner of Smith and Peel Streets) or the Yarra Bank degenerated into running battles, with off-duty soldiers and Catholic reactionaries attacking the speakers.

In 1940 the Communist Party maintained a centre in the Tattersalls Building in Swanston Street. Its youth organisation – previously the Young Communist League, now the League of Young Democrats – rented two floors and the basement for use as a co-operative cafe, gymnasium and printery. The Victorian State Committee of the CP occupied rooms 7, 8 and 9 on the third floor. In February 1940, a crowd of perhaps a hundred and fifty off-duty servicemen broke up the CP's Yarra Bank meeting, and moved down to Swanston Street. A small group of communists fought them back in a pitched battle at the base of the Tattersalls Building's staircase. The police, once more, refused to intervene.

Ultimately, though, attacks by the state proved more serious than those led by street hoodlums. From February 1940, the government demanded to inspect the copy of all radical newspapers prior to publication. The censor not only deleted whole articles but altered wording in individual sentences, and editors were forbidden to make any reference to the fact that this had been done. For example, the text for an article commenting on BHP's management in the mining union's paper *Common Cause* originally read:

> Mr T. Essington Lewis, chief general manager of BHP is now at the helm! Director of Munitions – munitions to be produced at a profit by his own company. Is this how 'equality of sacrifice' is to be guaranteed?

137

**Political Class of Young Democrats at which social problems are thrashed out.** Political demands include raising of school-leaving age, extensions of apprenticeship, equal pay for sexes, and increased recreational facilities.

When the article appeared it simply stated: 'Mr T. Essington Lewis, chief general manager of BHP is now Director of Munitions.'

Worse was to come. On 19 April, the Minister for Information Sir Henry Gullett announced that communist publications would not be permitted to comment at all on subjects relating to the war, Russia, or 'any strike within the Empire or any allied country' or 'any industrial unrest real or imaginary'. Since Gullett's list covered more or less the entirety of topics covered in CP publications, the May issue of *Communist Review* duly appeared with Jesus' Sermon on the Mount ('Blessed are the Peacemakers') as its principal article.

Shortly thereafter, communist publications were banned outright. A fortnight later, the government declared the Communist Party an illegal organisation. *The Argus* reported:

> Within a few minutes of Cabinet's decision, 40 police cars and more than 100 detectives from city and suburban stations were being summoned to Russell St. The offices of the Victorian branch of the Communist Party in Swanston St, and the League for Peace and Democracy in Collins Street were raided and searched. Documents were seized. Other parties of detectives went to the homes of more than sixty persons, most of them known communists in the city, suburbs and country.

Police estimated that they had seized some two truckloads of books from Swanston Street. Elsewhere, the raids proved less successful. When police arrived at the Party's International Bookshop in Exhibition Street, they blanched at the sight of so many heavy books and retreated to fetch a larger vehicle, allowing the staff time to hide two suitcases of literature in a nearby fish shop.

Indeed, the searches of party members' houses often suffered through the basic political illiteracy of the special police. Many party members managed to pass off the history of the Communist Party of the Soviet Union as an innocuous account of the Commonwealth Public Servants Union. Conversely, others lost harmless books, when the police simply confiscated any volumes with red covers.

The Party had made preparations for illegality, and so continued to operate underground. Its newspapers appeared, albeit in reduced form. But the repression took its toll. A number of militants were gaoled – some for simply letterboxing a socialist leaflet. In NSW, the communists Horace Ratliff and Max Thomas were sentenced to hard labour for possessing printing equipment, and then, after serving their time in gaol, interned in a detention camp.

On 22 June 1941, Germany launched a sudden attack on the Soviet Union. For the CP's Stalinist leadership, this necessitated an abrupt about-face. Now that Stalin was at war, the theoretical schema the Party had expounded in previous months suddenly became superfluous. Overnight, the Party declared the war to be just and progressive. Rather than agitating for peace, the CP now busied itself urging increases in production and preventing strikes (even, on occasion, supporting the use of scab labour). Any prospect of an independent working class movement against both fascism and war was thus snuffed out.

Not surprisingly, the government recognised the value of communist cadres drumming up enthusiasm for the war inside the main industrial centres. The Party regained its legality in 1942, and entered its biggest period of growth on the back of the popularity of Russia as a wartime ally.

The Tattersalls Building in Swanston Street still exists, though now renamed after John Curtin, the Prime Minister who led the country through the second half of the Second World War. It's a good place to visit when you need a reminder of how fragile our basic civil rights can be.

Curtin House.

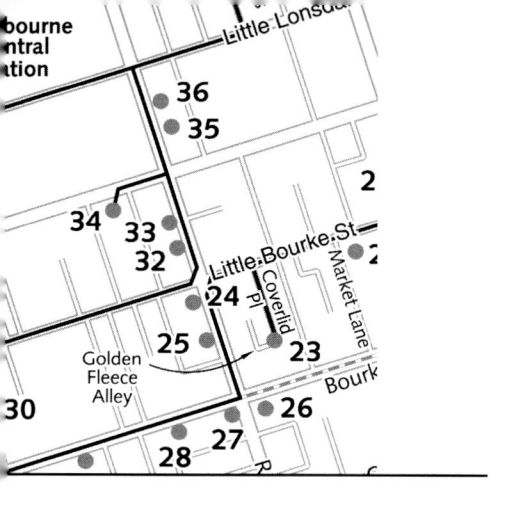

# 32. Anarchist Bookery

### 213 Russell Street

The pork and chicken-based menu of Singapore Kopitiam restaurant provides little hint that 213 Russell Street once housed Melbourne's first vegetarian restaurant. But in the 1890s, the building contained a radical bookstore (or 'bookery'), a hall for left-wing meetings *and* a flesh-free kitchen, combined into a kind of radical emporium.

Behind this extraordinary project stood the peculiar talents of David Alfred Andrade, one of the city's leading anarchists. Andrade's father had been a storekeeper, and both David and his younger brother William fell under the spell of a version of anarchism that relied less on working class revolution than on artisan-based co-operatives. For most of his life, David Andrade worked in shops – managing a short-lived stationery outlet in Sydney Road, Brunswick and then selling literature in E.W. Cole's famous Book Arcade.

His real talent, however, lay as a propagandist, holding forth at the Australasian Secular Association and then later the Melbourne Anarchist Club (an organisation in which he held the post of secretary). Throughout the 1880s and early 1890s, he penned a series of passionate and elegant articles for the Secular Association's *Liberator*, the Anarchist Club's *Honesty*, the *Australian Radical* and anywhere else that would print him, as well as a number of more theoretical pamphlets. To celebrate the second anniversary of the Melbourne Anarchist Club, Andrade composed and performed a version of 'I've got a little list' from Gilbert and Sullivan's *Mikado*, which culminated in:

> *The chap who says: 'You Anarchists are on the proper track,*
> *But as your goal's a long way off, you'd better turn back';*
> *Another who says Anarchy's not good enough for him,*
> *But while man robs his fellow-man, he'll be in with the swim*
> *And the namby-pamby, lack a-daisy, weak kneed Anarchist –*
> *They never can be missed, they never can be missed.*

Andrade himself never showed any inclination to turn back. The operation at 213 Russell Street is a case in point. Andrade's restaurant anticipated the Hare Krishnas' *modus operandi* by nearly a century, using cheap meals to draw in potential proselytes from amongst the down-at-heel. Its advertisements boasted of being 'unequalled in the city for meals of the very best quality, at exceedingly low prices to suit the times':

> It is a genuine vegetarian restaurant, pure and simple; no fish nor fowl being included in its choice and tasty dishes and yet the variety of them would surprise a meat eater and the taste of them would make him long to be a vegetarian. A plate of vegetarian soup can be obtained for 3d with three times the nutriment of an equal quantity of meat soup and a far pleasanter taste; a plate of delicious beans, vegetables, omelettes and other wholesome delicacies costs only 6d and is itself superior to a shilling meal in the best meat restaurants while the light and tasty puddings and the choice fruit, nuts and wholemeal bread are the best 3d dessert the most ardent epicure could desire; the thirsty can procure a cup of the best tea, coffee, cocoa or milk with bread and butter, for the modest sum of 3d while a dinner consisting of the whole three courses and a cup of tea can be obtained for one shilling!

From the outside, the two upper floors look much as they would have in the 1890s.

For those impressed by such fleshless fare, handily enough the shop also provided the headquarters for the Vegetarian Society of Australia.

Indeed, the building attempted to supply almost anything a radical might desire. Alongside his meeting room (which he defiantly named Liberty Hall), Andrade hosted a library, a reading room and his own printing press. The stock in the bookery reflected its proprietor's ecumenical enthusiasms, advertising 'literature upon Socialism (both Communist, Collectivist and Anarchist), Freethought, Spiritualism, Theosophy, Mesmerism, Chiromancy, Phrenology, Vegetarianism, Antivivisection, Hydropathy and so on', alongside heavy-duty tracts by Marx and Lassalle.

Thus, in 1892, a stroll into the bookery would enable you to read Wollstonecraft's *Vindication of the Rights of Women*, purchase a sex education title like *Plain Home Talk about the Human System; the Habits of Men and Women; the Causes and Prevention of Disease; our Sexual Relations and Social Natures* (with coloured illustrations), refresh yourself with a bowl of beans, and then wander up to Liberty Hall for a lecture series on free love.

Later that same year, Andrade produced his crowning effort, a utopian novel entitled *The Melbourne Riots and How Harry Holdfast and his friends emancipated the workers*, which his wife, Emily, typeset by hand. To a modern reader, it's a curious book – as a not unsympathetic reviewer declared at the time, 'the first ten [chapters of *The Melbourne Riots*] are records of conspiracy and gore, and the last ten are devoted to the elaboration of the scheme which the author has conceived to be the panacea for poverty'. The fairly thin plot involves Holdfast, an advocate of socialist co-operatives, spending years in gaol when the evil Felix Slymer incites an armed insurrection in Flinders Street. After serving his time, Harry emerges with a perfected scheme for co-operative land settlement which, once put in place, transforms rural Australia into a land of milk and honey – in the process inducing Slymer to abandon his wicked ways.

But Andrade aimed to do more than entertain his reader. The book complete, he formed his own Social Pioneering Company (quartered, naturally, at Liberty Hall) ready to enrol those enthused by Holdfast's exploits. To kick the process along, he posted an autographed copy of *The Melbourne Riots* to the Governor, the Earl of Hopetoun, with a note explaining:

> I am one of the representatives of the proletarian class which lives to wear out its life for the benefit of the ruling class; and you are the head representative of that oppressive ruling class in this colony . . . I have sent you by this post a copy of a little book which I have just written and published, entitled *The Melbourne Riots*, the aim of which is to lay bare the evils which now curse our civilisation . . . If you will honestly read the little book and conscientiously, boldly and fearlessly express your opinions on the proposals contained in it, perhaps you and I can work together to make the colony a little happier and more prosperous than we find it . . .

Alas, the only reply came from the great man's private secretary:

> Dear Sir, I am desired by his Excellency the Governor to acknowledge the receipt of and to express to you his grateful thanks for the copy of *The Melbourne Riots* which you have been so kind as to send him. His Excellency has read the work with much interest and though he fails to agree with you in your remark that 'He is the head representative of the oppressive ruling class in this colony' he is quite in accord with you as to the utility of getting people into the country districts, together with many other ideas which your work portrays.

Such faint praise did not generate sales. With the readers of radical literature failing to patronise the bookery in sufficent numbers, Andrade found himself in 1893 unable to make his rental payments. Emily had just given birth to their fourth child, a boy they named 'Proudhon' after the anarchist theoretician. With a young family in tow, the Andrades loaded their possessions onto a tip dray and left Melbourne to put David's enthusiasm for rural life into practice.

They established a property on a land settlement scheme in South Sassafras in the Dandenongs, where Andrade eked out a precarious living as a storekeeper and mailman. But in January 1898, the local paper reported:

On Wednesday 12 inst, Mr D.A. Andrade of South Sassafras, was awakened out of his sleep at about 5.30 am, by hearing one of the children crying out that the house was on fire. The family were all awakened, and every effort made to arrest the flames but in vain. In a short time everything was destroyed, the children narrowly escaping with their lives, for had not the youngest girl been awakened by the fire in time there is no doubt but what they would all have been burned in their beds. Besides the furniture and clothing the whole of the stock in the store and the books in the private library were destroyed, nothing being saved but the nightshirts which they were wearing at the time, Mrs Andrade having to throw hers off, as it was on fire.

The following week, the paper received a letter that was vintage Andrade. In it, he explains:

> Neighbours (some of whom have been heavy losers themselves by the fire) have rendered us aid, besides some from afar off, and I can only hope for the best.

Facing absolute destitution, with his house, shop and precious books gone, Andrade seems most concerned to record a nearby resident's prophetic dream about the fire:

> Whether ascribable to telepathic influence or otherwise, [the circumstances] will doubtless prove interesting to those who, like myself, are irresistibly drawn into the study of the mysteries of the universe which affords an illimitable field for investigation in physiology and theology.

Though Andrade's next years remain obscure, we know that the universe did not prove any kinder in the revelation of its mysteries. Some time around the turn of the century, one of Andrade's children – possibly his daughter, Gertrude – died. This finally proved more than Andrade could bear. Lapsing into madness, he was committed to the Ballarat Mental Hospital in 1903, where he remained until his death in 1928.

His medical records have not survived but a note from a nurse suggests he probably suffered from paranoid schizophrenia. She remembers him as an eccentric but very amusing old gentleman, given to writing humorous poetry.

Andrade's co-operative schemes seem even less viable now than they did in the 1890s. Yet a quick walk down Russell Street today makes it plain that the social evils he tried to fight still remain to be conquered. In that battle, we could do worse than recapture the enthusiasm and optimism that marked David Andrade's ventures.

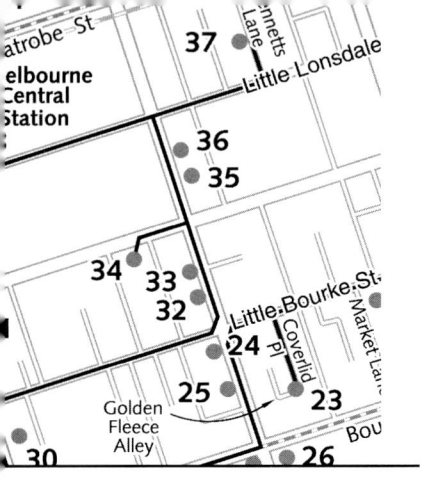

# 33. Communist Party Office

## 217 Russell Street

'It's only ten years since the Russian revolution and already the Soviet system has proven its superiority. In the capitalist world a great crisis is approaching . . .'

Thus does the writer Judah Waten's semi-autobiographical character Tom Graves begin a speech on a stump platform on the corner of Little Bourke and Russell Streets in the 1982 novel *Scenes of Revolutionary Life*.

After the first attempt to launch a Melbourne branch of the Communist Party collapsed in acrimony in 1922, two years passed before a second effort could be mounted. Initially, this 1924 branch did not seem promising. Several of the more experienced members (like the bookseller Percy Laidler and the theorist Guido Baracchi) flatly refused to rejoin, leaving the organisation largely dependent upon a middle-aged base, isolated from the working class. Indeed, the group seemed as much Bohemian as Bolshevik, a trend exemplified by one Mrs Young, who several years earlier had been stoned for wearing harem pants in Collins Street.

Nonetheless, the Party established an office in 122 Bourke Street (in an old grey 1880s building that, with some minor renovation, now trades as the Ito Noodle Bar). Fear of right-wing vandalism prevented the communists from advertising their whereabouts with a sign. In Waten's novel, a trip to the CP's Bourke Street headquarters involves travelling down a dark corridor past 'a warren of offices and rooms occupied by spiritualists, fortune tellers, palmists, Pelmanists, passport photographers, dentists, surgical bootmakers, tap dancers, barbers and an employment agency'.

In the mid-1920s, Party work consisted mostly of traditional socialist propagandising. The central role played by women in the campaign against conscription meant that the early Communist Party contained a largely female membership. Members conducted open air meetings in Russell Street (while the Salvation Army band prayed for their souls on the opposite pavement) or on the Yarra Bank, where they wheeled out an old piano to accompany revolutionary singing. Joe Shelley, the burly branch leader and sole full-timer, possessed a taxi donated by a Party sympathiser so as to enable him to supplement his meagre stipend. But Shelley – famously given to announcing to opponents that after the revolution they would have their throats cut, a task he would take great pleasure in performing personally – had no intention of wasting time on so prosaic an activity as collecting fares. Instead, he painted the cab red, adorned it with scarlet curtains, and then put it to use transporting members and propaganda on political missions around the city.

Despite such bravado, the branch's growth remained slow and painful. Internal wrangling culminated in a damaging split in 1925, which saw all but thirty of the members leave.

That same year the Party played a small role in supporting an important strike of British seamen, as well as participating in some mass work for the unemployed. By 1927 the CP felt sufficiently confident to expand its offices. While few landlords were enthusiastic about leasing to an organisation of professional revolutionaries, the branch eventually secured a lease on the second floor of 217 Russell Street, between Little Bourke and Lonsdale Streets.

Bill Murphy, an old IWW militant, acted as caretaker. Waten describes a Murphy-type figure sweeping up the cigarette butts left after meetings in order to fill a jar with tobacco, so as to allow the unemployed comrades to roll themselves a smoke. The optimism inherent in the move might have seemed somewhat misplaced, given that in 1928, a year later, Melbourne could still only boast of forty-eight members. Worse still, a mere fifteen of those remained fully financial.

217 Russell Street. The doorway to the upstairs office is below the round awning.

Nonetheless, changes were afoot. In 1928, vicious strikes broke out in the timber industry and the waterfront, sharply polarising the political atmosphere. Though the CP remained too small and isolated for serious interventions, it experienced its first real spurt of growth as the Great Depression began to bite.

By 1930, about 25 per cent of Melbourne's workers were unemployed. The next year, the jobless figure nationwide stood at close to 40 per cent. But while capitalism lurched into indisputable crisis, the first Five Year Plan for economic growth in communist Russia steamed ahead. Jobless workers literally lined up outside Russell Street to join the Australian representative of the Soviet system, the CP.

The reality of Russia in 1930 differed markedly from the appearance. By that time, the bureaucracy around Joseph Stalin had successfully crushed genuine workers' democracy to consolidate a stranglehold over the Bolsheviks. As a result, the international communist movement quickly restructured along more tightly disciplined and authoritarian lines. Within Australia, a new CP leadership (Joe Shelley was ousted as Melbourne branch secretary in 1928) began to

Noel Counihan's cage in the aftermath of the Brunswick free speech fight.

implement the dogma of the 'Third Period' – a peculiar piece of Stalinist idiocy under which the main fire of the communists was to be directed first and foremost at the Labor Party.

For the most part, this meant simply denouncing ALP and union leaders as 'social fascists' or, worse still, 'left social fascists'. In Melbourne on May Day in 1932, it culminated in an infamous incident when the Communist Party marched separately from the official rally, before a group led by the writer Jean Devanny stormed the speakers' platform and launched a physical attack upon Acting Premier Tunnecliffe!

Naturally, Moscow's Third Period schema made it more difficult for the Australian CP to overcome the traditional loyalty workers maintained for the union bureaucrats or ALP heads – most activists need to hear more than mere abuse before abandoning their traditional leadership. However, the Party suffered less of a problem in relating to the jobless, who provided the bulk of its recruits in the early 1930s. The unemployed belonged to no union, and retained no particular loyalty to Labor. Indeed, the angry hyperbole of the CP's new leadership often struck a chord amongst those who felt they had nothing to lose. Communists provided the leadership and the bulk of the activists for the militant Unemployed Workers Movement, an organisation dedicated to preventing evictions and winning better conditions for the jobless.

The new recruits resulted in qualitative as well as quantitative change. The influx of desperate unemployed produced a predominantly male organisation that was younger and far more determined.

Which was just as well, for the onset of the Depression ratcheted state repression up several notches. The Commonwealth Crimes Act of 1920 had defined sedition as including any actions intended to promote 'ill will and hostility between different classes of life'. During the 1930s, the Victoria Police took advantage of such laws not only to monitor the Party but to break up working class meetings with batons or fists, often with the assistance of openly fascist vigilante squads, like the Order of Silent Knights.

The Russell Street building came to official attention on a number of occasions, most notably after a militant unemployed demonstration outside Parliament developed into a riot in 1930. Police raided the CP headquarters, the nearby Matteotti Club and a number of houses belonging to known communists, confiscating banners, literature, Party files, an assortment of weapons and, according to *The Herald*, 'a woman's Russian handbag, bright red in colour'.

Nonetheless, the communists persisted. The struggle for the right to hold open-air meetings culminated in the famous free-speech battle in Phoenix Street, Brunswick in 1933. On 19 May, CP activist Shorty Patullo jumped on top of a tram and delivered a short speech to the crowd assembled near the corner of Sydney Road. As planned, the police followed him down an alley (although no-one had anticipated that, after beating him to the ground, they would also shoot him in the leg with their revolvers). The distraction allowed the artist Noel Counihan to clamber inside a steel cage bolted to a truck, and speak to a crowd of five thousand or more, while enraged police bashed at the bars with an enormous wooden battering ram in order to arrest him.

*Truth* keeping a close eye on the communists.

Towards the end of 1933, the CP – its ranks swelled with newly radicalised unemployed – shifted its base to the old Socialist Party building at 182 Exhibition Street (long since demolished). Shortly thereafter, in a belated recognition of the inadequacies of the Third Period analysis, the international communist movement changed its perspective. Communists were now instructed to operate through 'fronts' with respectable, middle class organisations – a move that marked a clear break with the Party's revolutionary traditions.

So the era embodied by the Russell Street headquarters marks, in many ways, the high point of communism in Australia. What was it like inside the building in the early 1930s? The best description comes again from Judah Waten:

> The new headquarters occupied the whole of the top floor of a single-fronted, two-storey building above a barber shop, with a sixpenny cafe on one side and a pawnbroker on the other.
>
> There was nothing musty about the new premises. New enlargements of Marx, Engels and Lenin hung on the freshly whitewashed walls. Most of the floorspace was given over to the meeting hall, with chairs placed in neat rows facing windows that overlooked Russell Street . . .

Waten is today best known for social realist novels like *The Unbending* and *Alien Son*. But the first public attention he received had nothing to do with his literary prowess. When the police raided 217 Russell Street in 1930, the newspaper reports mentioned a precocious 19-year-old named Judah Waten. He defiantly gave his occupation as 'journalist'. The police described him as a 'vagrant' – and took him into custody.

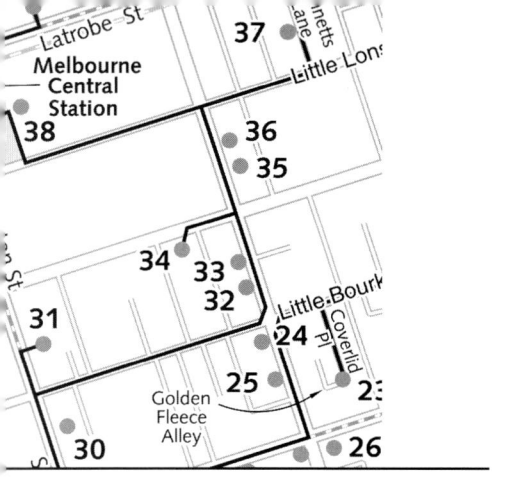

# 34. Greek Club Bombing

## 189 Lonsdale Street

On 1 December 1928, most members of the Lonsdale Street Greek Club were playing cards. A few years earlier, the building had been let to the Communist Party. Now it served as an apolitical social club. Uniformed waiters dispensed soft drinks, pies, cakes and cocoa. A competitor in the billiard tournament paused, his brow furrowed as he lined up his shot.

Then the bomb exploded.

Investigators later surmised that several sticks of gelignite had been placed in the floor above, in rooms empty since police raids on a Squizzy Taylor two-up school operating there. The explosion in the confined space sent a great sheet of flame shooting down from the ceiling above the card game. Shrapnel, bomb splinters and heavy wooden beams fell on the men, who staggered, dazed and bleeding, onto the street. When the dust settled, fifteen people had been injured (though none of the wounds proved fatal).

For the rest of the day, a large crowd surveying the damage blocked traffic between Swanston and Russell Streets. The noise from the bomb had woken all the patients convalescing in the hospital across the road. It even startled the audience in the Royal Theatre at a crucial juncture of the play *Interference* (the hero was poised to uncover a body). For the newspapers, the question of who was responsible for the outrage seemed as open and shut as any stage melodrama.

Earlier that year, eight blasts had rocked the city. The bombers had targeted the residences of shipping officials, strike breakers and others connected with the ongoing industrial tensions on the waterfront. Greek immigrants were said to be prominent among the volunteers used to break the wharfies' strike. So – despite furious denials issued by the ACTU, Trades Hall and the Port Phillip Stevedores Association – Melbourne's papers had no hesitation in blaming waterfront workers for the Greek Club blast.

*The Sun* – much the same kind of paper then as *The Herald Sun* is now – led the charge, proclaiming the existence of a 'gang backed by Red money' and a 'plot to cause racial and industrial strife'. The police, it declared, were already in possession of a confession, including an admission that 'large sums of money had been paid to the perpetrators'. Within a few hours, five men had been arrested – Timothy O'Connor, a dealer; Francis Delaney, a salesman; Stanley Williams, a bookmaker; and Norman and Sandy McIver, both stevedores.

Police uncovered no trace of *The Sun*'s 'Red money'. They did produce a bomb, which they claimed had been found in a car belonging to one of the men. But in essence, the police case boiled down to the word of the officers against that of the accused.

In 1928, the Victoria Police was a highly politicised organisation. Chief Commissioner Blamey was known to be so hostile to organised labour that the middle class magazine *Table Talk* admiringly described him as a fascist – and illustrated its point with a caricature of the Commissioner against a backdrop of stylised policemen forming swastikas with their batons. This was not hyperbole – it was an open secret that Blamey moonlighted as the supreme leader of the fascistic paramilitary outfit known as the White Army.

The rank-and-file police weren't much better. Five years earlier, the suppression of the police strike had seen unionised officers dismissed in favour of the volunteers who had scabbed on them. One Melbourne Club member described the police of the era as more or less a 'licensed basher squad'.

So a neutral arbiter might have taken the unsubstantiated testimony of the arresting officers in a political case with more than a pinch of salt. But Justice Sir William Irvine was not a neutral arbiter. A former Premier of Victoria, he had earned the nickname 'Iceberg' when he introduced the draconian Railway Strikes Suppression Act to smash the rail union. When it came time to sum up the evidence, Irvine phrased the matter in the classic formulation of the frame-up trial. In order to find the accused not guilty, he told the jury:

> you will, as reasonable men, have to believe that the three constables have deliberately fabricated this story, that the police put their heads together, determined to wrongly convict an innocent man, and that they maliciously and widely devised a plan to do it with long, false, perjured statements.

The three-story building nearest the right-hand side of the above photograph is that of the Greek Club, in which the bombs were placed. The floor on which the club room is situated is almost level with the line of the galvanised roofing. The bombs were placed on the floor above and burst downwards into the club room below. The picture shows all the windows shattered as the whole of the glass of the window panes was hurled into the street below. On Saturday night, immediately after the bombing, the roadway from Russell-street to Swanston-street was packed with a huge crowd of persons, who watched the extension ladders of the fire brigade swing upwards to the club rooms when firemen in the blackened structure explored the blackened interior for injured men who might not have been able to race from the building.

Top: the large white building is the Greek Club. Above: the aftermath of the bombing.

The only surprise in the outcome was that a couple of the men were not sent down. But three – O'Connor, Delaney and the union activist Sandy McIver – each received fifteen years' hard labour.

In disarray after its catastrophic defeat, the Stevedores Association was not well placed to campaign for the men. Nonetheless, a movement in their defence eventually took shape and began to hold meetings, lobby politicians and circulate leaflets outlining the circumstances of the case.

In the hysteria of the time, even a flier in defence of the men was treated by the authorities as tantamount to sedition. On 20 November 1931, *The Age* reported that when the Leader of the Opposition received the circular, he 'promptly sent his copy to the police for their information and consideration'. A month later, the police arrested the printer, and charged him with not registering his press.

Nonetheless, outrage at the sentences grew. In 1937, a petition by Dr Evatt (then a High Court judge), Brian Fitzpatrick, Maurice Blackburn and others succeeded in obtaining the release of O'Connor and Delaney.

McIver – the most political of the three – remained in Pentridge until 1939, a constant target of harassment by warders. Remission of sentence was refused him after he was caught with a matchbox crystal wireless he'd knocked together to listen to races, football and boxing.

After his release, McIver refused to speak about the bombing case, even when he became active in the union. Within labour circles, it was commonly accepted that he chose not to clear his own name for fear of compromising a family man. Furthermore, it was said that he had been denied an alibi by a well-known radio broadcaster, who had been with him on the night of the bombing but kept silent for fear of associating himself with the controversial case.

Years later, McIver still refused to discuss the issue:

> Too many people still alive. It would hurt too many people.

Still, he would never drink in the hotel operated by the broadcaster. When asked why, he said simply:

> He didn't shape up too well when I had my trouble.

Over seventy years later, the truth of the matter will probably never be known.

Today, the Greek Club's building is remarkably unchanged since the 1920s (the bombing did no structural damage). It's still a central part of the Greek precinct. And, though there's neither billiards nor cards, it's still operated as a club. Its name – the Apokalypsi – serves as an unintended reminder of the events of December 1928.

# 35. Unemployed Workers Movement

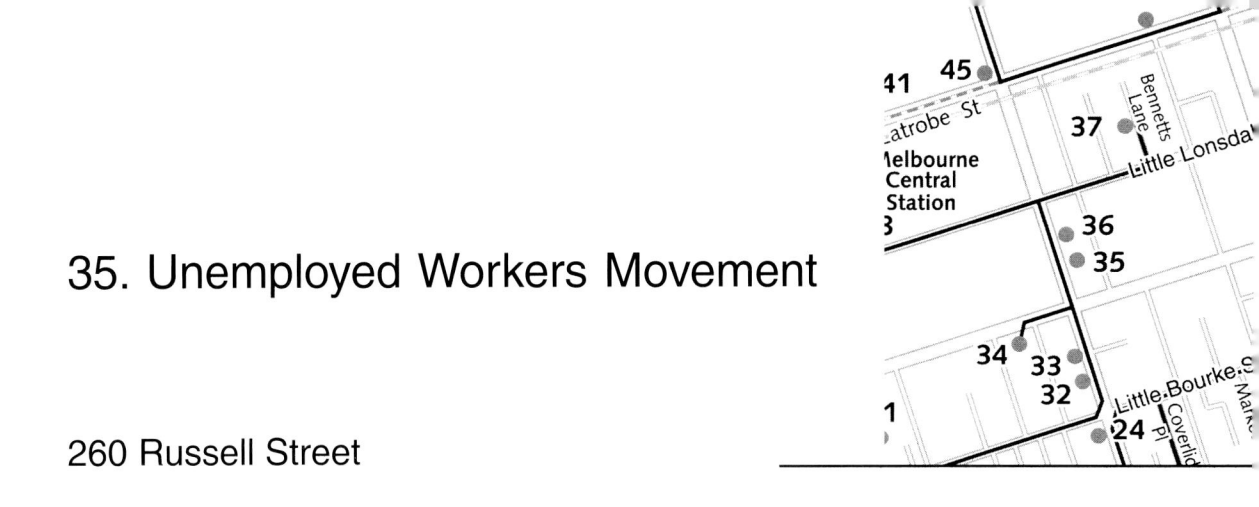

## 260 Russell Street

> The first eviction I saw gave me in many ways one of the biggest shocks of my life. It had a devastating effect on me, and I think probably it and a few other experiences were what finished the capitalist system as far as I was concerned, and I've never seen fit to change my view . . .

That's how Noel Counihan recalled the sight of a working class family forced onto the street during the Depression. And he, like many others, felt so angered that he joined the Unemployed Workers Movement – the organisation that had its headquarters in the three-storey building now known as Cafe Baloo.

The Melbourne branch of the UWM grew out of a committee of unemployed men who met in the courtyard at Trades Hall. Their first demonstration culminated in a brawl with police – and the battle to organise the jobless had begun.

The government introduced a form of dole (albeit in the form of orders from shops for specific foods) in mid 1930. To qualify you had to be a married man and had to register at the Labour Exchange, in the old Customs House on the corner of Flinders and William Streets. On the first day it opened, fifteen thousand men queued, entirely overwhelming the two clerks provided to process them. UWM members quickly took advantage of the situation, organising six separate impromptu meetings in the courtyard and on Bourke Street.

The tactic of utilising the lengthy queues in which the unemployed spent so much time (in soup kitchens and shelters) as forums for politics proved highly successful. By late 1930, seven UWM branches operated in working class suburbs like Fitzroy, Richmond and Brunswick. Many of the leading members of the organisation were Communist Party members, and it was common for branches to run classes in Marxism for both men and women. The organisation operated youth sections, and ran inter-branch sporting competitions. In the volatile and often violent political climate of the 1930s, it also provided a self-defence unit for working class organisations. Although the leaders and most of the members were male, the UWM featured women's sections and usually tried to have a female speaker on its platforms.

The struggle against evictions was probably the UWM's major activity. The

Noel Counihan's *At the Start of the March, 1932*, captures both the misery of unemployment and the anger it generated. Opposite top: a rare photo of an eviction of an entire street in Fitzroy. Below: Cafe Baloo.

organisation's tactics were simple. Activists would surround a house and physically prevent the police removing the tenants. Sometimes hundreds, and occasionally thousands, would turn up to these actions. One such memorable eviction fight took place in Brunswick:

> To the unemployed men the mention of the word bailiff was like waving a red rag at a bull. Without further parley the entire squad was on its way to Gold Street at the double.
>
> In her kitchen Mrs Curruthers had just heard the agent instruct the bailiff to mark certain furniture. At that moment there was a commotion and through the doors and windows appeared the modern knight errants. A push sent the bailiff reeling back into a chair where an enterprising gentleman tipped a dish of water over him. The agent and the bailiff were then subjected to some rough handling as they were bundled unceremoniously down the passage and thrown out of the house where they were seized upon by the crowd numbering several hundred who were waiting in the roadway. The agent and his clerk managed to escape in a motor car whilst the bailiff who was again roughly handled made a break for the South Brunswick railway station nearby. His progress was expedited by the avengers and he was almost thrown over a post and rail fence before he got out of the danger zone.

With little money and few resources at their disposal, the unemployed publicised eviction attempts however they could. One member recalls that 'the only method of advertising we had was a lump of chalk and we'd walk Melbourne of a night time chalking the footpaths from one end to the other'. Newspaper reports of the day record arrests for such crimes as chalking messages on footpaths such as 'Eviction case on the corner of Reilly and Forest Streets. Women and 8 children. Roll up'.

As the Depression wore on – and evictions became more common – a bicycle rider clanging a tin can usually proved enough of a signal to rally a street against a bailiff.

## EVICTION OF UNEMPLOYED MEN AT FITZROY.

The anti-eviction actions weren't always successful. One of the UWM members joked later: 'There were so many [activists] in Pentridge that they were holding study classes on political economy out there, and the Internationale was being whistled in the yards'.

But when the UWM couldn't save the tenants, it sometimes proved able to punish the real estate agents. In one case in Burnley:

> The evictions were instigated by the estate agents on behalf of the owner. They never let you know who owned the houses and we didn't know how to find out for ourselves, so we decided to take on the Richmond estate agents. On the Friday we met at a certain place and divided up into groups of two people to each estate agent. It was late shopping night and at a quarter to nine there were two of us outside each of the nine estate agents in Richmond. One chap in each group had a watch, and they were all synchronised. At a quarter to nine, 'Bang!' We wrecked every estate agent's window in Richmond with lumps of blue metal.

Bedding and other belongings of 75 Unemployed Men evicted from dwellings at corner of Fitzroy and James Sts., Fitzroy. Scene in James-st. shortly after eviction.

Two weeks after this action, Parliament granted rent allowance to the unemployed.

The UWM reached its peak towards the end of 1931, with some twenty-six branches (in both the city and the country) and an estimated Victorian membership of seven thousand. The building in Russell Street was known as the Proletarian Club, and provided a meeting place and central headquarters.

When the Depression ended, the UWM gradually became less and less relevant, and eventually disbanded. Many of its members, though, had become political activists for life. Today, Cafe Baloo stands as a reminder of the way the Depression destroyed lives – and also permanently changed the way many people looked at the world.

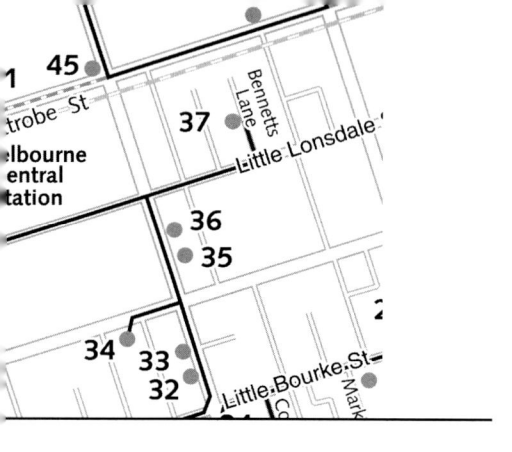

# 36. Cabinet Makers' Strike

## 264 Russell Street

Stand at the Lebanese House restaurant at 264 Russell Street (just up from Cafe Baloo). Look back up Russell Street to the old Magistrates Court on the corner of Latrobe Street. It's quite a distance. Yet on 17 November 1903, a running battle between Chinese workers and strike breakers extended that far and further, as an industrial dispute spilled over into a street brawl fought out with clubs, hammers and pieces of road metal.

'I do not suppose', wrote one journalist in the 1870s, 'any city in the world can show such foul neighbourhoods centred in its very heart'. Chinatown (the area around Little Bourke Street and its precincts) loomed in the imagination of white Australia as a sink of opium, gambling, sexual depravity – and cheap labour. Its narrow lanes housed over a hundred cabinet-making firms, turning out cut-price chairs, washstands, dressing tables and chests of drawers, and not least amongst the sins of John Chinaman (especially amongst white unionists) was his supposed eagerness to work for next to nothing.

In reality, Chinese workers resented poor conditions just as much as their white counterparts. Indeed, they'd been organised into their own union since the 1890s, surviving a dispute in 1893 and another in 1897.

The Chinese bosses were probably no worse than their white counterparts. But, in an era of industrial brutality, that meant that they were an extraordinarily ruthless lot. When, for instance, a reporter asked the factory owner Tye Shing whether the 1893 lockout had produced any hardship for his workers, his response was to laugh:

'No. Oh! No. Suffering? Ha, ha! No. There has been no suffering.'

The 1903 strike began when the bigger firms joined together to drive smaller competitors out of the market. The union struck in protest, and then mounted its own claim for higher wages.

Six weeks later, *The Herald* noted:

> The furniture men who went out from the shops in Little Bourke Street, Lonsdale and Little Lonsdale and Exhibition Streets and their intersecting lanes are for the most part still out, and apparently, as sturdily, though peacefully, determined to remain out, as if they had just begun.

In apparent desperation, the federated employers resorted to paying a contingent of fifty strike breakers exorbitant wages to come down from Sydney and start working. The scabs, adorned with 'Panama hats, crooked sticks and smart neckties' used knuckledusters to launch a vicious (and seemingly premeditated) attack upon the local workforce.

*The Age* reported, with the casual racism of the time, the police response to a disturbance in a furniture shop in Little Bourke Street that night:

> [Constable Fryer] found himself in the midst of a crowd of frenzied Chinese who were 'working themselves up' for a fight. Some were jumping about like kangaroos and shrieking like locomotives, while others were belabouring the furniture with sticks and making hideous grimaces.

Further down the street, the scabs' assault had already begun:

> No. 201 Little Bourke Street – a cookshop and fan-tan [i.e. gambling] bagnio – a battle was in progress. The place seemed to be in a state of siege, and a score of heathens raged furiously on the footpath. Chinese hats and torn garments lay scattered around, and several Chinese who had been put out of action were bemoaning their wounds.

Order was eventually restored – mostly through Constable Fryer and some passing members of the Scottish Regiment beating the bejesus out of all and sundry with their batons and rifle butts.

The next day, four of the scabs appeared in the Magistrates Court in Latrobe Street, charged with various counts of assault. The unionists had their own plans for justice. When the four left the building (accompanied by a pair of Europeans, who had helped arrange their passage from Sydney), they were attacked by a crowd of two or three hundred strikers. *The Herald* again took up the story:

> As soon as the four non-unionists and their European companions appeared, the crowd gave an appalling yell and precipitated itself on them. Instantly, pandemonium raged. Hammers, sticks and dumbbells rose and fell, yells rent the air, and very soon blood began to flow. In their efforts to escape, the non-unionists brought the tide of battle along with them, and in a minute or two heathen were raging from Little Lonsdale to Lonsdale Streets. Policemen came up at the double from all sides and the confusion was added to by Europeans running up to find out what the trouble was and other Europeans who had found what it was, and feared that it might be worse, rushing to get out of it.

This time, the unionists had the better of things. Many carried hammers and other tools of their trade, with which they quickly put the scabs to flight. The building at 264 Russell Street proved a godsend for one strikebreaker. *The Argus* recorded:

Top and Middle: sketches from the 1893 dispute. Bottom: cabinet makers at work.

Out of the scrambling press staggered a tall Chinese with a bleeding head, with a pack of his enemies in hue and cry after him, till Mr J.F. Stewart, who stood at the door of his printing works at No. 264 came to the hunted man's rescue. Mr Stewart confronted the angry crowd surging round his doorway and barred their entrance. With a happy inspiration, he lifted from a shelf a photograph of himself in military marching order (for he is a private in the Scottish Regiment), crying 'I am a soldier', and at the sight of the uniform which terrorised them on Saturday night the hunters decided not to 'tread upon the thistle'. The flying Chinese had taken refuge in the rearmost room of the premises, where sanguinary traces of his presence still remain.

The violence eventually died away (after a number of arrests), although Chinatown remained on edge well into the night. More court appearances the following day saw another melee, with one of the employers chased by his workers down Exhibition Street.

The strikers' refusal to be intimidated by the scabs achieved its purpose. In the end, none of the employers dared put the strikebreakers to work. As one explained to *The Argus*, they were: 'Too flightened [sic]; wait till all quiet.'

The dispute ultimately came to mediation with senior figures in the Chinese community. The result proved to be a partial victory for the workers. The union shared the costs of lost production, but was able to issue a new log of claims, on more favourable terms for the men.

In many ways, however, what the dispute represented most of all was a lost opportunity for the white union movement. If low Chinese wages menaced white conditions, wage improvements for the cabinet makers should have had the opposite effect. Thus the 1903 strike provided the material conditions to forge an alliance between Chinese and Australian workers to win improved conditions in all furniture shops, regardless of the race of the proprietor. Unfortunately, the Australian unions took no interest in the dispute – reinforcing the perception amongst Chinese employees that Australian unions were as much a part of the problem as the solution.

Ninety years later, John Stewart's printing shop – where the strike breaker cowered in fear – is now the Lebanese House restaurant. Number 201 Little Bourke Street still sells food – but it's doubtful whether the proprietors of Puccini's Bar and Bistro would refer to their establishment as a 'cookshop' (much less a 'bagnio'). There's even less trace of the cabinet manufacturers that once dotted the alleys of Little Bourke Street. One of Tye Shing's factories has been levelled; the other is now subsumed into a nightclub, trading, ironically enough, under the name 'International Bar'.

Lebanese House restaurant.

# 37. Salvation Army Picket

## 21 Bennetts Lane

Bennetts Lane today is primarily known for its jazz venue, which attracts a well-heeled and glamorous crowd to a small nightclub.

In the 1930s, though, there was precious little glamour to be found in the street. What the Bennetts Lane address meant to many at that time was a free meal at the Salvation Army. Here, on a daily basis, hundreds of men would queue up outside the grim-looking factory building at number 21 for a plate of mutton dished up by the charity-run soup kitchen inside.

By 1930, the jobless rate in Melbourne stood at around 25 per cent. Yet there was no national benefit scheme for the unemployed. A Royal Commission a few years earlier had briefly contemplated introducing a national unemployment insurance scheme to give the jobless a regular income – but had then ruled it unnecessary.

Instead, relief provision remained the responsibility of state governments which, for the most part, set up public works schemes to soak up a small part of the unemployed and left charity to cope with the rest. The result was a chaotic system of relief – hard to negotiate, and only ever available to a tiny proportion of those in need. For the most part, only married men received sustenance payments; single men and women had to apply to separate shelters for beds and meals.

Charity organisations (such as the Ladies Benevolent Fund) were generally operated by middle class women, the wives of businessmen, pastoralists and members of Parliament. They *did* run shelters and soup kitchens, and provide clothing, bedding and fuel, and occasionally some money towards rent. They also, however, subjected the unemployed to searching examinations, probing their cleanliness, their reputation with shopkeepers, their morals and even their sexual habits – and were not averse to maintaining blacklists of political agitators or the 'undeserving'.

And so, charity organisations were not universally regarded as favourably as one might have expected. By 1930, the Melbourne Trades Hall Council and the newly formed Central Unemployed Committee had organised a demonstration which demanded that sustenance provision be taken away from the Ladies

Benevolent Society, and distributed instead by the government or by councils. Some fifteen hundred men marched from the Exhibition Building to the Premier's Office, calling for the soup kitchens to be replaced with meal tickets, and free charity shelters with vouchers to registered lodging houses.

But the first direct action by the Melbourne unemployed took place in Bennetts Lane.

As the third largest charity in Melbourne, the Salvation Army operated five shelters in 1930, as well as the Bennetts Lane soup kitchen. The organisation was not regarded with much sympathy by radicals, who objected both to its insistence on religious surrender and to the licence given to the Salvos to march and sing in the streets in a time when working class processions were universally harassed.

The kitchen at Bennetts Lane, moreover, enjoyed a particularly poor reputation. The premises were overcrowded and unhygienic, the food often inedible, and the bowls rusty. Most of all, the men complained about the lack of variety. The unemployed queued, sometimes for hours, to receive a plate of boiled mutton or, on occasion, a saveloy.

Above: The warehouse today looks just as it did during the Depression (top) but perhaps not for much longer. The surrounding area is rapidly being developed for apartment blocks.

On 26 July, three hundred unemployed men conducted a meeting in the courtyard at Trades Hall. Bennetts Lane was discussed, and the men resolved to declare the kitchen 'black'. In effect, this meant a boycott. But it was not a peaceful resolve to seek food elsewhere that they had in mind. Rather, they agreed to set up a picket line outside the kitchen, disallowing any entry to the place until the food was improved. At the same time, the action would publicise the problems with charity-run relief and put pressure on the government to issue meal tickets for single men.

That Monday, a hundred men or so met in the lane at an early hour. A picket line was swiftly in place, and speeches were made on the need to fight for better treatment rather than meekly accepting whatever was dished out.

*The Argus* saw things in a somewhat different light:

## NO POT-LUCK FOR HIM!

"There has been a strike on the relief work at Maroubra (Sydney).... The Salvation Army's meals for the hungry in Melbourne have been declared black, the leaders complaining of the lack of variety in the food."

THE OLD LADY: "I'm tidying up the place; but if you like to step inside and take pot-luck, you're welcome to something to eat!"

THE DEADBEAT: "No pot-luck for me, Missus! When you're ready with three courses and a toothpick you can ring the blinking bell."

A *Bulletin* cartoon expresses the conservative response to unemployment.

at lunch time the disgruntled ones most of whom had lunches in paper bags gathered around the kitchen to prevent their less fortunate comrades in getting something to eat.

The day ended with police moving in on the picketers, arresting two men (and charging one of them with 'having insufficient means of support' – an unsurprising state of affairs for someone outside a soup kitchen!).

Over the next few days the picket grew in strength (from a hundred and fifty men to over four hundred), while the numbers eating at the kitchen dropped from almost a thousand to around two hundred. On the Tuesday, four hundred men marched through the city carrying banners, one of which read, succinctly enough: 'To Hell With the Soup Kitchen!'

Needless to say, reactions to the protest tended to vary depending upon the spectators' own experiences of unemployment. One gentleman, witnessing the demonstration, wrote to *The Argus*:

> What depths of moral degeneration are we as a nation sinking to when our men who are unfortunate enough to be in dire need of free meals provided at soup kitchens can turn round and complain lack of variety of the food and of the 'monotonous' mutton? . . . For the common good, I sincerely hope that steps will be taken (if not already) to prevent further such flagrant banner displays and the public parading of such sinister sentiments as expressed in that degrading language – 'To Hell With the Soup Kitchen!'

Despite such condemnation, the action ultimately proved successful. By the end of the week – with the picket still in place – Lieutenant Colonel John Blake, the Social Secretary for the Salvation Army, met with the Premier, who promised that the government would provide funds for the purchase of beef as well as mutton, and would help the Salvation Army find a larger premises for the kitchen. Despite this, Blake still managed to convey his personal contempt for the unemployed when he commented to *The Herald*: 'We have been putting mutton on every day until some of the men started going around bleating like sheep. We are now going to try some beef for a change.'

The main demand – the provision of food vouchers – was not won until later. But the black ban helped to shake the passivity of the unemployed and to kick-start the protest movement. Through the remaining years of the Depression, the jobless became increasingly militant. The organisations they formed demonstrated that, even in the most difficult circumstances, it's always better to fight than to surrender.

# 38. Public Library

## 328 Swanston Street

In 1883, *The Argus* published an article condemning the presence of the poor in the Public Library on Swanston Street:

> A visitor to the library may test the matter first by his nose. He can smell vagrancy the moment he crosses the threshold. Using his eyes, he can see it right up and down the long hall; peering curiously about, he can find it in any of the alcoves, nicely sheltered and walled about with books. If he chooses to particularise, he may see an unmistakable specimen enter, shuffle up to a bookcase, select a volume of light literature, choose a seat, set up his elbows as supports to his head, and bend his eyes on the print. In a little while he spits. In an hour he will sleep; if he snores an attendant may disturb him; then he will read and spit again.

*The Argus* proposed two solutions – regulations forcing potential entrants to show a letter of introduction from a 'respectable' household or, failing that, the division of the building into distinct areas for different classes. By name, the library might have been 'Public' (or 'Free'), but there was more than a suggestion from Melbourne's elite that the building and its collection remained rather too good for the populace, since 'the books . . . are handled, and soiled, and spoiled, and frequently mutilated, by creatures who would be better bestowed within Her Majesty's gaols'.

In reality, *The Argus* needn't have worried. After all, the Library remained closed on Sundays – the only day most people had free – thus effectively limiting its use to those with leisure enough to visit during the working week.

Indeed, the strict enforcement of the Presbyterian Sabbath rendered most of Melbourne notorious for wowserism during the 1880s and 1890s. On the seventh day, official regulations closed theatres, barred newspapers and allowed trains to run only on the condition that they carried worshippers to church – thus ensuring that working people could find almost no entertainment on their single free day.

And, as a speaker at a public meeting on the topic declared:

> all these irritating and annoying restrictions [are] solely due to an outside lot of self-elected, impertinent, meddlesome busybodies, who being in themselves a combination of meanness and misery, [are] endeavouring to render other people as miserable as themselves on Sundays, and [have] succeeded, to a great extent, in doing so.

But the ban on the library particularly galled Melbourne's left-wing activists. The Melbourne radical tradition had largely developed from the secular and free-thought organisations, where activists took books and their contents very seriously. The anarchist Chummy Fleming, for instance, described his own discovery of the delights of reading as coming 'like a flash of light one Summer's morning'. So the idea of a religious superstition barring the mass of working people from the knowledge contained in a library paid for with public taxes seemed utterly outrageous.

Almost as soon as the Library began operations in 1856, the issue of Sunday closing caused controversy. In 1883, the Museum and Gallery relented for two months, opening their doors on the Sabbath – and the turnstiles recorded nearly six thousand visits on the first Sunday.

The conservatives struck back by forming the Sunday Observance League, an organisation dedicated to maintaining the ban on any public activity during the Sabbath. Though progressives countered with the Sunday Liberation Society, and a series of public meetings defending the Library (one of which culminated in a riot), the forces of reaction temporarily triumphed – Parliament bowed to pressure and legislated to force the Library's closure.

In 1889, a large mass meeting convened at Queens Wharf, with different organisations and individuals merging their separate 'stumps' to allow for a joint discussion of the Public Library issue. Before long, Chummy Fleming took to the platform, and declared:

> After the meeting is over, I shall be going up to that Library to look at it from the outside, and think about how much I should like to be inside reading, instead of loafing about in the street.

Several other speeches followed, but at the close of the meeting:

> it seemed that the whole crowd as one man was seized with an impulse to go and do what Fleming had said he was going to do; instead of as usual scattering in all directions, the whole mass went surging up solidly to view the Library and devoutly wish to be inside.

A pattern for the next months had been established. Each Sunday, people assembled at the Wharf to listen to speeches, before a crowd (sometimes numbering as many as four or five thousand people) strolled through the streets cheering:

> for a Free Sunday, for a Social Revolution, the opening of the library etc. on Sundays . . . When they reached Swanston Street, the throng gave 'three hearty cheers for the opening of it'.

Meetings concluded at the Working Men's College (today's RMIT), where each week they resolved to continue the agitation.

When Parliament met to consider the matter, the assembly outside the Working Men's College elected a delegation to present its views to the legislators. The chosen five promptly set out to Bourke Street, with the rest of the meeting following. However:

> when they arrived at Bourke Street the crowd there, seeing a small crowd come along with well-known agitators in it, became excited and rushed to see what was going on. In a few moments some six thousand people, at a moderate estimate, were surging towards Parliament House.

The unexpected arrival of such a throng – with troublemakers like Chummy at the head – naturally alarmed the police, who prepared for battle. Just when a riot seemed imminent, 'a sudden downpour of rain occasioned a precipitate retreat to the shelter of the Bourke Street verandahs, while the deputation went quietly in'.

State Library, now open on Sundays.

After a month or so of the Sunday processions, police arrested Fleming and two other prominent agitators, Sam Rosa and John White. Chummy and Rosa faced charges of 'insulting behaviour' and 'loitering'; White, 'insulting behaviour' and 'taking part in a procession'. Rosa's account in *The Liberator* (the newspaper of the Australian Secular Association) details their court appearance the next day:

> the policemen retailed certain interesting little fictions of their own invention, to the effect that we said the Prince of Wales was no good, and that the queen ought to take in washing (the magistrates were struck with horror at the idea of the queen turning laundry-woman) and that the poor were plundered by the rich. 'They don't confine themselves to the Public Library at all, your worship,' said one sapient bobby, 'but they denounce capitalists and even magistrates, your worship.'

Despite their obvious outrage, the police lost the 'insulting behaviour' charges. The activists, however, copped a guilty verdict on the other charges and were duly sentenced to pay a fine of three pounds or face gaol for one month. Declaring that they had done nothing wrong, the three chose gaol.

In gaol, they continued to do what they could to keep the campaign alive. White reminded readers of *The Liberator*:

> I have been a constant agitator for Reform for 40 years, and am the same now as when I stood along side of my dear father in the old country during the Chartist troubles in '48, in the cause of Freedom. I do all I do calmly and deliberately, and regret nothing I do. Though I am ill in body, I am strong in mind.

For his part, Chummy bemoaned that the 'reading matter supplied me [in prison] consisted of the bible, *Sunday at Home*, and a hymn book, which disappointed me, as I thought I should have a month's enjoyment, rest and reading'. But he found scope for political work by campaigning to improve conditions for prisoners. He also continued to express his commitment to the Sunday campaign, waxing philosophical on the issue:

> What is life? – tomorrow it may have passed. So, after all, to do courageous and noble deeds – helping the dawning of the universal Brotherhood of Humanity, is worthy of us all.

His letter ended, however, on a somewhat plaintive note. 'If any of my friends could visit me,' he wrote, 'I should be delighted to see them . . .'

After the three were released, other issues moved to the fore, and the campaign gradually died away. Public opinion, however, continued to swing against Sunday closing.

On 22 September 1904, Parliament relented – making Melbourne the last city throughout the length and breadth of the British Empire to throw open the doors of its public institutions on Sundays.

Right: Premier Gillies watches public opinion battering down the gates of the Public Library in a *Bulletin* cartoon.

## SUNDAY OPENING.

*WORKING MAN:* "IF YOU DON'T OPEN THE DOOR WE'LL HAVE TO BREAK IT OPEN."
*GILLIES:* "DON'T ASK ME TO OPEN THE DOOR FOR A CONTINENTAL SUNDAY. WHY NOT STOP AT THE ATHENÆUM CLUB AND READ THE STORY OF JONAH AND THE WHALE?"

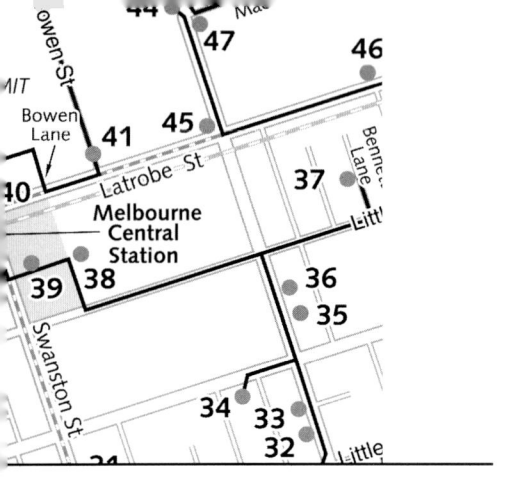

# 39. Sir Redmond Barry Statue

## State Library Steps

The statue of Sir Redmond Barry – the man who hanged Ned Kelly – on the steps of the State Library does more than immortalise a particularly nasty specimen of establishment Melbourne. It also captures some sense of an age when power delighted in display, when authority depended more or less overtly on physical repression and when portly, middle-aged gentlemen thought they cut fine figures in skin-tight ceremonial stockings.

Sir Redmond Barry descended from a wealthy family of Anglo-Irish aristocrats. He arrived in Sydney in 1839 and then quickly moved to Melbourne. Despite the relatively small number of people in the new colony with legal training, it took Barry some time to fully integrate himself into Melbourne society (the contemporary historian Garryowen suggests that he was 'never a favourite with the Attorneys [since] his solemn starchness and profuse punctiliousness overpowered them').

Barry first came to prominence providing legal representation for Aborigines, a task which (perhaps surprisingly) he performed with some diligence (although his clients were almost always found guilty). He soon climbed up the ladder, becoming the first Solicitor General of Victoria in 1851 and joining the bench of the Supreme Court in 1852.

Once entrenched in power, he rapidly won a reputation as a 'hanging judge'. He presided over the farce of the Eureka trials, at which the government proved unable to convince any jury to convict the rebels, leading *The Age* to remark, 'the heart of the people is sound; it is only the heart of the Government that is rotten'.

Barry also tried the fifteen prisoners accused of murdering the brutal Inspector-General of Convicts, John Price. He refused any legal counsel for the accused who then, according to the law of the day, were not permitted to give sworn evidence in their own defence. Not surprisingly, most were found guilty. Barry ignored the jury's recommendation for clemency, and sentenced all the men to die.

Indeed, Barry – as an owner of large tracts of Irish land – possessed an especial antipathy towards transported convicts, many of whom came from that class of rebellious peasants whom his family had traditionally oppressed. *The Argus* commented in February 1853:

> So convinced is [Barry] of the hideousness of having the land overridden with fugitive convicts, that he doles out to every bondman that comes under his lash nearly one half more punishment than he awards to those who, having come to the country free, have deserted the path of virtue.

'I'll see you there where I go'; Ned Kelly and Redmond Barry in court.

Most official histories lavish praise on Barry's efforts to improve the tone of Melbourne society. He was a Chancellor and early patron of Melbourne University, he helped establish the Public Library, and lent his support to the Horticultural Society. Yet his aim seems to have been not so much to foster knowledge in the population at large as refinement among the well-to-do. As Manning Clark notes, 'for [Barry], civilization meant the Melbourne Club, the best seats at the theatre, the bowing and scrapings of the law courts, all the "Yes Your Honour" and "If Your Honour Pleases", and brass bands on Sunday to give the people pleasure'.

So, for instance, when asked to speak at the Mechanics Institute on 'The Art of Agriculture', Barry's idea of an appropriate presentation involved lengthy speculations on the agriculture carried on in the garden of Eden – a dissertation, which, as a contemporary noted, threw 'very little light on the conversion of gum tree forests into cornfields'.

Similarly, when the Public Library reached completion, Barry took it on himself to address the workmen on the site with 'a strange compound of classic history, obscure philology and mediaeval gleanings . . . surely not the matter to lay before an assemblage of hard-working mechanics as a sort of festivity on the completion of their labours'.

As a judge, the harshness of Barry's sentencing was resented all the more for his tendency to leaven his judgements with this kind of aristocratic pomposity. In one instance, he advised an unfortunate woman, weeping in the dock, 'Dry your tears, madam, and proceed to gaol for eighteen months with hard labour'.

Barry's partiality for post-sentence moralising came most famously to the fore during the trial of Ned Kelly. As soon as Kelly had been captured, Barry lent his assistance to the prosecution, allowing, for instance, the authorities to move the trial from Beechworth (the jurisdiction in which Kelly's crimes had been committed) to Melbourne, purely on the basis that sitting in a region where people knew the truth behind Kelly's outlawry rendered the prospect of a conviction more remote.

When the hearing began, Barry made public his desire to wrap the trial up in a single session, a prospect that even the prosecution found difficult to take seriously. Then, in his summing up, Barry told the jury to discount the applicability of Kelly's claims of self-defence – an extraordinary piece of misdirection which, many years later, led the former Chief Justice of Victoria to declare that 'Edward Kelly was not offered a trial according to the law'.

Once the jury reached its predictable guilty verdict, Barry took it upon himself to deliver Kelly a lecture: 'You appear', he said, 'to revel in the idea of having put men to death'.

The outlaw shot back: 'More men than I have put men to death', an apparent reference to Sir Redmond's partiality for capital sentencing. Then, with singular dignity, Kelly continued: 'The day will come when we shall all have to go to a bigger court than this. Then we will see who is right and who is wrong.'

Barry – no doubt taken aback – cut the dialogue short and intoned a sentence of death that concluded with the usual formula, 'May the Lord have mercy on your soul'.

Kelly again intervened: 'I will go further than that, and say I will see you there where I go'.

Ned Kelly met the executioner on 11 November 1880. Barry subsequently took ill, and died – surviving Kelly by only twelve days. Medical records put his death down to diabetes, a condition worsened by obesity (Manning Clark later wrote: 'He was a man of huge appetites, swallowing oysters and champagne in such quantities that not even the ample robes of a judge could conceal the effects of such gluttony on his figure'). But the notion of a Kelly curse has passed down into folklore.

The Barry statue was completed – at a cost of £1000 – some seven years later. *The Age* described it on its unveiling as 'an exquisite representation of the late judge . . . posed in a dignified attitude' – a curious assessment of a monument that fixes the rotund Sir Redmond standing with knees turned slightly outward, like a flasher preparing to open his coat.

In any case, it's doubtful whether any of the kids performing skateboard stunts know the name of the corpulent gentleman standing (in a bizarre juxtaposition) alongside statues of Joan of Arc and St George and his dragon. Most of them, however, could tell you the story of Ned Kelly.

The Redmond Barry statue.

# 40. Guild Hall

## RMIT University

The stolid Victorian columns of RMIT's Storey Hall sit somewhat uneasily beside the postmodern exuberance of the neighbouring buildings. Yet despite surface impressions, the building boasts perhaps the most interesting history of the entire campus. It was here, in 1917, that Melbourne's first-wave feminists established a workers' commune with the men from the city's waterfront.

Storey Hall began life in 1884 as the Hibernian Hall, intended to bolster the presence of Irish Catholicism in the face of the growing organisation of Protestant Loyalist groups. From 1904 it held services for Central Zion Tabernacle, before becoming the secular Guild Hall in 1907 – a site for dances, exhibitions, meetings and the like.

But in late 1916, the Women's Political Association took up the lease. The WPA had been founded by Vida Goldstein, who in 1903 had become the first female in the British Empire to stand for Parliament. She spent the next decade agitating for women's rights – demanding female suffrage in Victoria, representing Australian women in international conferences and contesting federal elections (unsuccessfully) on four more occasions. In the process, her political views shifted sharply to the left. By the time of the First World War, the WPA's paper *Woman Voter* consistently campaigned for equal pay, international female suffrage, equal rights to divorce, and – perhaps most significantly – opposition to militarism.

From a distance of nearly ninety years, it's hard to imagine the impact of the First World War on the Australian political scene. But perhaps the death of Princess Diana provides something of an analogy. In the same way as a fatal car crash transformed Diana from a faintly ridiculous aristocrat to the ubiquitous Queen of Hearts, the declaration of war in 1914 generated a wave of patriotism that overnight turned most of Melbourne's radicals into ardent jingoists.

But while, all around her, former socialists declared their adherence to King and Country, Vida Goldstein stood against the tide. She explained to the press that she hoped 'women in all parts of the world will stand together, demanding a more reasonable and civilised way of dealing with international disputes'. Three days later, she founded the Women's Peace Army, an anti-war auxiliary to the WPA, under the slogan: 'We war against war'.

The socialist activist May Francis's memoirs illustrate the courage that a principled anti-war stance required:

> With another young member of the Women's Political Association, I was selling their weekly paper at the corner of Swanston and Flinders Streets on a Saturday morning a few months after the war started. To draw attention to the small paper, we had a stencilled poster. On this Saturday the poster read 'Germany Wants Peace'. Within minutes [my companion's] poster and papers were torn from her at the corner of St Paul's. Although only nineteen years old, she had taken part in the suffragette movement in England, arriving in Australia just before the outbreak of war. Realising that this would be a new experience for me, she rushed across the road and told me to drop the poster and papers quickly and slip away into the large crowd making their way into the railway station. I refused to do this and we were both attacked by the crowd. Police got through and seemed almost as angry because we had disrupted the peak hour traffic. The word was passed around that we were pro-Germans. I had no hope of saving the poster but fought and succeeded in saving the papers. The crowd behaved more like wild animals than human beings and it was only with difficulty that the police got us out of the crowd.

Naturally, those in authority did all they could to encourage the nationalist hysteria. *The Argus*, for instance, informed its readers in December 1915 that, although Christmas traditionally meant a time of goodwill, such seasonal sentiments did not apply to Germans – nor to those who campaigned against the war.

Despite the hostility, the WPA's stand found support from a galaxy of talented female activists. WPA agitators included Bella Lavender (the first woman to take a degree from Melbourne University), Elizabeth Wallace (a veteran of the Prahran free speech fight), Jennie Baines (later to become the first Australian political prisoner to engage in a hunger strike) and Adela Pankhurst (subsequently a foundation member of the Communist Party).

The WPA was also fortunate to possess in the person of Cecilia John not only a capable financial secretary but an operatic singer of some talent. Her rendition of the anti-war anthem 'I Didn't Raise My Son to Be a Soldier' became so popular that the government actually banned the tune under the War Precautions Act of 1915. Undaunted, WPA activists handed out copies of the lyrics to encourage the crowd to sing along, on the theory that the police wouldn't dare arrest the entire audience.

The WPA moved into the Swanston Street hall in 1916 – a space at that time boasting 'besides offices and club committee rooms . . . two halls, one accommodating 300, the other 1700 persons'. It provided the perfect platform from which to fight a mass campaign. As *Woman Voter* commented: 'The new offices give us what we have long desired in the way of light, air and roominess. We give all our friends a cordial invitation to visit us in our new quarters'.

The women quickly moved to signal their occupancy. The WPA boasted its own flag of purple ('for the royalty of international justice'), white ('for the purity of international life') and green ('for the springing hope of international peace'), and *Woman Voter* reported:

> On Friday afternoon our flag was hoisted at the Guild Hall to fling its message of peace and goodwill to Australia and the world. A large number of members and friends made the journey to the roof of the hall, where our president Miss Vida Goldstein, with the aid of Miss Cecilia John, after dedicating the flag to the cause of Internationalism, hoisted it to the accompaniment of ringing cheers from the spectators.

The celebration acted as a spur to an organisation now embroiled in the biggest campaign of its life. The Labor Prime Minister Billy Hughes had returned from a trip abroad with renewed enthusiasm for the conflict in Europe, exulting that 'war prevents us from slipping into the abyss of degeneracy and from becoming flabby'. More particularly, he decided that victory for the British Empire depended upon providing more soldiers – and so declared that a referendum on conscription would be held as soon as possible.

Storey Hall.

Yet even as news of Hughes' intention appeared in the press, opposition was organising. That day, the No Conscription Fellowship held a mass meeting in the Guild Hall. Afterwards, hundreds of demonstrators carried their banners down Swanston Street and up Bourke Street to Parliament House. In a pattern that would become common, police combined with off-duty soldiers in a vicious baton charge that left scores of marchers injured.

The anti-conscription movement brought women into Australian political life in a way previously never seen. Vida Goldstein and other WPA members regularly addressed the huge meetings on the Yarra Bank. Their Women's Peace Army helped build the stop-work rally called by the unions on 4 October that brought forty thousand onto the streets. Many demonstrators subsequently found their way back to a special meeting held afterwards in the WPA's hall.

A few weeks later, WPA activists mobilised for a Women's No-Conscription Demonstration and Procession that began at the Guild Hall and then marched down Swanston Street behind an 8-year-old standing in front of a banner proclaiming: 'A Little Child Shall Lead Them'. When drunken soldiers threatened

**SENATE ELECTION.**

# Vote for the Woman Candidate

WHO POLLED 51,497 VOTES IN 1903.

## VIDA GOLDSTEIN

Every woman of every political party should endeavour to secure the return of the Woman Candidate, as **All the Men** in Parliament cannot represent **One Woman** as adequately as **One Woman** can represent **All Women**.

to attack the march, a group of wharf labourers interceded to provide protection.

The eventual defeat of the referendum led to a new political polarisation. Prime Minister Hughes walked out of the ALP, forming a national government with the aid of the conservatives. Meanwhile, the WPA continued its evolution to the left. The censorship of *Woman Voter* (at one point Goldstein resorted to filling the blank pages of the paper with the message: 'MR HUGHES SAYS WE MAY HAVE A FREE PRESS'), the police surveillance of meetings and the overt press lies about WPA members brought the organisation closer to other groups under attack from the authorities. So when waterside workers walked off the job in 1917 in protest against rising prices, Goldstein and her comrades threw their complete support behind the strike.

Again, this was an act of remarkable courage – not simply because respectable Melbourne regarded a strike during wartime as tantamount to treason, but also because there was no guarantee that predominantly middle class suffragettes would be welcomed on rough, male-dominated sites like the waterfront. Nonetheless, the WPA's key agitators soon made themselves a familiar fixture at strike meetings, urging the men not only to continue the struggle but to broaden and politicise their demands. Years later, waterfront families remembered the impact of the WPA's Jennie Baines:

> She could talk – the biggest thing about Jennie was her mouth! Jennie was only tiny, but didn't she stir us up, didn't she give us a bit of curry!

Realising that wartime shortages would make it difficult for the strikers to hold out for a prolonged dispute, the WPA sought to provide immediate material aid. But rather than fulfilling the traditional female role of serving tea and cakes, the women conceived of a plan to turn the Guild Hall into a strike support centre or, as *Woman Voter* somewhat grandiloquently put it:

a Workers Commune ... with the object of befriending the women and children, who are always the greatest sufferers in an industrial conflict, and helping the men to win out in their fight against the unendurable exploitation and oppression of their class and lay the foundation of Industrial Democracy in Australia.

Funds came from collections at the Yarra Bank and at other workers' meetings, while local businesses were pressed into donating supplies. Before long, the women had established a registration depot, kitchens, restaurants, dining rooms, boot factory, grocer's shop, recreation hall and barber's saloon ('one of the first essentials for victory in an industrial fight is that the men shall keep their self respect and nothing tends to break a man's spirit so much as being unkempt. And so the barber's saloon plays its part in the strike by keeping the men well shaved and their heads well trimmed'). In the evenings, regular socials, movie and card nights helped bolster strikers' morale.

Yet as well as providing support, the WPA members intended the Guild Hall commune to be a political intervention. Along with food and shelter, it also offered political debate and discussion. *Woman Voter* explained:

Opposite: Vida Goldstein. Above: this collection of supplies (assembled a few months later for another dispute) gives a sense of what the Guild Hall commune must have looked like.

> We are also helping to organise women into strong trade unions and to form a Women's Union – One Big Union for Women – the condition of membership to be membership in a Trade Union, if eligible, or that the applicant shall be the wife, daughter, mother, sister of a Trade Unionist, or a woman who actively supports Trade Unionism, who shall be organised with the object of inspiring them with a sense of women's responsibility for Industrial and International Solidarity, Justice and Peace.

After all, great events were in the air. The Bolsheviks had just taken power in Russia, an event Goldstein described as 'the Sign of the Times, of the approaching social and industrial revolution'. At home, Billy Hughes announced another conscription referendum, plunging the WPA into a fresh round of campaigning. That December saw another women's peace procession leave from Trades Hall to march down Swanston Street. According to *The Argus*, they sang 'revolutionary songs and shouted defiance' before becoming embroiled in a melee with returned soldiers. Indeed, the second referendum proved just as bitter as the first, with anti-war activists regularly facing physical attacks. At one meeting, soldiers attempted to tear down the WPA flag from the Guild Hall, before Cecilia John drove them back with a fire hose.

Yet while the anti-conscription campaign once again proved successful (the second referendum was decisively defeated), the waterside workers were less fortunate, with the strike ending in a rout. Victorian wharfies held out longer than elsewhere, and the WPA commune continued operation until February 1919. By the time the men returned to work, the Guild Hall had supplied 60,000 food parcels, prepared 30,000 meals, provided 6500 haircuts, distributed 30,000 items of clothing, repaired 2000 pairs of boots and collected nearly £1500 in donations. Just as importantly, it had shown in concrete terms the potential for unity between the women's movement and a combative working class. On the traditional celebration of the Eight-Hour Day, the wharfies marched to Guild Hall and showed their gratitude with a salute to the WPA.

The incident marked the high point of the movement. After the war, Vida Goldstein travelled abroad. Increasingly interested in Christian Science, she dropped out of active politics. The WPA disbanded shortly afterwards, though many of its agitators ultimately found their way into other organisations, such as the Victorian Socialist Party and later the Communist Party.

# 41. Working Men's College

## RMIT University

On a December afternoon in 1881, the Honorable Francis Ormond, a wealthy Melbourne squatter with an interest in education and a bent for philanthropy, chaired the annual Scotch College speech day. In the course of his remarks, he declared to the assembled worthies that Melbourne would benefit from what he described as a 'Working Men's College', and then boasted that, if the government provided a site and the public raised money, he would personally donate funds to match those raised by subscription.

What provoked this extravagant gesture?

Ormond, perhaps more farsighted than his peers, recognised that, until provided with some mobility within society, working class people would continue to rebel against their exploitation. The promotion of 'culture' – the values and beliefs of their masters – would, he hoped, inoculate them against pernicious ideas like unionism and socialism. Furthermore, Ormond knew that an increasingly complex industrial economy could no longer rely on training its workforce through an apprentice system based on 'learning on the job'. After all, as he explained, 'the necessity for the scientific and technical training of the working classes is now prominent in the minds of thinking people'.

To Ormond's mind, these 'thinking people' were to be found largely amongst the ranks of those establishment figures nodding sagely along to his speech. Much to his chagrin, though, Melbourne's upper class initially displayed little interest in the proposal.

Support instead came from the opposite end of town. William Murphy, a self-educated cabinet maker elected Secretary of Melbourne's Trades Hall, heard of the offer, and promptly determined to raise the requisite money. The trade union movement regarded education with a great deal of seriousness. The achievement of the eight-hour day in 1857 meant that some workers possessed a few hours for educational pursuits. With higher education almost exclusively the preserve of the privileged, Trades Hall had attempted to provide classes run by workers for workers, with a voluntary teaching staff of 'men who, through the day had performed their eight hours of labour at the 'banker', the foundry, the workshop or the scaffold, and then gave up their evenings to improve the

Above: the Ormond statue today, looking decidedly sinister. Opposite: *Melbourne Punch*: for large sections of respectable society, the idea of working class education remained inherently comical.

position of the rising generation about to enter upon the battle of life'.

In the wake of Ormond's offer, Murphy recognised that a formal college would provide a more thorough-going curriculum. He thus committed Trades Hall to a series of fundraisers – including a special Carlton-Collingwood football match – to raise Ormond's £5000. Unions called public meetings in the Town Hall and working class suburbs like North Melbourne, Collingwood and Brunswick, generating substantial interest in the idea.

Support began to flow in from unions representing dozens of trades – including blue-collar workers like bricklayers, bootmakers, printers and masons. Twelve hundred subscription lists circulated around factories and workplaces in Melbourne, bringing in donations from 11,700 workers and their families. Workers and their unions raised £3383 for the cause of education – enabling the union movement to boast that it had contributed five pounds to the project for every one pound contributed by employers.

It quickly became apparent, however, that Ormond's 'Working Men's College' differed substantially from the institution dreamed of by Murphy. The first Council of the College in 1882 neatly embodied the differences in their visions. Workers' representatives found themselves outnumbered by Ormond's unelected appointees and sundry government officials. Further class divisions opened when Ormond tried to enlarge the council at the expense of the unionists, and then declared that the college should be christened after Queen Victoria's youngest son, Prince Leopold – even tying an offer of further donations to acceptance of the new name.

Despite continuing conflicts, the Working Men's College managed to open in 1887 – and enrolled two hundred students within the first week. Nevertheless, the idea of providing distinctively working class education – with workers having some say as to what they learned – had been all but discarded. Ormond's much vaunted interest in the working class (prompted, according to one biographer, by 'a heart full of longing to uplift all toilers and to fling open to them doors of technical knowledge in order to contribute to the elevation of their social condition') did not lead to any desire to put workers actually in charge of anything – even an educational syllabus. As first Director of the College, the Council appointed a middle class gentleman (the son of one of Ormond's cronies), selected at a meeting at which all Trades Hall representatives were conveniently absent.

**THE END CROWNS THE WORK.**

*1st (alleged) Working-man.*—"Blooming fine lectchah, eh, Bill?"
*2nd (alleged) Working-man.*—"Oh! blooming, but when's the light refreshments a coming round?"

In the end, Ormond knew the class to which he belonged. Indeed, while he gave £20,500 to the Working Men's College, he also forked out £112,000 to Ormond College at Melbourne University, an institution that to this day specialises in providing live-in accommodation for the sons and daughters of the wealthy.

What was once the Working Men's College is today RMIT University. RMIT – with campuses and property scattered across Melbourne and Victoria – has ditched all historical ties to the working class movement and boasts the distinction of being the first tertiary institution to charge up-front fees for degrees. The campus naturally honours Francis Ormond as its founder, with a statue and a building named after him. No memorial stands for William Murphy, who ended his days as caretaker of the institution he'd fought so hard to build, picking up rubbish and locking the buildings after hours, before dying penniless in 1921.

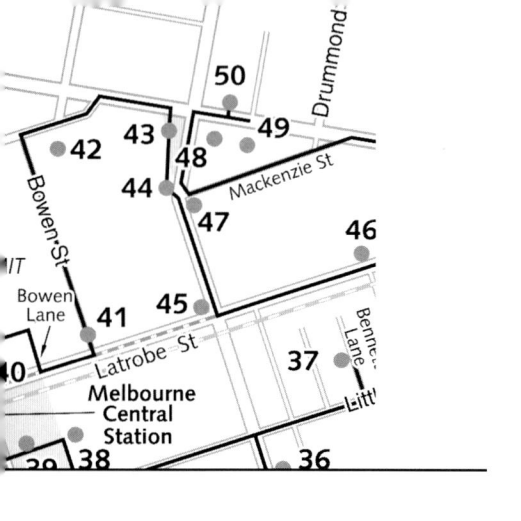

# 42. Gallows Hill

## Corner Franklin and Bowen Streets

In 1842, huge crowds watched six men die on a scaffold erected on a small rise, outside the partially constructed walls of the Melbourne Gaol. Three were hanged for bushranging. The others died because they were black.

When the white armed robbers Charles Ellis, Martin Fogarty and Daniel Jepps went to the gallows on 28 June, the proceedings were undertaken with the kind of well-mannered grotesquery characteristic of the English judicial system. On the scaffold the men shook hands with each other, and then each shook hands (twice!) with the executioner. Jepps' final speech to the huge crowd followed a familiar tradition of gallows exhortation:

> Fellow Christians, you see before you three young men in the prime of life and strength about to suffer on the scaffold for the crime of bushranging. I trust you will take warning by our untimely fate, and avoid those crimes which have brought us to this end. Good people, I most humbly beg your prayers to the Almighty on our behalf. I die in the faith of our Salvation through the blood of our Divine Redeemer.

Even the more macabre elements of the ceremony (the transportation of the men to the gallows seated on their own coffins, the stricture that their bodies should remain hanging for an hour, the acknowledgement of the hangman's right to their clothes) followed a pattern hallowed by Tyburn tradition, reassuring respectable Melburnians (and warning the lower orders) that civilised justice still operated in this strange continent.

The other two hangings that year served an additional purpose. In 1842, an undeclared war still simmered between the colonists and indigenous people. The public execution of Aboriginal men in January and September aimed to terrorise the native population into submission.

In 1841, George Robinson, the Chief Protector of Aborigines in Tasmania, had brought a party of Aboriginal people from Flinders Island to Port Phillip, hoping they would help pacify the local Aborigines. Instead, five of Robinson's party took to the bush to launch a desperate guerrilla struggle.

All were survivors of the notorious Black Wars. The band's leader, Jack

*The condemned men leaving the gaol, en route to the first execution.*

Napoleon Tunermenerwail, had been born in north-eastern Tasmania, near the site of a notorious massacre. William Thomas, the son of an assistant Protector, later recalled:

> There was a man among them a man superior in every respect to the others, he had been a leading man, a chief, in his own country, and he was the leader of the malcontents here – his name was Napoleon. He talked about how they had suffered at the hands of the white man, how many of their tribe had been slain, how they had been hunted down in Tasmania – now was the time for revenge . . .

Early in October 1841, Tunermenerwail, Robert Smallboy and three women (including Trugernanner, later erroneously declared – under the name Truganini – to be the 'last of the Tasmanians') stole two guns and some ammunition from Sam Anderson and Robert Massie's hut at Bass River. They robbed seven stations, wounded four whites and killed two whalers they encountered at Cape Paterson.

The settler Henry Meyrick described in a letter home how 'the whole neighbourhood has been thrown into the utmost confusion' by the Tasmanians' campaign. They easily evaded pursuers – until the authorities lit upon the idea of using the skills of local black trackers. Tunermenerwail and Smallboy gave themselves up when the contingent of border police held pistols to the heads of the Tasmanian women and threatened to shoot unless they surrendered.

In the ensuing murder trial in Melbourne, the defence counsel revealed that one of the dead whalers had earlier abducted Trugernanner and killed her husband. Remarkably, the three women were acquitted. Though the jury found the men guilty, it recommended mercy 'on account of general good character and the peculiar circumstances under which they are placed'. But Judge Willis – a man later described by NSW Governor Gipps as an 'apologist of the cruellest practices by some of the least respectable of the settlers on the Aborigines' – had a different agenda. He told the Tasmanians: 'The punishment that awaits you is not one of vengeance but of terror . . . to deter similar transgressions.' On 21 January 1842, a horse-drawn cart collected Tunermenerwail and Smallboy from the Collins Street gaol, and paraded them in a circuit around Collins, William, Lonsdale and Swanston Streets.

This was the first execution in the new colony, and a crowd of six thousand gathered around the gallows hill (near the intersection of Franklin and Bowen Streets). Smallboy's terror was unmistakeable (*The Gazette* records that 'Bob's feelings broke out in the most heartrending groans; the terrified and piteous looks he threw around him, pressing against every one that spoke to him as if to catch at some chance of salvation, was terrible to witness'). Tunermenerwail, however, remained impassive, conducting himself with remarkable dignity in front of a mob that 'shouted and yelled and vented [its] gratification in explosions of uproarious merriment'.

The scaffold was badly constructed; the hangman unfamiliar with his work. When the moment came, the clumsily constructed trap opened and then caught, leaving the men to dangle and choke. Eventually, a spectator managed to remove the obstruction. Tunermenerwail died instantly. Smallboy slowly asphyxiated.

The third execution that year stemmed from the vicious campaign waged against indigenous people on John Cox's holdings in the Mount Rouse area. Cox himself later boasted to the author 'Rolf Boldrewood' of shooting Aborigines for stealing sheep:

> It was the first time I had ever levelled a gun at my fellow man. I did so without regret or hesitation . . . I distinctly remember knocking over three blacks, two men and a boy, with one discharge of my double barrel.

In 1840, Cox's employee Patrick Codd died from head wounds inflicted by Aboriginal warriors. Three or four Aborigines were immediately killed in reprisals, and another twenty-five massacred in an unconnected slaughter in nearby Hamilton.

Above: the view today from the gates of the gaol overlooking Gallows Hill. Opposite top: Jack Napoleon Tunermenerwail. Below: Robert Smallboy.

Codd's death would have been forgotten. But in February 1842, Governor La Trobe brought charges against six white men for murdering four Aboriginal women and a child. Naturally, an all-white jury brought down an acquittal. But Judge Willis's criticism of the government for allowing an action against those responsible for the deaths of 'lubras' while white deaths remained unpunished spurred a renewed interest in the Cox case. In mid-April, an Aborigine identified as 'Roger' was charged with murder.

No translator was made available for Roger's 'trial'. *The Port Phillip Herald* later reported him as claiming that Codd had molested black women and killed black men. Governor La Trobe himself suggested that Codd had brought his death on himself through conduct 'criminal in the highest possible degree'. La Trobe even argued that that by Codd's death 'the sly murder of many of that [Aboriginal] race was avenged'.

But none of this mattered. A jury took ten minutes to find Roger guilty. Judge Willis then sentenced him to death, again making the political significance of the punishment clear by suggesting that the sentence be conducted at Mount Rouse rather than Melbourne.

This particular piece of judicial wisdom remained unacted on. Once more, the scaffold darkened the Melbourne skyline. A cart brought Roger to the execution ground – and then the proceedings paused, when a necessary official was found absent. In an extra piece of cruelty, Roger was left to wait for fifteen minutes at the foot of the gallows before the hangman did his work.

Thereafter, public executions fell out of favour in Victoria. For the authorities, outdoor hangings contained an element of danger, in that they encouraged large numbers of ordinary people to gather in one place. Once Aboriginal resistance had been crushed, Melbourne's rulers took an increasingly dim view of crowds, particularly those likely to be stirred by the passions of an execution, and further judicial killings were moved inside the walls of the gaol.

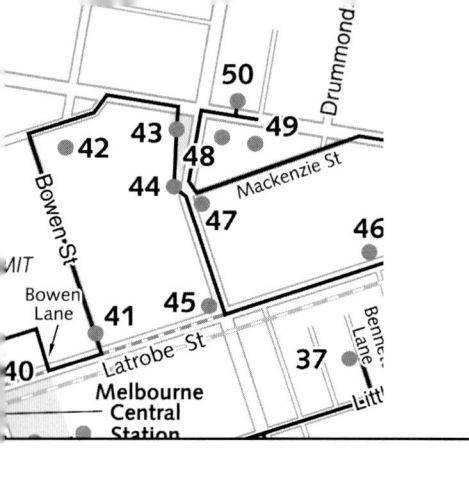

# 43. Eight-Hour Day Monument

## Corner Victoria and Russell Streets

> Some stupid mischievous blockhead – the worst enemy [the workers] ever had in this colony – set this agitation going; and the result will be that the whole fabric of their prosperity will be blown to the winds. Who will believe in any tale of distress of scarcity of labour, when he reads of processions first, and jollifications afterwards, to enforce a reduction of the day's work to eight hours, and without any diminution in the amount of wages?

So wrote *The Herald* on 22 April 1856, in response to the first eight-hour day procession.

The establishment of the eight-hour day was one of the great victories of the working class movement in the nineteenth century. Following from the success of workers in New Zealand and New South Wales, Victorian stonemasons began agitation over the question of shorter working hours in 1856.

On 5 March, the Melbourne Lodge of the Operative Masons met at the Belvedere Hotel, on the corner of Victoria and Brunswick Streets. After consultation with employers, a public meeting of the building trade was convened at the Queen's Theatre in Queen Street on 26 March. The meeting resolved that the eight-hour day be introduced on 21 April.

James Stephens, a stonemason and union activist working on the construction of Melbourne University, recorded what happened:

> I called a meeting during 'Smoko' time, viz., between ten and eleven o'clock in the forenoon, and reported our interviews with the employers, but that Mr Cornish, contractor for the Parliament Houses, would not give in. I then insisted that the resolution of the society should be carried by physical force if necessary.
>
> The majority of masons employed are society men, and we can easily coerce the minority. It was a burning hot day and I thought the occasion a good one, so I called upon the men to follow me, to which they immediately consented, when I marched them to a new building then being erected in Madeline Street, thence to Temple Court and on to the Parliament House, the men at all these works immediately dropping their tools and joining the procession.

*The Herald* described the ensuing march as nothing more than 'childish and useless perambulations'. But by 1 May, it was forced to concede:

> They have succeeded, at least in all the building trades in enforcing [the eight-hour day] without an effort. The employers have found it necessary and politic to give in, and without a struggle; agreeing, we believe, to pay the same amount of wages as formerly for ten hours' labour.

The stonemasons' example gradually spread – but not without struggle – to other trades. By 1876, Marcus Clarke – author of *For the Term of His Natural Life* – could celebrate in verse:

> Our children's tend'rest memories,
> Round Austral April grow,
> 'Twas the month we won our freedom, boys,
> Just twenty years ago.

The memorial to the eight-hour victory now standing outside Trades Hall was funded by public subscription. The collection initially failed to reach the required sum of £3000, and the original site at Spring Street (between Parliament House and Treasury) consisted only of the pedestal.

The monument was completed in 1903. A thousand people – including fourteen veterans of the original campaign – gathered to hear the socialist Tom Mann speak at the unveiling ceremony. The three eights bounded by a circle at the top of its pillar represent the division of the day into

Top: Tom Mann speaking at the unveiling of the Eight-Hour Day monument (above).

183

*The eight-hour day march at its peak.*

equal portions for rest, recreation and labour.

After 1856, the anniversary of the stonemasons' strike became a regular celebration, with each trade that observed the eight-hour day marching behind its banner from Trades Hall to Parliament.

The original eight-hour day campaigners had made much of the opportunities shorter hours would offer to workers for self-improvement (one activist had assured *The Sydney Morning Herald* that 'the majority of masons are men of a different stamp, and if they had time, many, I doubt not, would have their names enrolled as members of that valuable Institution – the Mechanics School of Arts'). The annual procession – rarely failing to pause for the singing of the National Anthem – became dominated by respectable, skilled unionists. After the 1890s, it was supplanted by the more radical May Day march as the pre-eminent event on the union calendar.

# 44. Old Melbourne Gaol

## Russell Street

When taking a tour through the Old Melbourne Gaol, it's difficult not to concentrate on the more morbid relics of convict life. But the flagellator's lash and the hangman's rope tell only one part of the gaol's story. The penitentiary also became on occasion a site of resistance, both within and without its walls.

From its earliest days, the Melbourne prison provoked controversy. When construction began in 1841, the prospect of an enormous grey gaol perching atop the Russell Street hill caused the citizenry not a little alarm.

Some went so far as to voice suspicions that the government intended the penitentiary to serve as a colossal concentration camp into which the entire population might be herded. Others – more plausibly – saw the gaol as evidence that authorities intended to recommence transportation to Port Phillip. At a public meeting called to agitate for separation from NSW, Edward Curr urged his audience to:

> Look next at the gaol, that hideous mass of deformity which stands so conspicuous before you, and which [has] been so correctly designated as a libel on our colony. It has cost you £25,000! And why and wherefore was the monster, huge as it is hideous erected? I will tell you. Your rulers dwell in a convict colony where it is calculated that a number of persons equal to the whole number of the inhabitants are passed through the gaols once every three years. This explains their ideas in erecting here the libellous monster.

In the event, the government decided against renewed transportation (in part, at least, due to popular protest). The inmates received by the completed prison on 1 January 1845 were entirely local – a mixed assortment of old lags and first-time offenders of both genders, as well as a small company of the mentally ill for whom no other accommodation could be found.

Not surprisingly, the first escape attempt took place almost as soon as the gaol opened. It was foiled by an informer but subsequent efforts proved more successful. In 1847, Jacob Jacobs, a Launceston convict, managed to scale the wall. The following year, William Booth hid in the labour yard and then used a rope to clamber to freedom. Then in 1851, two inmates made an astonishing escape from the privies, by clambering down the sewerage pipe. One headed for the bush (then still to be found in Victoria Street), with soldiers in hot pursuit. Though he was eventually recaptured, his companion successfully found his way into the city where he disappeared in the slums of Little Lonsdale Street before high-tailing it to Sydney.

Those in charge of the Melbourne gaol regarded themselves as reformers, committed to scientific methods of penology. But their attempts to construct a model system succeeded only in creating a regime in which brutality was more thoroughly and systematically applied.

The remaining wing of the gaol.

Take, for instance, the treadmill – an enormous cylinder attached to a set of steps, upon which a number of prisoners could be forced to mount. Once set in motion, the mill revolved inexorably, and the resultant force could be used to crush stone into gravel. Throughout the nineteenth century, the treadmill captivated reform-minded penal governors, since it enabled hard labour to be administered in mathematically precise quantities. It was hated by the men for exactly the same reason. Traditional prison labour at least allowed inmates some latitude in the speed at which they worked. The unvarying exertion the mill forced on unfit and ill-nourished prisoners amounted to something little short of torture.

In 1851, twenty-eight prisoners scheduled for a session on the Melbourne gaol's treadmill declared a strike. The prison chaplain implored them to submit; they told him to 'delay his _____ clapper, and keep his _____ preachments for Sunday'.

E.P. Sturt, the Visiting Justice, supposedly a 'humane and good natured man', examined the case and promptly sentenced all the strikers to seven days solitary confinement with bread and water. At the end of that period, only two men – Nobby Smith and Bob Newell – held out. According to Garryowen:

> Nobby bullyragged Mr Sturt in a style of such profane Billingsgate as would make the most foul-tongued bullock driver blush; and 'Bob' not only slang-whanged but took to hammering a turnkey.

Smith received thirty-five lashes, Newell fifty, and the strike collapsed in disarray.

As well as confining prisoners, the old gaol provided facilities to kill them. Though the first Melbourne executions took place outside its walls, the completion of the prison coincided with a move away from public hangings. When the murderer Jeremiah Connell was put to death on 27 January 1847, it was on gallows erected within the treadmill yard.

That same year, the hangman despatched two Aboriginal men charged with killing the settler Andrew Beveridge. The Beveridge clan had been expressly refused permission to establish their holdings near Swan Hill, the land having already been set aside for an Aboriginal reserve. Nonetheless, Beveridge squatted on thirty thousand acres, and then, in flagrant violation of both white and black law, threatened to shoot Aboriginal people for butchering his cattle. According to some reports, he had also been sleeping with an Aboriginal woman. On 23 August, Aboriginal warriors fatally speared him.

Local settlers brought three men to Melbourne for trial, identifying them only as 'Bobby', 'Ptolemy' and 'Bullet-eye'. A jury found Ptolemy and Bobby guilty within three minutes of deliberation. The extent of the white concern for justice may be gauged by the apparent inability of the assembled journalists to distinguish between the two men on the scaffold – *The Argus* report has Bobby dying instantly and Ptolemy slowly asphyxiating, in complete reversal of the accounts in *The Herald* and *The Patriot*.

This gruesome double execution generated a sequel, the irony of which is only too apparent. Though the jury found Bullet-eye innocent, the court commanded him to watch his friends die, apparently in order that he appreciate the workings of British justice. A short time after Bullet-eye's return to the Murray district, he seems to have seized an opportunity to demonstrate how well the lesson had been learnt. His people came into conflict with a man named McTier, a shepherd working on the notorious blackbirder Benjamin Boyd's station. When the bodies of McTier and his two sons were later recovered, it was found that the men had been killed by strangulation, with homemade nooses still dangling from their necks.

*The Patriot* had bewailed how the assemblage at Bobby and Ptolemy's deaths included women with infants in their arms, who had 'conducted themselves with most unbecoming levity'. But while some crowds did take a ghoulish relish in watching men die, on other occasions large numbers rallied for precisely the opposite reason. In fact, a number of the executions in the gaol took place in the face of angry demonstrations.

The most famous instance involved the legendary bushranger Ned Kelly, the man for whom the Melbourne gaol is today perhaps best remembered. While the outline of Kelly's career remains well known, the politics behind his case is often forgotten. His gang remained at large for as long as it did only because it enjoyed the active support of much of the population in northern Victoria, who identified far more with the son of an Irish-born small landowner than with the hirelings of the moneyed Anglican establishment sent to hunt him down.

With Ned on sentence of death in the Melbourne gaol, the extent of his support even in the city became apparent when, on 5 November 1880 – less than a week before his scheduled execution – some six or seven thousand gathered to protest the sentence in the Hippodrome in Exhibition Street.

*The Bendigo Independent* made the extent of the political polarisation generated by the case clear when, with remarkable candour, it noted:

Inside the gaol, 1905.

In revolutions and on occasions when executions take place in Paris, a new element appears in the mobs . . . male and female beasts – and these came out of their holes and were at the Kelly meeting, and shocking the respectable classes, and enabling them to comprehend upon what a fearful volcano society stands.

A few days later, a thousand people (*The Age* described them as 'the unwashed-looking mob') gathered at Government House to present a petition with 32,000 names calling for Ned's life to be spared. Eventually, almost double that number would be collected. On Tuesday 9 November, another demonstration on the corner of Latrobe and Swanston Streets nearly developed into a fully fledged riot, with police reinforcements arriving to prevent the fifteen hundred protesters reaching the Supreme Court reserve.

Finally, on the day of Kelly's death, some five thousand (according to *The Telegraph*, 'a mob of nondescript idlers') gathered outside the gaol. When the hangman pulled the lever and the clang of the trap reverberated around the gaol, the other inmates expressed their solidarity in a great howl of rage that emerged simultaneously from every cell.

Forty years later, the case of Angus Murray provoked a very similar reaction. Murray, an associate of the notorious gangster Squizzy Taylor, was sentenced to death in 1924 for his part in the murder of a bank manager during an armed robbery. Murray certainly didn't fire the fatal shot and, given the dubiousness of the evidence against him, may not have even been involved in the hold-up.

The Trades Hall Council, the Victorian Socialist Party and the Melbourne Branch of the ALP combined in a campaign to prevent the execution. Protest meetings took place simultaneously at the Exhibition Building and the Town Hall, with an attendance estimated at twelve thousand people.

Shortly afterwards, ten thousand gathered at a union rally at the Yarra Bank, while a petition with seventy thousand signatures reached the state Governor. On the day of the hanging, the Port Phillip Stevedores held a stopwork. Several thousand people – mostly working class housewives – assembled in Russell and Victoria Streets. Many were weeping, while others sang 'Nearer My God to Thee'. The mood gradually turned to anger, and the women marched on the gaol gates. Forty police and ten mounted troopers held the crowd back, ignoring

AS THE PRISON BELL TOLLED, many in this gathering outside the Melbourne Gaol yesterday fell on their knees and prayed, while others commenced singing hymns. Mounted police had to be summoned to push back the big crowd from the gaol enclosure.

*The Sun*, the day of Angus Murray's hanging.

repeated demands to remove their helmets as a mark of respect. At 10.00 a.m. – the time set for Murray's death – the crowd enforced a complete silence, which lasted for almost five minutes.

Murray repeated his innocence on the scaffold. According to *The Herald*, when the trap fell, another prisoner was heard to yell, 'You murderers!'

Afterwards, some of those gathered outside proposed to march upon Parliament. The crowd made its way over to the nearby Trades Hall, where Percy Laidler – hastily summoned at the behest of right-wing union leaders – eventually managed to convince the throng to disperse.

While the demonstrations didn't save Murray, they did help to foster public opposition to capital punishment. Forty years later, mass protests against the hanging of Ronald Ryan achieved the abolition of capital punishment throughout Victoria.

As for the Melbourne gaol, it was gradually superseded by Coburg's Pentridge as the city's primary penitentiary. Mindful of the value of the site as a prime piece of real estate, the authorities gradually demolished the boundary walls, the cemetery, the hospital and several cell blocks. The gaol closed in 1929; less than half of the original complex remains.

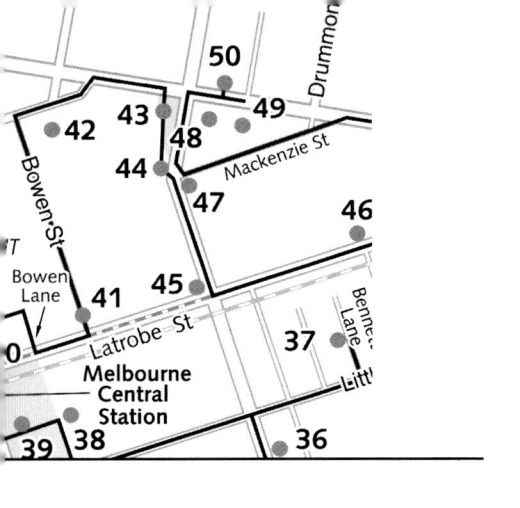

# 45. City Court

## Corner Latrobe and Russell Streets

The area surrounding the old Magistrates Court in Russell Street (now owned by RMIT) retains an association with law and order from Melbourne's earliest days. The acquittal of the Eureka rebels took place on the site (in the forerunner to the present building), with the infamous Redmond Barry presiding in handy proximity to both the police station and the Melbourne gaol. The demolition of the old court in 1910 allowed the construction of larger premises, styled – as *The Argus* noted with approval – to represent 'the grim majesty of the law'.

The strangest events associated with the City Court building took place in 1918 – the year a lengthy battle raged in Melbourne over the right to fly red flags.

The outbreak of the First World War in 1914 saw the government introduce a series of repressive laws, aimed at curbing the anti-war activities of radicals and socialist organisations. The security forces banned literature, undertook widespread surveillance and raided the homes, offices and meeting halls of left-wing activists. The bulwark of the government's campaign against subversion came from the War Precautions Act, a draconian piece of legislation which the authorities amended to suit the prevailing circumstances. One such amendment gave the Minister of Defence power to prohibit the flying of any flag without permission. A later regulation related specifically to the red flag, prohibiting the exhibition or use of any red emblem on any building, ship or public place, or on any demonstration.

The red flag had represented the aspirations of radicals of all persuasions since time immemorial. Probably originating as an emblem of naval mutiny, the flag had flown during the French revolution and later the Paris Commune. After the Russian revolution, it began an association with Bolsheviks, but retained its weight as the central icon of the mainstream labour movement. The anthem 'The Red Flag' (which still brings a tear to the eye of many old rebels today) invites workers to:

> *Raise the scarlet standard high,*
> *Within its shade we'll live or die.*
> *Though cowards flinch and traitors sneer,*
> *We'll keep the red flag flying here.*

The flagpole at Trades Hall formed the original target of governmental ire. When word of an imminent ban leaked out, the Trades Hall Council responded by hoisting a flag to celebrate the fall of the Bastille (during the French revolution) and the anniversary of the Great London Dock Strike. *The Argus* countered with a denunciation of

> the peace-at-any price section of the council, the members of which regard the Union Jack with undisguised contempt . . . [I]n the minds of these men the flying of the red flag proclaims that the Trades Hall has cut itself adrift from the British Empire and has no sympathy with the aims of the Allies in the war.

But when the law eventually came into effect, the Trades Hall Council quailed at the prospect of deliberately flouting it. Though left-wing unionists called for an immediate twenty-four-hour strike, Trades Hall prevaricated and then eventually capitulated to the law.

The radical left, however, would not be so easily cowed. The Victorian Socialist Party's members had been among those putting the most pressure on Trades Hall to resist. The VSP's orator Bella Lavender declared to a mass meeting: 'I was never prouder than when the little Red Flag fluttered from the Trades Hall in hypocritical old Melbourne.'

The organisation's newspaper *The Socialist* repeated the gist of Bella's remarks to readers:

> 'Oh, fools!' she said, after making eulogistic references to the inter-State Labor Conference which took place at Perth and expressing the view that she did not care if the political side – the vote-catching side, the 'keep-your-weather-open side', as Joe Cook had said – of the Labor movement, were consigned to the proverbial scrap heap, 'to think that by formulating a regulation under the War Precautions Act, and bringing out a statement that certain flags can be flown and others cannot be flown, unless under a special permit, it is possible to keep a free people back!'

Certainly, it didn't seem possible to keep the VSP back. The socialists immediately embarked upon a spirited campaign of civil disobedience, centred around publicly flying the red flag as often as possible.

The Yarra Bank and the City Court provided the fields of battle, with public flag wavings at the first inevitably provoking court cases at the second. The impassioned scenes at the Yarra Bank battles often verged on the farcical. For instance, *The Argus* reported:

> Yesterday afternoon . . . the red flag fluttered in the breeze, until [Plainclothes Constable] Kiernan took possession of it. There were a few hoots, and the crowd joined in singing 'The Red Flag'. Meanwhile, with persistence worthy of a better cause, the despoiled party obtained another red flag from somewhere and nailed it to a piece of moulding. This in turn was seized by Senior

Above: Dick Long (left) inside the 'Red Flag Cafe' with visiting VSP members. Opposite: Violet Clarke – another flag flier – poses for the camera.

Constable Proudfoot. Still defiant, the red-flaggers obtained a wisp of red material which looked like a woman's gossamer, and displayed that. This time the uniformed police, under Senior Constable Thompson, took action and in the light skirmish which ensued the substitute for a flag was trampled underfoot, much to the indignation of those who had displayed it.

While the daily papers reported events in scandalised tones, *The Socialist* gleefully recounted each battle, with a running commentary ('the speakers were in excellent trim, and felt – as they indeed were – crusaders in a Cause') on the successes of its side. Inevitably, however, the focus tended to shift to the City Court, where a lengthy procession of socialists stood in the dock on flag-related charges. One of the first (and indeed the most regular) was Dick Long, a bewhiskered carpenter and poet from Sandringham. Unlike most of his flamboyant VSP comrades, Long suffered from shyness – yet his opposition to the ban on the flag catapulted him into public prominence.

Presenting at the City Court on the extraordinary charge that he did 'contrary to the War Precautions Regulations, 1915, made under the War Precautions Act, 1914–1916, exhibit a flag, namely, a Red Flag, in contravention of a prohibition made in pursuance of sub-regulation (1) or Regulation 27BB of the said Regulations, in a public place, to wit, Flinders Park, Melbourne', Long's defence rested on the claim that he had flown the flag as a protest 'as the emblem meant more to him than anything else'. In the course of a long and impassioned statement, he disclaimed any desire for clemency, saying that he had deliberately flown the flag and accepted full responsibility for his action. Initially avoiding gaol, he almost immediately made his way back to the Bank, where repeated flag-waving led to his imprisonment (an event reported by *The Socialist* under the headline: 'Long Still Keeps it Flying: Persistent Poet Pounced on by Police; He Goes to Gaol Rather than Sign a Bond').

The VSP's Women's Socialist League took up the campaign with gusto. Jennie Baines – a leading member of the VSP and the Women's Peace Army – had no hesitation in throwing herself into the struggle, having already faced gaol fifteen times since arriving in Australia.

In the subsequent court hearings, Baines – a gifted orator – made a striking impression in the dock. Possessing 'a face ashen white [with] dark, blazing eyes' and a powerful voice 'which no opposition could drown', she used one City Court session to explain how 'the people of Germany, by the action for the Red Flag, had been the means of ending the war', before advising the judge to read the VSP pamphlet *The Story of the Red Flag* and then being (according to *The Socialist*) 'admiringly congratulated by friends upon [her] fine attitude throughout and upon [her] declarations in court'.

In March 1919, Jennie Baines received a sentence of six months' imprisonment for repeated violations of the War Precautions Act. As she left the dock, she turned to the magistrate and:

> cried out in sepulchral tones, into which she infused a wealth of feeling, 'If I do not obtain a speedy release my death will lie at your door!'

Once incarcerated, she immediately embarked on a hunger strike – reputedly the first ever to take place in Australia. Her stance further publicised and polarised the issue. One supporter went so far as to pen a poem under the title 'Jennie Baines (at the City Court)':

*Here cunning reigns,*
*While Mrs Baines*
*Pluckily pits*
*A rebel's wits*
*Against the Dogberry that sits –*
*Supported by dull legal lights,*
*And brief-bad rites –*
*Keeping intact*
*A War Precautions Act*

Despite attempts to induce Baines to capitulate (according to a disgusted *Socialist*, her captors offered her 'the daintiest and most appetising food'), she held out for four days – at which point the authorities, clearly feeling that they had met their match, released her.

By June that year, the VSP attracted three thousand people to a meeting at the Auditorium to sing 'The Red Flag' 'with a depth of feeling and volume of sound that stirred the conservative atmosphere of Collins Street as it had never been stirred before'. Baines, one of the evening's star speakers, concluded her remarks by asking the audience to accompany her to serenade Dick Long from outside the gaol (Long had told the prison Governor that he 'was an outdoor man and couldn't stand this type of life', and had therefore been allowed to build himself a hut in the prison yard, which he called 'The Red Flag Cafe'. The VSP organised a regime of meetings and song singing within earshot to keep his spirits up). About seven hundred people accepted Baines' invitation but found that the police had blocked the road to the prison. Nonetheless, they demonstrated 'by song and speech' their support for the incarcerated poet.

When the wartime powers of the government expired, Parliament eventually rescinded the War Precautions Act – allowing the ban on the red flag to lapse. Today, the flag still remains the emblem of radicalism – just as it was for Dick Long, Jennie Baines and the rest of the red-flaggers in the City Court of 1918.

The old Magistrates Court today.

# 46. Turn Verein Hall

## 30–34 Latrobe Street

In the early 1870s, William Maloney, a talented young man with a penchant for snappy dressing, worked as a teller in the Colonial Bank of Australia. Enraged by a rude customer, the always hot-tempered Maloney invited the man to step outside. Bad move. Maloney stood barely over five feet. The man casually beat him to a pulp.

Like the classic ninety-pound weakling, Maloney dreamed of revenge. To prepare himself, he enrolled in a gym – the Melbourne Deutscher Turn Verein, a German physical culture club in Latrobe Street. It was a decision that changed his life.

In the wake of the Gold Rush, Melbourne housed some ten thousand German immigrants. The foundation of the Turn Verein in 1860 provided a meeting place and cultural centre, a club that aimed at the development of the body through exercise, and the mind by the promotion of literature, music and social entertainments.

Just as importantly, the Turn Verein acted as a meeting place for the many German socialists driven out of Europe in the repression following the defeated revolutions of 1848 and 1849. A number of quite important revolutionaries found their way to Melbourne. They included the poet and journalist Hermann Puttmann, one of the leading theorists of the 'True Socialism' that Karl Marx polemicises against in the *Communist Manifesto*.

The military leader of the revolutionary forces in Baden, Gustav Techow, also found exile in Melbourne. Techow had escaped fifteen years' imprisonment, written a history of the movement and then participated in an ambitious attempt to raise money in America to fund a second uprising. Like Puttmann, Techow knew both Marx and Engels personally, and corresponded with both of them from Australia. He later wrote, 'Marx impressed me not only by his unusual superiority, but also by his very considerable personality. If his heart were as big as his brain and his love as great as his hate I would go through fire for him'.

For men like these, the Turn Verein provided an important link with their revolutionary past. Techow, a skilled gymnast who made a living instructing the Education Department in physical education, exercised on the Turn Verein's

'Sefton', the former Turn Verein Hall.

parallel bars, while Puttmann used the club as an outlet for poetry and music. His 1862 book *Deutsches Liederbuch für Australien* consisted of classical poetry, patriotic, Masonic and drinking songs, many of which were lustily performed by the Turn Verein choir.

Indeed, by the time Maloney came on the scene, the Turn Verein premises in Latrobe Street contained a concert hall and a dining room where members could avail themselves of sausages and beer (German delicacies that doubtless put something of a dent in many training programs) while discussing issues of concern to their community. As he worked on his pecs and his abs, Maloney found himself listening to debates on the latest developments in the European labour movement.

By the 1870s, many of the '48ers had shifted somewhat to the right. Both Puttmann and Techow, for instance, enthusiastically supported a German victory in the Franco-Prussian war. At the same time, however, a new German left had emerged in Australia, spurred by the mounting achievements of the socialist movement back home. Melbourne's German-speaking socialists had cohered into a group known as the Verein Vorwärts.

The Vorwärts organisation formed in the late 1880s to read and discuss the latest socialist newspapers from Germany. But the group also involved itself in local politics. In 1887, Verein Vorwärts contacted the nascent Australian Socialist League about the possibility of joint work. Though the ASL was too small and unstable for a continuing alliance to be viable, the two bodies did manage to combine with local anarchists and some French socialists for a celebration of the Paris Commune. According to a report in the *Australian Radical*, one of the Vorwärts group addressed the meeting in English:

> He would not say much, but he wanted to emphasise the necessity of there being no more nations but one country – the world!

A certain Comrade Graewe later took the stand, and explained that the socialists in Germany could:

> already count numbers equal to the rest of Europe and the time would come when their aspirations would be realised. In the meantime, it behoved all those in sympathy with the cause to unite and spread true ideas far and wide.

That meeting between Australian, German and French revolutionaries naturally

A SOCIAL EVENING AT THE MELBOURNE TURN VEREIN.

concluded with a ringing rendition of the 'Internationale', with all standing for the chorus.

We don't know much about the Verein Vorwärts' subsequent development. Some three hundred people attended its anniversary dance in 1895 in the Turn Verein building. The same hall hosted its twenty-third anniversary in 1909, an event involving dancing, a concert and speeches. An invitation had been extended to the Victorian Socialist Party to send delegates, whose speeches were well received. Shortly thereafter, the Vorwärts group amalgamated with the VSP, whilst retaining its own library.

The Turn Verein – like most German associations – became a target for jingoism with the outbreak of the First World War. Forced to sell its premises, it amalgamated with another German club in 1921.

As for Maloney, the exposure to the left-wingers in the Turn Verein gym recruited him to European-style socialism. As he later reminisced, it was from the German '48ers he met there that he 'learned most of his democracy'. After studying medicine in Europe, he returned to Melbourne to become a familiar part of the radical scene. Throughout the 1890s, the 'Little Doctor' remained ecumenical with his enthusiasms, associating at various times with the Social

Democrats, the semi-secret Knights of Labour, the Single Taxers and, ultimately, the Labor Party. He first won a seat in federal Parliament in 1904, in a decision the conservative *Argus* interpreted as signifying that 'at present, a great many crank feelings prevail'. But crank feelings or not, Maloney remained in office until his death in 1940, never rising to any great prominence but remaining one of Victoria's best loved Labor members.

But what of Maloney's original goal? Did he achieve his revenge? Suffice to say that becoming a convinced friend of the labouring masses did not divert our youthful bank clerk from his purpose. Long hours with the bar-bells eventually furnished Maloney with 'the greatest chest expansion of any one connected with [the Turn Verein]' (a boast he later voiced in Parliament). Thus equipped, he sought out his old enemy and suggested they resume combat.

*The Melbourne Punch* later recorded:

> for many months Maloney trained himself into Tip-Top condition, forced his conqueror into a second fight and had the satisfaction of giving him a sound drubbing.

The old Turn Verein building has now been extended and divided up to form a block of apartments called Sefton. It still stands more or less intact in Latrobe Street, a monument to the early German socialists – and to William Maloney's eventual vengeance.

# 47. Police Strike

## Old Russell Street Police Complex

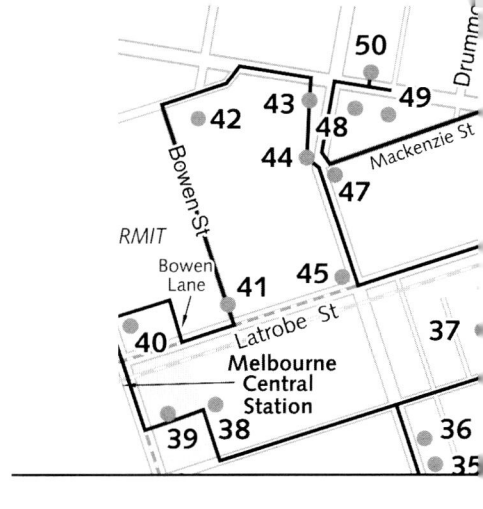

> It is Cup night. It is 10 pm and though the streets are almost deserted, there is a soldier, fully equipped ready for action, with bayonet fixed, on duty inside the door of the post office. Armed blue jackets guard the Federal Treasury and armed men guard other Federal property. Coming from the post office, a distance of two blocks, fourteen motor cars containing special police passed slowly by. All night long, through the city streets, scores of these motor patrol cars glide slowly in and out, up and down. . . . Guarding the city's property we have also tramping up and down all night long companies of specials, batons swinging, and squads of Light Horsemen. Newspaper reports say there are 8000 specials. In one city block at the one time I have counted 200 in company formation, all bearing the arm bands and swinging their batons.

That's *The Workers Weekly* of November 1923. The article details Melbourne in turmoil over a strike – a strike centred on the old Russell Street police barracks.

Most of the time, the powers-that-be remain acutely conscious of the importance of the constabulary in protecting the status quo – and so, as a matter of course, ensure that police have little to complain about. As for the officers themselves, the task of monitoring the population in an industrialised country quickly teaches them to despise the working class as a source of criminality, and their experience of industrial disputation is more likely to involve breaking picket lines than forming them.

But in the early 1920s, with modern policing still in its infancy, the situation was different. In the midst of an austerity drive, the authorities calculated that the force need receive remuneration no greater than (as the government bluntly put it) 'lower grades of employment in the trades and callings'. As a result, Victorian police enjoyed neither adequate pensions nor overtime rates, and suffered the worst officer-to-population ratio of any of the states.

In 1922, the state government appointed a new Chief Commissioner – Alexander Nicholson, a country policeman employed largely on the basis of a personal friendship with the Police Minister. Nicholson responded to the discontent in the ranks by setting four plainclothes police to supervise the uniformed constables, a move he justified on the basis of having witnessed 'men idling about the streets, leaning against lamp posts, gossiping – actually smoking in uniform, and in broad daylight'.

The introduction of these 'spooks' took place in the context of a world still shaken by the Russian revolution. The radicalism fostered by 1917 found echoes even within the ranks of Victorian police. In April 1923, Constable William Brooks circulated a petition among his fellows (whom he addressed as 'Comrades and Fellow Workers') demanding the withdrawal of supervisors, the restoration of pensions, and parity with police conditions in NSW. Furious, Commissioner Nicholson tried to transfer Brooks to Geelong and then Colac. Brooks' refusal led to an insubordination charge, generating substantial publicity and confirming him as the unofficial leader of the discontent within the force.

For the rebellious police, Russell Street served as a natural organising centre. Regulations forced single constables to live in the police building, in tiny rooms lacking the most basic facilities – thus adding another grievance to the list of demands. A subsequent investigation found that 'shabbiness and congestion were the features most in evidence [in] the Russell Street barracks . . . Many of the rooms are badly in need of renovation . . . while the overcrowding of others is serious enough to constitute a menace to the health of the occupants.'

On 31 October 1923, Brooks called a barracks meeting. Twenty-eight constables resolved not to go out on their scheduled beat unless the spooks were removed. Nicholson responded by dismissing the strikers, and thus dramatically escalating the dispute. Brooks promptly embarked on a tour of suburban police stations, advertising a strike meeting in the Temperance Hall in Russell Street. By Friday, 2 November – with the spring racing carnival set to draw thousands into the city – some six hundred police had walked off the job.

That evening, striking constables gathered at the gates of Russell Street to greet police replacements arriving from the country. Those reporting for work were greeted with hoots and cries of 'scab' and 'blackleg', while the surprisingly large number that chose instead to join the strike received enthusiastic cheers. A crowd of onlookers watched the strikers come to blows with loyalist police, before a baton charge cleared the street.

The news of the strike brought thousands of curious Melburnians pouring into the city. For the most part, they shared the strikers' hostility towards the scabs. On the corner of Bourke and Swanston Streets, a police loyalist (described by *The Argus* as 'a stoutly built middle aged man') became the centre of an angry mob until he was eventually forced to seek shelter in the doorway of a building occupied by the Society for the Protection of Animals.

In Elizabeth Street, tramway staff directed traffic. Uniformed sailors did the same elsewhere. In Swanston Street, cars lined up bumper to bumper, as the angry crowd chased police on point duty back to the Town Hall, which then remained in a virtual state of siege for the rest of the evening. The appearance of

*Mounted police disperse a crowd outside Flinders Street Station.*

police or their sympathisers served as a signal for fusillades of bottles and eggs. Police inside used high-pressure fire hoses in an attempt to clear the Town Hall doors, before resorting to baton charges at around 9.00 p.m.

Despite sporadic violence, a strange atmosphere of carnival prevailed. Several two-up schools operated openly in Collins Street, the largest attracting some three hundred people. One man took to the roof of a stranded tram, where he performed a brief, impromptu dance.

The throng dispersed around midnight, with the last trains running back to the suburbs. But the authorities remained apprehensive about what Saturday might bring. A hasty conference of the chiefs of the Navy, Army and Airforce resolved to cancel all leave and place all staff on standby. Army personnel were placed on guard at strategic locations like the Commonwealth Treasury and the Federal Printing Office, while soldiers in the Victoria Barracks assembled an arsenal suitable for street fighting (machine guns mounted on RAAF motor lorries, reserves of pistol ammunition and twenty Vickers machineguns).

Meanwhile, a meeting of prominent politicians, military leaders and businessmen set about establishing a force of strike breakers capable of policing the city. The resulting 'Special Constabulary Forces' were drawn overwhelmingly from the representatives of the privileged classes, especially those with service experience. The public-school spirit that prevailed amongst the squatters, Stock Exchange men and bankers who joined the SCF was nicely expressed in an interview one volunteer gave *The Herald*. He explained:

> I've had some rough times on the other side with Fritz but I must confess that the battle of Bourke Street today had plenty of 'ginger' in it. Fritz gave us a fair go but the mob today went about like packs of wolves and disgraced the name of Australian manhood.

Despite the enthusiasm of the specials, mustering sufficient numbers to patrol the entire city took time. And neither the volunteers nor the loyalists commanded any respect from the crowds that continued to flock to the city. Taxi drivers refused to carry 'specials' to their base in the Town Hall, and the cars used for patrols had to cover their number plates for fear of recognition. Even within Russell Street police headquarters, the three waitresses working in the canteen announced their refusal to serve constables who had not gone on strike.

Unfortunately, the strikers proved incapable of seizing the initiative. Many workers distrusted the striking police almost as much as the scabs – they remembered the brutal police attacks in the waterfront dispute of 1917 and couldn't hide a certain satisfaction in seeing police receive some of the same treatment themselves. But, more importantly, Brooks and his fellows lacked a clear strategy. They were not affiliated to the Trades Hall Council (indeed, the official police association refused to support the strike), and found it hard to call for solidarity from other workers. Lacking any tradition of collective action, many rebellious police simply joined the throng milling about the city.

Late Saturday evening, the press of the crowd smashed the glass of the Ezywalkin building in Swanston Street. As the window fell away, the mob suddenly realised that there was no-one to prevent them taking the goods on display. With the racing carnival in full swing, the major department stores all advertised expensive spring fashions. Suddenly, these were accessible to everyone. *The Argus* reported:

> Women gathered skirts in hand, turned them into capacious holders, filled them and scuttled north, south and west. Small boys, too, were busy, and youths stacked tinned foods in piles and bore them down the lanes. A touch of the grotesque marked the orgy. Young men headed a cheering troupe and, for the moment, appeared to be carrying women in a startling unconventional manner. They were really bearing over their shoulders silk stockinged and daintily shod dummy figures.

The looting spread from the Leviathan Clothing building to Kermodes Jewellers, Charles Jeffries footwear and other shops in Swanston Street between Bourke and Collins Streets. Buckley and Nunn, Myers, Rundles, London Stores, Danks and Thos Evans all had windows smashed and stock seized. In total, significant damage occurred to thirty shops in Bourke Street, fourteen in Elizabeth Street, twelve in Swanston Street, eleven in Little Collins Street, five in Collins Street, two in Russell Street and one each in Queen, Exhibition and Spring Streets.

Though authorities quickly blamed the looting (which *The Argus* described as a 'Bolshevist orgy') on the city's criminal element, most of those arrested proved to be perfectly ordinary working class people. *The Herald* later observed: 'A remarkable feature was the number of women and girls who took part in the demonstrations against the police'.

Indeed, the majority of injuries suffered that night came not from the mob turning on itself, but from the forces protecting private property. After police baton charges, ambulances carried nearly two hundred people off to nearby hospitals. And once police numbers grew (with an influx of specials and country police), the loyalists took delight in punishing the crowd. A plainclothes constable later boasted to *The Herald*:

*The remainder of the Victorian era police building on the corner of McKenzie and Russell Streets.*

> We gave the 'bucks' [larrikins] the hiding of their lives tonight. We had to take a hiding from them on Friday night, but, by the Lord Harry, we got our own back tonight. They'll be sore for a week. I think I saw and cracked half the 'bucks' I know.

By Sunday, Melbourne swarmed with specials. *The Workers Weekly* described Melbourne as 'under *fascisti* rule' – a not totally inappropriate description of a city in which teams of returned servicemen and vigilantes patrolled with batons.

The strike gradually petered out. By 17 November, the special constables had been demobilised to make way for an interim auxiliary force. Despite attempts to organise a Police Reinstatement Association, not one of the 636 strikers dismissed or discharged from the force was ever allowed back into the ranks of the Victoria Police.

Alongside the official vindictiveness to the strikers, the authorities took steps to prevent further disputes by conceding almost all of the strikers' demands. Increased funding allowed better accommodation, better equipment and the introduction of a pension plan. There was no attempt to revive the spooks.

The combination of carrot and stick has proved effective. In the eight decades since, the police have never again gone on strike. The force now operates from a new, state-of-the-art building near the Crown Casino. Yet the old building in Russell Street remains as a reminder of the one time that the police turned against their masters.

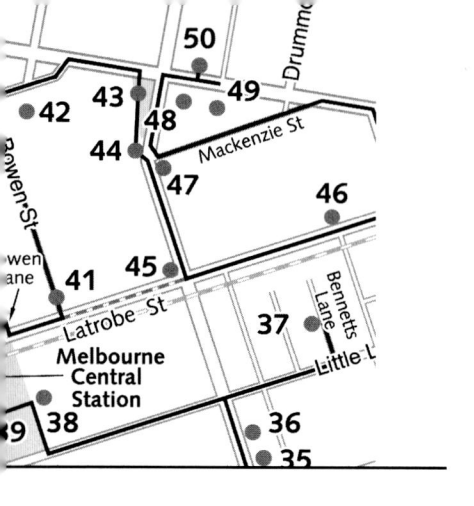

# 48. Progressive Spiritualist Lyceum

## Corner Victoria and Lygon Streets

The mutual benefit society known as the Independent Order of Odd Fellows constructed the solid hall on the south-east corner of Victoria and Russell Streets as its Melbourne headquarters in 1887. For the next hundred years, the Odd Fellows supplemented their income by hiring out the building to all comers. The capacity of the hall, and its proximity to Trades Hall, meant that it found favour with a succession of radical organisations – from the Victorian Socialist Party to the communists, the IOOF building hosted anyone who wanted room for a dance, concert or meeting.

But perhaps the oddest set of fellows to gather there did so under the banner of the Victorian Association of Progressive Spiritualists. That is, for a brief period, the VAPS's Spiritualist Lyceum used the hall for an alternative Sunday school that combined advanced educational theories with a fervent belief in physical communication with the dead.

Spiritualism travelled to Australia in the 1860s, on the crest of extraordinary popularity in the United States. It found its local advocate in William Henry Terry, a mild-mannered Unitarian who abandoned his drapery business after uncovering latent psychic abilities during a seance. Terry's enthusiasm for matters spiritualistic set him at odds with his more conventionally religious wife, Martha, who took to yanking on his whiskers and knocking off his hat whenever she found him perusing occult literature. Their eventual judicial separation left Terry with custody of eight of his nine children.

Fortunately, he managed to make a success of a spiritualist bookshop in Russell Street – a mystical emporium stocking everything from ouija boards to Egyptian lentils – while practising successfully as a psychic healer. With his flowing white beard lending an appropriately otherworldly appearance, he became a leading proselytiser for the new faith.

What did spiritualists believe? First and foremost, that the psychic manifestations of various parlour mediums provided empirical proof of the reality of human survival beyond the grave. In its own perverse way, spiritualism appealed as a kind of rationalism, with its doctrines emanating from discoveries made during seances in much the same way as laboratory experimentation buttressed the hypotheses of chemists. The new religion was also profoundly democratic. Unmediated access to the great beyond rendered the hierarchical institutions of traditional churches superfluous. Anyone could hold a seance – as Terry enthusiastically announced, all that was required was a drawing room and a few friends.

Spiritualism seemed to many like a reform campaign, opposed to clerical superstition and, by extension, many conventions of Victorian society. Terry, for instance, espoused liberal views on the status of women (many mediums were, after all, female) and appealed to the Brotherhood of Man that prevailed in the afterlife to oppose mounting anti-Chinese racism. He also revealed that the spirits shared his enthusiasm for temperance and vegetarianism, a happy coincidence that added authority to his diagnosis of Martha Terry's ill-temper as stemming from a surfeit of 'pork and porter'.

The IOOF building today.

The first meeting to attempt to organise the new movement took place in Trades Hall in 1870. The group eventually became known as the Victorian Association of Progressive Spiritualists (after the alternative 'Association of Friends of Spiritual, Moral and Social Progress' had been rejected as too long-winded). The banner of its publication *Harbinger of Light* ('A Monthly Journal Devoted to Zoistic Science, Freethought, Spiritualism and the Harmonial Philosophy') proudly proclaimed that 'dawn approaches, error is passing away, men arising shall hail the day'.

Within a year, the VAPS boasted a membership of over three hundred and claimed a thousand or more people had attended its meetings. Its ranks included radicals like Monty Miller, a veteran of the Eureka Stockade and later a member of both the Melbourne Anarchist Club and the Industrial Workers of the World. The poet Bernard O'Dowd – who would go on to edit the socialist paper *Tocsin* – showed early enthusiasm for spiritualism, while George Manns acted as Secretary both for the Spiritualists and for the Democratic Association of Victoria, the Australian section of Karl Marx's International Working Men's Association.

A *Harbinger* correspondent styling himself 'A Working Man' encapsulated this radical trend by declaring: 'spiritualists are thorough progressionists and have decided to throw to the winds all old foolish ideas, creeds and dogmas and to free themselves at once from the iron grasp of priestcraft'. Indeed, in 1872, spiritualists and DAV members pooled their resources in an attempt to establish a 'Co-operative Association' – a utopian rural commune intended to be both socialist and spiritualist. Unfortunately, though the 'Working Man' declared the foundation of 'Aurelia' to be one of the wisest steps the spiritualists had taken, the project never really got off the ground. Manns – apparently without irony – attributed the venture's failure to 'some discordant spirits' amongst the colonists.

The spiritualists' other major reform took place in the sphere of education. To shield their children from the clergy's baleful influence, they established their own Sunday school – the Progressive Spiritualist Lyceum. The *Harbinger* explained, 'A full Lyceum consists of twelve groups of twelve members each . . . The children are taught songs and recitations which they deliver in chorus while performing intricate chain marches and other pleasant drills'.

For the most part, the Lyceum involved the substitution of church rites with practices more in tune with common sense. The Spiritualist liturgy, for instance, entailed the following dialogue between the pupils and the Lyceum conductor (an office held for some time by Alfred Deakin, later Prime Minister):

> *What is our baptism?*
> *Frequent ablutions in hot water.*
> *What is our eucharist?*
> *Nutritious food and cold water.*
> *What is our inspiration?*
> *Plenty of sunlight and fresh air.*

But if such homely rituals seemed too prosaic, the Lyceum also offered pupils considerable licence to debate and discuss matters political and religious – as well as the opportunity to witness the conductor lapse into a trance and deliver a lecture in the voice of a disembodied phantom (a prospect unlikely to be available in more traditional Sunday schools).

The pupils produced their own magazine, *The Lyceum Miniature*, in which they published creative writing, essays and poetry. It was assumed that children would flourish if given freedom to grow, a philosophy considerably indebted to the New Lanark schools operated by the utopian socialist Robert Owen (and, it should be stressed, in stark contrast to the prevailing educational wisdom).

At its peak in the 1870s and 1880s, the movement spread throughout the state, with Lyceums established at Richmond, Bendigo, Stawell and elsewhere. In Castlemaine, pupils gathered in a hall decorated with the poetic (but perhaps somewhat disconcerting) assurance:

> *It is a beautiful belief,*
> *That ever round your head*
> *Are hovering on viewing wings*
> *The Spirits of the Dead.*

An account of a presentation night at the Melbourne Lyceum in May 1878 illustrates how thoroughly the syllabus combined its admirable emphasis on performance and free expression with out-and-out Spiritualist bunkum. According to *The Harbinger*, the evening began with:

> the song 'Life's Beautiful Sea' . . . sung by the whole Lyceum, this was followed by a selection of golden and silver chain recitations and choral responses . . . At the conclusion of the musical reading, the Lyceum . . . led by the conductor performed a series of calisthenics to the music of the piano; these were executed with energy and precision and were applauded by the audience. An ornamental march by the Lyceum brought the more active

CALISTHENICS.

The Lyceum students perform their calisthenics.

portion of the proceedings to a close, and seats being arranged a number of recitations and songs were creditably given by members of the groups. [The visiting spiritualist lecturer] Mrs Britten eulogised the Lyceum system and impressed upon the children the fact that with her spiritual eyes she could see present with them children and teachers from the spirit-world inspiring them and sympathising with their thought and actions . . .

Unfortunately, the regularity with which visiting mediums like Mrs Britten suffered exposure as frauds removed much of the gloss from the movement, as did the chronic inability of the spiritualists to refrain from depressingly mundane personal feuds and organisational splits. Furthermore, as the century drew to a close, the growth and politicisation of the international workers' movement meant that the vague rationalism offered by the Progressive Spiritualists no longer beckoned with the same force. Terry died in 1913, leaving his books and the little money he possessed to the 'Cause of Higher Spiritualism'. The movement limped on, but increasingly became the preserve of conmen and cranks.

The Lyceum occupied a variety of buildings during its existence – a room in Stephen (Exhibition) Street, the Horticultural Hall opposite Trades Hall, a (now demolished) building in Swanston Street and elsewhere. The last trace we can find of it is in the 1920s, when a much reduced Melbourne Progressive Spiritualistic Lyceum shared the Odd Fellows premises in Victoria Street with the IOOF's Grand Lodge of Victoria.

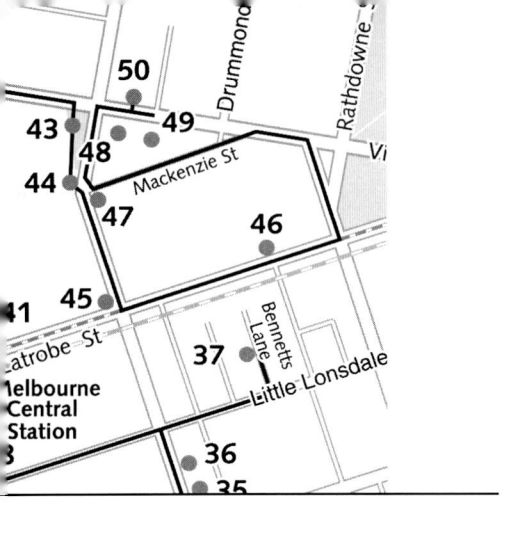

# 49. Matteotti Club

## Horticultural Hall

**Prosecutor:** Do you believe in assaulting people?
**Carmagnola:** No, I believe in freedom and justice for everyone, not like the Fascists who create tyranny.
**Prosecutor:** You say and apparently believe that the Fascists should be assaulted and spat upon.
**Carmagnola:** If you knew what the Fascist Party do, you would agree with me.
**Prosecutor:** Then if you took such a big interest in the welfare of your country and your people, why did you come to Australia, and why don't you go back?
**Carmagnola:** Because I am ashamed to call myself an Italian under the present Regime.
**Prosecutor:** Do you think any decent Australian is proud of you?
**Carmagnola:** Yes, they should be, because I stand for the freedom and justice of the Italian people, and also for the Australian people. I would be prepared to fight for Australia if her people were under a tyrant.
**Prosecutor:** We don't want you.

The year is 1932, and the place is Townsville, Queensland. Italian anarchist Francesco Carmagnola is on trial for ripping the Fascist Party badge from the coat of the Italian Vice-Consul, Mario Melano.

Carmagnola had arrived in Melbourne in 1927. Immediately, he founded an anti-fascist social club which he named after Matteotti, the Italian parliamentarian murdered by Mussolini.

The original building in Spring Street quickly proved too small. The Victorian Horticultural Society – an eminently respectable organisation – was then in financial difficulty, and the Matteotti Club moved into its premises on Victoria Street, opposite Trades Hall.

The site was perfect for Carmagnola and his comrades. The huge downstairs hall held five hundred people for meetings or dances. Bocce (Italian bowls) could be played in a courtyard. In the smaller rooms, members could read radical papers from around the world, play cards, eat or simply chat with other Italian-Australians.

The Matteotti Club, May Day, 1931.

But the central focus of the club was anti-fascism. Many members had first-hand experiences of Mussolini, and believed that the only way to deal with fascists was to physically intimidate them. Their paper *La Riscossa* declared its intention to 'hinder, make difficult, if not prevent, the life of the diplomats of Fascism, and for every crime which is committed in Italy against one of ours, we can take revenge on one of them abroad'.

As good as their word, Matteotti Club members regularly descended upon clubs and restaurants where fascist sympathisers gathered, and contemptuously ripped off their Party badges. On 2 February 1929, they disrupted the first talking picture screening at the Melbourne Auditorium, in protest at footage of Mussolini delivering a speech. Later that year, they gathered outside the Temperance Hall in Russell Street, where a group of about a hundred and fifty fascists – many wearing the famous black shirt – had assembled to celebrate the anniversary of Mussolini's March on Rome. Sneaking inside in small groups, the Matteotti Club supporters fell upon the fascists with iron bars, knives and pieces of wood, and then made a hasty retreat. The incident severely dented the confidence of Fascists in Australia – many chose not to attend a similar celebration in Sydney, and those that did decided against wearing their black shirts.

The Matteotti Club also made determined efforts to link up with the Australian trade union movement. In 1930, Carmagnola wrote to the ACTU warning that Italian Consuls in Australia coerced Italians to work as strike breakers:

209

We know Consuls advised our countrymen, 'Don't be fools; here is your opportunity to get work at good wages.' It is necessary here to show that 'advice' tendered by a fascist consul is not advice in the usual sense of the word. Any Italian worker who disregards such 'advice' is put on the list of anti-fascists and the Government of Italy is advised, which leads to the persecution of any relatives or friends there.

On May Day rallies, the Matteotti Club supporters marched through the streets of Melbourne in their red shirts, carrying posters with the slogan 'Down with Mussolini, the assassin of the Italian people'. On May Day 1931, Carmagnola addressed seven thousand workers by the banks of the Yarra, encouraging them to chant 'Death to Mussolini'.

In October 1930, the police raided the Matteotti Club and the Communist Party (in nearby Russell Street) after a militant demonstration against unemployment. While officers managed to arrest plenty of Party members and to 'find' an assortment of weapons underneath its building, their raid on the Matteotti Club netted only Valentine Ciotti, later charged with possessing an unregistered pistol, and with 'having unlawfully had in his possession 62 opossum skins and two kangaroo skins'.

By the end of 1933 the Club had collapsed. The Depression hit Melbourne hard, and Italian radicals had scattered across Australia in search of work. Infighting between some of the central figures in the Matteotti Club and *La Riscossa* also contributed to the Club's decline, and possession of its premises reverted to

Opposite: Frank Carmagnola with a group of Club members. Top: an evening at the Matteotti Club. Left: the VHS hall as it stands today. In the foreground is the yard where Club members once played bocce.

the Horticultural Society.

In the late 1990s the building was privatised. The choir rehearsals and occasional exhibitions and shows came to an end. Though the ceiling is cracked and peeling, the flagpole upon which the Matteotti Club defiantly flew a red flag still stands. If you make your way down the west side at the back of the building, you can see in peeling paint the name of the club – still visible after all these years.

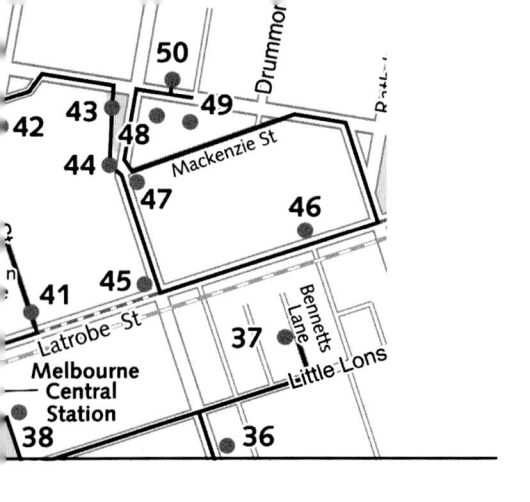

# 50. Trades Hall

## 54 Victoria Street

*A place where workmen may their minds engage*
*To useful purpose o'er the printed page*
*– One which the tints of age may haply show*
*Or one which caught the ink an hour ago: –*
*A Hall where wife and children may be found*
*To listen to a concert of sweet sound,*
*Or hear the lecturer and quickly learn*
*What years of study teach him to discern: –*
*Science, with pleasure mingled – happy task!*
*Minerva speaking through a Momus mask.*
*All those, and more than these this hall will yield:*
*We guess the crop before we reap the field.*

Where lies this magical place? Believe it or not, on the corner of Victoria and Lygon Streets. The poem by journalist Charles Bright describes – or rather predicts, for it dates from several years before the building's construction – Trades Hall, the centre of Melbourne unionism.

The first Trades Hall arose directly out of the 1856 struggle for the eight-hour day. With victory achieved, the unions – mostly representing the more skilled and confident workers – decided they needed a hall of their own as a space for discussions, but also (and perhaps more importantly) to provide a centre for working class education and advancement.

In recognition of these aims, their co-ordinating committee renamed itself the Melbourne Trades Hall and Literary Institute and embarked on an ambitious fundraising campaign, culminating in a gala night at the Princess Theatre (where the verse above made its debut, recited by the theatrical star Miss Provost). The main entertainment came from a special performance of 'The Hunchback', which was received with considerable enthusiasm from the worker audience (although *The Herald* noted that the applause 'came in where it was least expected, and the laughter excited by some of the most pathetic portions was immense'). At the end of the evening, the national anthem played, and the curtain rose to display unionists assembled with the banners of the various trades flying, before the entertainment concluded with a comedy routine entitled: 'How to Make Home Happy'.

By 1859, the unions possessed sufficient money to commence construction of their own happy home. The stress on the educative rather than industrial function of their project encouraged a surprising degree of support from establishment Melbourne. The liberal Berry government, attracted by the prospect of workers humbly seeking self-improvement, provided Crown land on the corner of Victoria and Lygon Streets, on the condition that it never be traded for gain.

The original Trades Hall.

When the completed building – a timber construction with a galvanised iron roof, containing a large hall and four committee rooms – opened with a grand tea for some two thousand, the conservative *Argus* joined in the festivities, declaiming, 'In wishing [Trades Hall] prosperity there can be no diversity of opinion' (although it could not refrain from sneering at celebratory table settings that included flowers 'stuck into tumblers and white earthenware jugs with imitation iron hoops').

None of the original building remains. The oldest part of today's structure dates from 1875. John Reed, the architect responsible, had previously designed the Public Library, the Wesley Church in Lonsdale Street, the Melbourne Town Hall and other Victorian landmarks. With a brief to construct a hall worthy to stand as 'the working man's parliament', he produced a squarish, two-storey edifice facing Victoria Street. Additions over subsequent years mostly retained the same style.

In 1882, for instance, the growth of the movement necessitated the addition of a north extension. The wall above the stone staircase built at this time was adorned with the names of the 'Eight-Hour Men' – the leaders of unions that successfully won the shorter working day. The construction of an elaborate council chamber two years later reinforced the image of a parliament of labour.

The original model was explicitly gendered – the building was to be a parliament belonging to working-*men*. Bright's ode to Trades Hall's future successes that night in the Princess Theatre reflected a traditional conception of what unionism could offer females:

> *As a woman, in the strife I cannot share*
> *But still may praise the men who nobly dare*
> *Let man in battle wield the dreadful sword!*
> *Let woman sympathise, – respect, – reward!*

In 1882, however, five hundred women and girls showed their willingness to do more than sympathise and respect by striking against the appalling conditions in the Melbourne clothing industry (one of their leaders, Helen Robertson, recalled many years later that 'working girls were treated like animals and every ounce of their vitality was sapped up in long hours at the employers' profit'). A delegation made contact with Trades Hall to form the Victorian Tailoresses Union – the first union for women workers in Australia, and one of the earliest in the world. The incident marked a significant development in Trades Hall's history. The widely publicised dispute encouraged more workers' organisations to affiliate to the Trades Hall Council, and helped win legal recognition for unions, as well as adding the phrase 'log of claims' – from the Tailoresses' cata*log*ue of fair prices – to common usage.

The male union leaders still regarded the corridors of Trades Hall as no place for a woman. The construction of the Female Operatives Hall in the aftermath of the Tailoresses' dispute aimed to provide female workers with lectures and meetings, in part to draw them into the movement, but also to safeguard their morality by keeping them off the street. In 1960, it was replaced by the so-called 'new building', a modernist monstrosity about which the less said the better.

The ugliness of the new building seems all the more regrettable given Trades Hall's close association with the arts. In its early years, it functioned as a kind of educational centre for workers, providing classes in mathematics, English, economics, public speaking, history and politics. In 1867, the Painters and Decorators Union threw its support behind an Artisans School of Design. Artists of the calibre of the landscapist Louis Buvelot instructed a generation of young painters within the building, including future giants such as Frederick McCubbin and Tom Roberts.

Until 1971, the Victorian Branch of the ALP also maintained its headquarters in Trades Hall. Though today Labor does its best to minimise its association with the working class, the Party initially formed directly out of the defeat suffered by unions during the Great Strikes of the 1890s. Indeed, the resulting Political Progressive League (the forerunner of the Labor Party) often found itself described simply as 'the Trades Hall Party', a tag that today's ALP leaders would regard with horror.

The organisation's proximity to the union movement did not, however, make it any fonder of radicalism – as became apparent when the Fitzroy Branch of the PPL decided upon the activist Sam Rosa as its candidate in the election of 1892. Rosa had featured prominently in the unemployed agitation of 1890, in the course of which he had delivered the following advice to the jobless:

> When the pinch of poverty was overcome and they secured work, they ought to reserve a certain sum out of their weekly earnings for the purpose of buying muskets. It would be well, too, if they went out into the outlying districts and there practised military drill and firing exercises.

The prospect of a candidate espousing armed insurrection proved too much for the PPL to swallow. The Party's central committee flatly refused to endorse Rosa's candidature, despite the branch's decision. The Trades Hall paper *Commonweal* reasoned that 'a man who exhorted his hearers to loot the shops, and talked about drilling the unemployed, could never command the support of workers and liberals who desire to effect reform in a peaceful manner'.

*The Commonweal*'s desire for liberal support did not prove sufficient to placate *The Argus* which – having long since renounced the good wishes it had bestowed on Trades Hall – thundered:

> The natural consequence of every movement such as that inaugurated by the Progressive League is to bring to the front rash and mischievous men who are a danger to society.

A discussion of the experience of Labor in power would take us too far afield. Suffice to say that many unionists found that, rather than offering any danger to society, their elected representatives have displayed a marked tendency to degenerate into, as the socialist magazine *Tocsin* once noted, 'a heterogeneous pledgeless, irresponsible body, bereft of vertebra and spinal marrow'.

The battle for control of the ALP and the unions has traditionally been fought within the environs of Trades Hall – on occasion, quite literally. The main staircase of the building still bears bullet holes from what may have been one such incident. In October 1915, police investigating suspicious noises discovered an open window near the Victoria Street entrance. In the darkness, they encountered John Jackson, Richard Buckley and Alexander Ward in the act of robbing a safe. During the ensuing gun battle, twenty-six shots ricocheted around the corridors. Two of the intruders received bullet wounds; Constable David McGrath bled to death in the rooms of the Typographical Society on the second floor. Buckley and Ward possessed long criminal records. Nonetheless, a court found John Jackson guilty of the murder. He became the last man to face the gallows of the Old Melbourne Gaol, across the road from where the shoot-out took place.

In his novel *Power Without Glory*, Frank Hardy connects the affair to an attempt by the corrupt businessman John Wren (a major powerbroker within Victorian Labor) to rig a union election. In Hardy's version, Wren and the gangster Squizzy Taylor wait outside in a car, while the three safe-crackers try to grab ballot papers and membership lists. When the operation goes wrong, Wren selects Jackson to take the fall while Taylor pays off juries to ensure the others receive light sentences.

Certainly, we know that the Typographical Society's safe contained membership cards but little money, while Jackson worked for a bookmaker on a racetrack controlled by John Wren. Whatever the truth, within Trades Hall, the scars from the gun battle are shown to visitors as 'Squizzy Taylor's bullets'.

The building contains memorials to some prouder moments, too. Near the Lygon Street entrance, a plaque commemorates the part played by the trade union movement in the anti-conscription struggles of 1916 and 1917. By 1916,

Opposite: Trades Hall decorated with anti-conscription banners in 1917. Above: Trades Hall, 2001.

initial union enthusiasm for the First World War had dimmed, and a gathering of the Congress of Australian Trade Unions in Melbourne in May resolved to oppose any attempt to introduce military conscription, widely tipped to be on the horizon. A few months later Prime Minister Hughes returned from Britain and announced a referendum on the question. When the unions formulated their conference decisions into an anti-conscription manifesto, an increasingly dictatorial Hughes determined to suppress it. Military police destroyed the type at the printers, before arriving at Trades Hall with a warrant proclaiming their right to 'enter and search, if needs be by force'.

E.J. Holloway, the Secretary of Trades Hall, later recollected how the officer in charge announced:

> he would have to break down the door [of Trades Hall] with the butts of their rifles if I continued to refuse to open it. [But] the caretaker opened it because he said that it was at any rate his duty to protect the property.

The troops confiscated ten thousand copies of the manifesto. Later, the Minister for Defence slapped a ban on the document. But Holloway commented:

> the raid and the ban were manna from Heaven for our Executive. Indifference in many was suddenly turned to curiosity and interest. All the world wanted copies. We and our work and our Manifesto all took on an air of martyrdom in spite of ourselves.

The 1916 referendum went down to defeat, a result Hughes described as 'a triumph for the unworthy, the selfish and treacherous in our midst'. But despite the government's best efforts, a second referendum the following year received the same treatment.

Towards the end of the war, rumours began to circulate that the government intended to use the War Precautions Act to ban the display of the most famous emblem of workers' struggle, the red flag. At a series of Trades Hall Council meetings, delegates declared it necessary to protest such legislation – by immediately hoisting the red flag from the Trades Hall flag pole. A discussion of days and dates to be celebrated produced a list that included 18 March (the proclamation of the Paris Commune in 1871), 1 May (May Day), 14 July (fall of the Bastille in 1789), 13 August (Great London Dock Strike of 1889), 28 September (the organisation of the First International in 1864), 11 November (the hanging of the Chicago martyrs in 1887), and 4 December (Eureka Stockade in 1854).

Other more left-wing delegates promptly moved that the red flag should also be flown on all election days, referendum days, every day during the continuance of a strike, as well as the anniversary of the Russian revolution. A last-minute amendment suggested that, in addition to the days enumerated, the flag should fly every other day of the year!

Unfortunately, the delegates then discovered that Trades Hall didn't actually possess its own flag. A borrowed ensign celebrated Bastille Day and the Dock Strike anniversary, while the Sail and Tent Makers Union received a hurried commission to sew the THC its own red flag.

But when the mooted flag ban eventually passed into law, Trades Hall buckled – and chose not to fly its flag until the government repealed the War Precautions Act shortly after the war ended.

A casual visitor to Trades Hall today might note the security on the doors in the main building. When iron grilles first made their appearance in the building, they functioned solely to keep out supporters of the Communist Party during the bitter unemployment struggles of the 1930s.

In 1930, the Communist Party could muster up to four delegates on the Trades Hall Council. Its representatives inevitably invited rowdy supporters (mostly unemployed activists) to join in their denunciations of union bureaucrats' unwillingness to mount a serious fight for the jobless. In July 1931, right-wing officials announced a ban on visitors to meetings. The communists responded by calling on supporters to force admission. Subsequent meetings became wild melees, with police attacking the unemployed in the hall, and a group of activists occupying the Council Chamber.

When the Trades Hall leaders eventually suspended two communist activists, the CP brought out a leaflet headed 'Smash Trades Hall bureaucracy'. Denouncing 'the Trades Hall outfit' as 'the boss's tools within our own ranks', it announced a demonstration outside the building. The communists prepared for what both sides expected to be a bloody confrontation by establishing their own first aid station in Cardigan Street, equipped with a Party doctor and nurses. But, though a thousand people assembled (and a CP organiser purportedly boasted that 'there'll be Soviet power in Melbourne tomorrow'), a massive police presence succeeded in shepherding demonstrators away from the THC delegates.

The continuing hostility between communists and the union leaders eventually came to a head at the May Day procession the next year when CP supporters physically attacked the Acting Premier Tom Tunnecliffe (who had been Police Minister during a period of great police brutality to the unemployed). The incident resulted in a decades-long THC ban on May Day celebrations.

Nonetheless, while eschewing the traditional day for radical propaganda, Trades Hall sought other channels to disseminate the official union message. In May 1926, the Industrial Printing and Publicity Group – an organisation associated with both the THC and the Labor Party – applied to the Postmaster General's Department to operate a radio station. Resistance from the Melbourne establishment meant that the licence did not arrive for four years. In early 1930, the union leader J.F. Chapple pointed out to federal parliamentarians that 'radio propaganda is essential to the promulgation of democratic views and that the progress of our party is wrapped up in the venture'. The point had occurred to conservatives, too – the rabidly reactionary Police Commissioner Thomas Blamey mounted a last ditch attempt to halt the venture, claiming that the transmission mast would interfere with police radio.

Nonetheless, eventually radio 3KZ went to air, operating out of a tiny studio inside one of the Trades Hall towers. In 1931, the THC secretary Bill Duggan delivered the inaugural Labor program, explaining:

> Unionism stands like one of the giant gum trees of our forests – its roots are embedded in the soil of the country; its branches spread throughout the length and breadth of Australia!

For the most part, 3KZ presented standard radio fare – music, variety shows, quiz competitions and the like – with the occasional scheduled Labor broadcasts. It became a commercial success; its contribution to propagandising for democracy remains less clear.

Today, 3KZ is no more. Its degenerate successor, GOLD FM, presents a staple of 'good time oldies'. But though it's a long time since Trades Hall ran its own radio, many of the hits and memories of trade unionism can still be traced back one way or another to the mighty old building in Victoria Street.

# Further reading

In the interest of readability, we have neither sourced nor footnoted *Radical Melbourne*. The list below is intended as a starting point for those wanting more information.

Any book by Henry Reynolds makes a good introduction to the growing literature about Aboriginal people. For a guide along similar lines to *Radical Melbourne*, try Meyer Eidelson's *The Melbourne Dreaming* (Aboriginal Studies Press, 1997), a walking tour through Aboriginal sites within the city and its surrounds.

Robyn Annear's book *Bearbrass: Imagining Early Melbourne* (Mandarin, 1995) provides a sense of the geography of the first years of white settlement. But it's hard to go past Michael Cannon's work, especially *Melbourne after the Gold Rush* (Loch Haven Books, 1993) and *Old Melbourne Town before the Gold Rush* (Loch Haven Books, 1991). Of course, the classic contemporary account (not always historically reliable, but consistently entertaining) is Edmund Finn's *Chronicles of Early Melbourne, 1835 to 1852,* (Heritage Publications, 1976).

Unfortunately, there's no single, up-to-date history of the working class movement in Australia. If you can find a copy of *The Bitter Fight: A Pictorial History of the Australian Labour Movement* by Joe Harris (University of Queensland Press, 1970), it gives a reasonable overview, with some fantastic illustrations. You might also try Brian Fitzpatrick's *Short History of the Australian Labour Movement* (Rawson's Bookshop, 1944), although it's rather dated now.

For the struggles of wharf labourers, there's Rupert Lockwood's *Ship to Shore* (Hale & Iremonger, 1990) or Wendy Lowenstein and Tom Hill's collection of interviews *Under the Hook* (Melbourne Bookworkers, 1992).

Verity Burgmann's *In Our Time* (Allen and Unwin, 1985) provides the best introduction to the early Australian socialist movement, while Bruce Scates' *A New Australia* (Cambridge University Press, 1997) covers some of the same ground with an emphasis on non-socialist radicals. Bob James has painstakingly documented the careers of the main Melbourne anarchists – see, in particular, *Chummy Fleming: A Brief Biography* (Monty Miller Press, 1986) and *J. A. Andrews: A Brief Biography* (Monty Miller Press, 1986).

For the Industrial Workers of the World, see Verity Burgmann's *Revolutionary Industrial Unionism* (Cambridge University Press, 1995) and Frank Cain's *The Wobblies at War: A History of the IWW and the Great War in Australia* (Spectrum Publications, 1993).

Though there's no general history of the Victorian Socialist Party (in book form, at least), David Day's biography of John Curtin (Harper Collins, 1999) provides some information (and a guide to other sources). Another starting point is *Solidarity Forever* (National Press, 1972), Bertha Walker's idiosyncratic but fascinating biography of her father Percy Laidler, which deals with the VSP alongside the IWW, the the Communist Party, and many other organisations. It also touches upon the Victoria Police strike providing a good counterpoint to the more thorough (and conservative) account in Brown and Haldane's *Days of Violence* (Hybrid, 1998).

You can find details of the Chinese cabinet makers' strike and the Yee Hing riot in *The New Gold Mountain: The Chinese in Australia, 1901–1921* (C.F. Yong, Raphael Arts, 1977), while Gianfranco Cresciani's *Fascism, Anti-Fascism and Italians in Australia, 1922–1945* (Australian National University Press, 1980) covers the Matteotti Club and its opponents.

The best single source of information about the Communist Party comes from *The Reds: The Communist Party of Australia from Origins to Illegality* (Allen & Unwin, 1999) by Stuart Macintyre. For more personal accounts, look for some of the many published books of reminiscences (for instance, Ralph Gibson's *My Years in the Communist Party*, International Bookshop, 1966 or Judah Waten's – fictionalised – account in *Scenes of Revolutionary Life*). Though centred around Sydney, Hall Greenland's biography of veteran Trotskyist Nick Origlass (Wellington Lane Press, 1998) gives a sense of how the CP seemed to its left-wing critics.

For the Depression years, see Wendy Lowenstein's oral history *Weevils in the Flour* (Scribe, 1998). Charlie Fox's *Fighting Back* (Melbourne University Press, 2000) is a brilliant history of the unemployed struggles of the time, while Frank Huelin's *Keep Moving* (a shamefully neglected Australian novel) gives a sense of life for the jobless on the track. Arthur Howell's memoir *Against the Stream* (Hyland House, 1983) provides a record of the anti-war struggle of the period, which nicely supplements Egon Kisch's side-splitting notes about his Australian tour (*Australian Landfall*, Australasian Book Society, 1969).

The collection above, of course, does nothing more than touch the surface of what's available. For more references, we recommend two compilations of source material – Andrew Scott's *Rediscovering Labor* (Australian Labor Party, Victorian Branch, c.1991), and Beverley Symons' resource *Communism in Australia* (National Library of Australia, 1994).

# Index

Aborigines (execution & incarceration) 13, 18–20, 26, 43, 44, 166, 178–81, 187; (other) 11, 16, 17, 24, 46, 64–5, 67, 91, 123, 129, 220
*Age, The* 27, 30, 42, 48, 60, 62, 69–70, 73, 74, 77–8, 86, 94, 96, 101, 102–3, 117, 118, 131, 136, 150, 155, 168, 188
Ahern, Elizabeth (Lizzie) 34
Anarchism (see also Melbourne Anarchists Club) 12, 13, 52, 58, 72, 74, 86, 113, 119, 134, 142, 162, 196, 208; (media and police constructions) 73, 77, 83, 94
Anarchist Bookery 140–2
Andrade's Bookshop 13, 100, 125–8
Andrade, David 13, 58, 99, 100, 125, 140–3
Andrade, William 13, 99, 100, 125–6, 127–8, 140
Andrews, John Arthur 13, 99, 100, 220
anti-fascist protest 71–2, 80–2, 86, 123–4, 136, 208–10
*Argus, The* 28, 30, 31, 32, 40, 42, 51, 53, 59, 60, 61, 63, 66, 72, 74, 76, 77–8, 85, 86, 94, 96, 108, 138, 155–6, 158, 160, 161, 166–7, 170, 174, 187, 190, 191, 198, 200, 202, 213, 215
Athenaeum 68–70
*Australian Communist* 133–4
Australian Labor Party (ALP) 11, 34, 48, 52, 59, 73, 77, 82, 110, 111, 115–6, 117, 132, 135, 136, 146, 172, 188, 198, 214–9
*Australian Radical* 140, 196
Australian Secular Association 140, 163
Australian Socialist League (ASL) 104–6, 196
Australian Socialist Party (ASP) 132, 134, 135
Baines, Jennie 13, 170, 172, 193–4
Baker, Carl 133, 134
Baracchi, Guido 134, 144
Barker, Tom 111
Barry, Sir Redmond 12, 13, 15, 68, 90, 166–8, 190
Batman, Henry 19–20
Batman, John 15, 19, 24, 43–6
*Beacon, The* 52–3, 54
Blamey, Thomas 13, 15, 149, 219
Bo Leong 102–3
'Bobby' 187
Bone, William 43
Bourke House 80, 122–4
Brooks, Constable William 200, 202
'Bullet-eye' 187
*Bulletin* 60, 78, 106, 159, 165, 179
Burke and Wills statue 65–7, 86
Burke, Robert O'Hara 64–67
Café Baloo 151, 153, 154
Carmagnola, Francesco 208, 209–10
Casimir, Chris 114–5
Catholic Worker 81
Chinatown 12, 79, 100–3, 154–6
City Court 11, 12, 61, 190, 191–194
Cole, Edward William 13, 55–8
Coles Book Arcade 13, 55–8
Collins Street Gaol 44–46, 180
Colored Idea 129–31
Common Cause 137
*Commonweal* 52, 53, 215
Commonwealth Crimes Act 146
Communist Party of Australia (CP) 12, 13, 27, 29, 79–82, 84, 86–7, 103, 112, 118, 119, 121, 122, 127, 132–5, 136–9, 144–7, 148, 151, 170, 174, 204, 210, 218, 220
Communist Review 138
conscription 13, 34, 84, 86, 112, 136, 137, 144, 171, 174, 216
Coull, Jim 86–7
Counihan, Noel 13, 119, 121, 146, 147, 151, 152
Coverlid Place 104
Curr, Edward 35, 185
Curtin, John 84, 139, 221
Customs House 39, 40, 42, 60, 151
Delaney, Francis 149–50
depressions 50, 54, 80, 82, 83, 94, 106, 145, 146, 151–3, 160, 210, 221
Devanny, Jean 146
Dickinson, Ted 81
*Direct Action* 111–2
Don, Charles Jardine 10, 92–3
Dugdale, Harriet 14
Duke of Kent Hotel 27–30
Earsman, William 133, 134–5
Eastern Market 10, 11, 83, 93
Eight hour day 10, 12, 86, 92, 174, 175, 182–4, 212, 214
Engels, Friedrich 121, 195
Eureka Stockade 11, 13, 69–70, 91, 99, 166, 190, 218
executions 12, 26, 166, 168, 178–81, 186–9, 215
Fabian Society 73, 113, 114
*Farrago* 119
fascism (see also anti-fascist protest) 61, 63, 136, 139, 146, 203
Fawkner, John Pascoe 17–20, 24, 43–5
feminism 14, 15, 169–74
Finn, Edmund (see also Garryowen) 21, 220
Flagstaff Gardens 11, 17–24, 37
Flanigan Lane Theatre 27–30

Fleming, Chummy   13, 52–3, 74, 76–7, 86–7, 99, 100, 104, 105, 107, 134, 162–4, 220
Fox, Len   80, 82
Francis, May   125, 126, 135, 170
Franks, Charles   17–8
free speech fights   (Prahran) 33–4, 116, 170; (Brunswick) 147
free thought   13, 56, 125, 141, 162, 205
Garden, Jock   103, 133, 134, 135
Garryowen (Finn, Edmund)   21, 22, 26, 35, 37, 38, 45, 46, 88, 89, 166, 186, 220
George, Henry   51, 52, 53, 54
Gibson, Ralph   13, 79, 80, 82, 87, 221
Golden Fleece Hotel   104–5, 106, 108
Goldstein, Vida   169, 171, 172, 174
Gray, Charles   64–7
Greek Club (Apokalypsi)   13, 148, 150
Griffin, Gerald   123–4
Guild Hall   169–74
*Harbinger of Light*   205
Her Majesty's Theatre   97, 100
Hirsch, Max   51–54
*Honesty*   98, 99, 140
Hosier Lane   79, 80, 82
Immigration Act   123
Industrial Workers of the World (IWW or Wobblies)   12, 13, 100, 109–12, 113, 116–7, 132, 145, 205, 220–1
Irvine, Sir William   149
Jarvis, Leah   116
John, Cecilia   170, 171, 174
Kelly, Ned   12, 68, 166, 167–8, 187–8
King, John   64–6
Kisch, Egon   13, 122–4, 221
Knights of Labour   52–3, 198
La Trobe, Superintendent (also Governor)   14, 21, 22, 23, 36, 37, 181
Laidler, Percy   13, 47–50, 126, 127, 128, 144, 189, 220
Land Convention   90, 93–4
Lane, Ernie   115
Lane, William   58
*La Riscossa*   209, 210
Lavender, Bella   170, 191

League of Young Democrats (formerly Young Communist League)   79, 137
Lenin, V.I.   15, 121, 127, 132, 133
*Liberator*   140, 163
Liberty Hall   141, 142
Long, Dick   192–3, 194
*Lyceum Miniature*   206
McIver, Sandy   149, 150
Maloney, Dr William   13, 106, 195, 196, 197–8
Mann, Tom   13, 32, 33, 34, 47, 73, 74, 76–7, 115, 183
Marshall, (Rev) Dr   74, 76–7, 78
Marx, Karl   34, 56, 121, 141, 195, 205
*Masses*   121
Masters and Servants Act   45
Matteotti Club   71–2, 146–7, 208–11, 221
Maughan, Jack   29, 30, 118, 121
May Day   10, 32, 34, 52, 81, 84, 86, 87, 121, 146, 184, 209–10, 217, 218
Mechanics Institute   12, 13, 68–70, 167
Melbourne Anarchist Club (MAC)   97, 100, 104, 105, 106, 116, 125, 140, 205
Melbourne Club   11, 12, 13, 64, 67, 88–90, 149, 167
Melbourne Cricket Ground (MCG)   81–2
*Melbourne Punch*   75, 95, 107, 126, 177, 198
Melbourne University Labour Club   119–20
Menzies, Robert   27, 122, 123, 136, 137
Mercantile Chambers   52, 54
Miller, Monty   13, 99, 100, 116, 117, 205, 220
Movement Against War and Fascism (MAWF)   12, 80, 122
Murphy, William   175–7
Murray, Angus   188–9
New Theatre   27, 28–30, 80, 121
O'Connor, Timothy   149–150
O'Dowd, Bernard   113, 115, 205
O'Dowd, Monty   116
Old Cemetery   11, 12, 24–26
Old Melbourne Gaol   12, 37, 46, 178, 185–9, 190, 194, 215
One Big Union (OBU)   110; (for women) 174

Orange Lodge (Protestant Loyalist Society)   35–7
Ormond, Francis   175–7
Palmer, Vance   30
Pankhurst, Adela   13, 94, 96, 134, 170
Parliament House   11, 12, 13, 48, 50, 67, 79, 90, 91–4, 146, 163, 171, 182, 183, 184, 189
Party Processions Act   37
Pastoral Hotel   36, 37, 38
Patullo, Shorty   147
Petrie, Larry   99, 100, 104, 105, 106, 107
Police Strike   12, 62–3, 149, 199–203, 220
Political Progressive League (PPL)   52, 53, 214–5
*Port Phillip Herald* (as *Port Phillip Herald*) 21–23, 36, 46, 181; (as *Herald*) 35, 55, 58, 60, 62, 66–7, 118, 147, 154, 155, 160, 182, 183, 187, 189, 201–2, 203, 212
*Port Phillip Patriot*   21, 23, 35, 36, 187
Price, Tom   85–86
Prichard, Katharine Susannah   29
Progressive Spiritualist Lyceum   13, 204, 205–7
Proletarian Club   118, 153
*Proletarian Review*   127
Prostitution   95, 99, 123
'Ptolemy'   187
Public Library (see also State Library)   13, 60, 161–3
Puttmann, Hermann   195–6
Queens Wharf   83, 105, 162
Quong Tart   58
racism   17, 21–2, 46, 58, 64–5, 102, 111, 123, 124, 129–31, 154, 155, 178–81, 205
radio (3KZ)   219
Red Flag Campaign   190–4, 217–8
Riot Act   22, 37, 96
Rosa, Sam   104, 105, 106–8, 163–4, 215
Russian revolution   10, 71, 127, 132, 174, 190, 200, 218
St. John, Major   22–3
St John's Lane   37, 38
Salvation Army   11, 111, 144, 157–60

Scots Church   11, 73, 74–8
Shelley, Joe   144–5
Smallboy, Robert   26, 179–81
*Smith's Weekly*   121
Social Democratic League (SDL)   86, 106, 108, 197
Social Democratic Party (SDP)   113, 115–6
Social Pioneering Company   142
Social Questions Committee   32, 73
*Socialist, The*   32, 33, 48, 49, 50, 74, 76, 77, 191, 192, 193, 194
Socialist Hall   31, 32
*Socialist Melbourne*   79
Socialist Party choir   31, 32
Socialist Sunday School   33
Spanish Civil War   81–2
Special Constabulary Force (SCF or Specials)   36, 59, 60–3, 69, 85, 96, 201–2, 203
spiritualism (see also Victorian Association of Progressive Spiritualists and Progressive Spiritualist Lyceum)   12, 141, 144
Stalin, Joseph   79, 121, 124, 136, 137, 139, 145
Stalinism   79–80, 82, 124, 134, 139, 145–6
State Library of Victoria (see also Public Library)   11, 12, 41, 87, 97, 166, 167, 213
Stephens, James   182
Stock Exchange   12, 47–50
Storey Hall   15, 169, 171
Strikes (see also Police Strike)   (waterside workers/dock strikes) 15, 39–42, 59, 80, 84, 86, 94, 96, 145, 148, 172–4; (other) 21–3, 59–61, 84, 86, 92, 94, 111–2, 145, 154–6, 182–4, 186, 188, 191, 214
Strong, Reverend Charles   74
*Sun, The*   148, 149, 189
Sunday Liberation Society   162–4
Sunday Observance League   162
Swebleses, Joe   34
Table Talk   95, 149
Tattersalls Building (Curtin House) 137, 139
Techow, Gustav   195–6
*Telegraph, The*   188

Temperance Hall   113, 120, 200, 209
Tennant, Kylie   118, 119
Terry, William Henry   204–5
Theatrical Employees Hall (Apokalypsi)   132, 134
Tivoli Theatre   129–30, 131
*Tocsin*   73, 100, 125, 205, 215
Town Hall   11, 12, 13, 51, 59, 60–1, 62, 63, 96, 176, 188, 200, 201, 202, 213
Trades Hall Council (THC)   59, 61, 103, 108, 148, 157, 175–6, 188, 191, 202, 214, 217–219
Trades Hall Building   13, 70, 83, 96, 106, 124, 151, 158, 174, 183, 184, 189, 191, 204, 205, 207, 208, 212–219
Trotsky, Leon   15, 127
*Truth*   26, 130, 131, 147
Tunermenerwail, Jack Napoleon   26, 178–181
Turn Verein   13, 195–6, 197, 198
Turner, Frederick   50
Unemployed Workers Movement (UWM)   12, 146, 151–3
unemployment   21–3, 31, 47–50, 73–4, 76–8, 86, 96, 106–7, 111, 145, 146, 151–3, 157–60, 215, 218, 221
unions (waterfront workers)   39–42, 148–150; (stonemasons) 92, (Australian Workers Union) 100, (Amalgamated Engineering Union) 133, (ACTU) 136, 148, (mining union) 137; (general)   11, 23, 59–61, 64, 85, 86, 110, 111, 115, 116, 131, 132, 146, 154–6, 171, 174, 175–6, 182–4, 188, 189, 191, 209, 212–3, 214–9
Unlawful Assemblies and Processions Act   94
Vegetarian Society of Australia   141
Verein Vorwärts   106, 196–7
Victoria Market   11, 12, 24–26
Victorian Association of Progressive Spiritualists (VAPS)   204–207
Victorian Council Against War and Fascism (VACWF)   81, 122, 124

Victorian Single Tax League (VSTL)   51–54, 198
Victorian Socialists League (VSL)   12, 113–5, 117
Victorian Socialist Party (VSP)   13, 31, 32–4, 47–9, 73, 74, 78, (Women's Peace League) 94, 116, 133, 147, 174, 188, 191, 193–4, 197, 204, 220–1
Walker, Bertha   13, 126, 220
Wallace, Elizabeth   170
War Precautions Act   170, 190–4, 217–8
*War! What For?*   122
Waten, Judah   12, 144, 145, 147, 221
Webb, Sidney and Beatrice   52, 114
Western Market   40, 44–5
wharfies (see also strikes: waterfront workers)   109, 220
White Army   149
White, John   163, 164
White, Sam   119–20
Williams, Stanley   149
Wills, William   64–7
*Woman Voter*   169, 170, 171, 172–4
Women's Peace Army   13, 169, 171, 193
Women's Political Association (WPA)   15, 169–174
Workers Art Club (WAC)   12, 13, 27, 29, 30, 118–21
*Workers Voice*   29, 30, 79–82
*Workers Weekly*   199, 203
Working Men's College   12, 106, 163, 175–7
Yarra Bank   12, 34, 52, 60, 74, 77, 81, 83–7, 96, 105, 107, 114, 124, 133, 137, 144, 171, 173, 188, 191, 193
Yee Hing (now Chinese Masonic Society)   101–3, 221
Young Comrades Contingent (Socialist Army)   33

# RADICAL MELBOURNE

- ● Tour Stop
- ── Walking Tour
- ─ ─ Tram